The North of England Ghost Trail

THE NORTH OF ENGLAND
GHOST TRAIL

Liz Linahan

Constable · London

First published in Great Britain 1997
by Constable and Company Limited
3 The Lanchesters, 162 Fulham Palace Road
London W6 9ER
Copyright © Liz Linahan 1997
The right of Liz Linahan to be identified as the author
of this work has been asserted by her
in accordance with the Copyright, Designs and Patents Act 1988
ISBN 0 09 476910 9
Set in Linotron Sabon 10.5 pt by
SetSystems Ltd, Saffron Walden, Essex
Printed in Great Britain by
St Edmundsbury Press Ltd
Bury St Edmunds, Suffolk

A CIP catalogue record for this book
is available from the British Library

CONTENTS

Foreword by David Clarke   11
Introduction   15

DERBYSHIRE   18

The Village of Eyam   19
Wingfield Manor   22
The Royal Oak   24
Norbury Old Manor   25
The Town of Castleton   26
Nine Ladies Stone Circle   32
Ringwood Hall Hotel   34
Sudbury Hall   35
Arbour Low Stone Circle and Gib Hill Barrow   36
The City of Derby   37
The Chesterfield Canal   39
The Village of Ashover   40

Contents

CHESHIRE   46

Dunham Massey Hall   47
The Lion and Swan Hotel   50
Higher Huxley Hall   51
Little Moreton Hall   53
The Red Cow   54
Heathercliffe Country House   58
Llyndir Hall Hotel   59
The Blue Bell Inn   61
Bramall Hall   62

NOTTINGHAMSHIRE   66

Nottingham Castle   67
Clumber Park and Sherwood Forest   70
Upton Hall   73
Worksop Priory Gatehouse   75
The Salutation Inn   76
The Beeston-Mansfield Road   77
Newstead Abbey   80
Ye Olde Trip to Jerusalem   82
Rufford Country Park and Abbey   83

LINCOLNSHIRE   89

The Sun Inn   89
Church Farm Museum   92
Blackfriars Arts Centre   94
Gainsborough Old Hall   95
Tattershall Castle   97
The White Hart Hotel   98

Contents

Gunby Hall 99
St Wulfram's Church 100
Lincoln Castle 103
Stragglethorpe Hall 105
The Barn Gallery 107
Branston Hall Hotel 108

SOUTH YORKSHIRE 112

Conisbrough Castle 113
Mosborough Hall Hotel 116
The Stocksbridge Bypass 118
Hickleton Churchyard 121
Carbrook Hall Hotel 121
Roche Abbey 124
Packman Lane 126
Cromwell's Eating House 128
Hellaby Hall Hotel 129
Junction 31, M1 131
The Lindholme Area 132

EAST YORKSHIRE 135

Burton Agnes Manor 135
The Town of Hessle 138
Fort Paull 141
The City of Hull 142
Skipsea Castle 144
Elsham Hall Country and Wildlife Park 145
The Town of Beverley 146
The Rudston Monolith 149
Burton Constable Hall 150

Contents

WEST YORKSHIRE   153

Temple Newsam House   153
The Ackworth-Pontefract Road   158
The Town of Haworth   159
The Three Houses Inn   161
Oakwell Hall and Country Park   163
Abbey House Museum   166
The Leeds-Farsley Road   167
Rogerthorpe Manor   168
Nostell Priory   170

NORTH YORKSHIRE   175

The Theatre Royal   175
Ripley Castle   178
Beningbrough Hall   181
Duncombe Park   182
Richmond Castle   184
Bolton Abbey   187
Scarborough Castle   189
Byland Abbey   190
Bolton Castle   192
Whitby Abbey   194
The City of York   195

LANCASHIRE   201

Chingle Hall   201
The Punch Bowl   208
Brandlesholme Old Hall   209

Contents

Guy's Thatched Hamlet   211
Mitton Hall   212
Pendle Witch Country   213
Lancaster Castle   217
Wardley Hall   218
Stubley Old Hall   220
Rufford Old Hall   221
The Red Pump   221

CUMBRIA   224

Workington Hall   225
The Kirkstone Pass Inn   229
Overwater Hall Hotel   230
Lake Windermere   231
Wardrew House   232
Levens Hall   234
The Village of Croglin   236
Castlerigg Stone Circle   238
Dalston Hall Hotel   239
Brougham Hall   243
Gosforth Hall Hotel   245

COUNTY DURHAM and TYNE AND WEAR   248

Redworth Hall Hotel   249
The Cooperage   252
Lumley Castle Hotel   254
Tynemouth Priory and Castle   257
Hylton Castle   257
The Theatre Royal   260

Contents

The Oak Tree Inn   262
Preston Hall Museum and The Green
   Dragon Museum   264
The Lord Crewe Arms Hotel   266
The Eden Arms Swallow Hotel   268
The Dorman Museum   269
Washington Arts Centre   270

NORTHUMBERLAND   273

Bamburgh Castle   273
Beadnell House   278
Warkworth Castle and Warkworth Hermitage   279
Meldon Park   282
Broomlee Lough   285
Chillingham Castle   285

Acknowledgements   293
Bibliography   295
Index   297

FOREWORD

Prowling around windswept moors and ancient ruins looking for ghosts and phantoms in the dead of night is not everyone's cup of tea. But some of us – like you, dear reader – will always be fascinated by the mysteries which lurk on the edge of the known world, and are always searching for that one bit of evidence which might prove something is out there . . .

Back on Hallowe'en night 1994 I was hot on the trail of a ghostly presence which was said to haunt a stretch of new road running over the Pennine hills above the steelworks at Stocksbridge, near Sheffield. Dozens of local folk, including policemen and security guards, had spotted the phantom figure of a monk on the Stocksbridge bypass, which opened in 1987 and quickly became a notorious accident blackspot.

The ghost story had been featured extensively in the local press and on national TV, and many sincere witnesses had come forward with strikingly similar stories which they told with impressive honesty. After years on the trail of spooks, flying saucers and assorted oddities I had become jaded and cynical about the physical reality of the paranormal – but this series of events struck me as different. The Stocksbridge haunting was one of the few occasions where I had managed to chart an outbreak of paranormal events from day one, speaking directly to witnesses and watching the growth of folklore around one or two inexplicable happenings which I found completely baffling.

On this particular freezing cold, windswept night I was parked up on Pearoyd Bridge which runs across the bypass and drops down into the little town in the valley below. One of the sightings had taken place on what has now become known as 'the Ghost Bridge', which continues to attract legions of ghost-hunters who sit watching and waiting for the phantom monk to approach and tap on the window.

With me this night was Liz Linahan whom I had met for the first time two weeks previously, following the publication of her first book *Pit Ghosts, Padfeet and Poltergeists*. The press release promoting her new volume of ghost stories collected in the collieries and villages of the South Yorkshire and North Nottinghamshire coalfield had landed on my desk and immediately struck a chord with me. Reading about sightings and happenings in popular books, many of which are rehashes of earlier books, discussing people and events which have never been properly recorded or investigated is one thing. It might be fireside entertainment while the wind howls outside, but in my journalistic experience it's no substitute for getting out in the field and finding out what's *really* going on – and that's exactly what Liz has set about doing in her writings.

We didn't track down the phantom monk of the Stocksbridge bypass that night, but we did decide it was time we put the paranormal world on the map and discovered exactly what was prowling our stately homes, haunted houses and ancient ruins. That's partly where the idea for this book was originally conceived, and the rest, as they say, is history.

Foreword

The North of England Ghost Trail will introduce you to a host of original material and stories collected and recorded for the first time in recent years – much of it never before featured in print. You will find poltergeists, ghost dogs and phantom horsemen, spectral monks, weird sounds, cursed objects and multiple hauntings galore, all in places which are accessible to the public and easy to find via the maps and directions included alongside the text.

Although the majority of the stories are attached to places with a great deal of history, like ancient castles, old halls and monuments, some, like Stocksbridge's 'Ghost Bridge', are a product of the twentieth century. As will become clear, ghost stories – like the folklore they are – are continually evolving and changing with the times. Many famously haunted locations are still host to little-known paranormal happenings in the present day, and the guide includes updates on a number of these. Many towns and cities like York, Chester and Derby now have their own conducted ghost-tours of historic buildings, and ghostlore often blends so well with history it has become an ideal hook for the tourist industry to promote the delights of the North.

The world of the paranormal is big business. Twenty years ago ghosts and phantoms were the stuff of paperback writers and wide-eyed believers – and the worlds of science and academia regarded the subject as a lunatic fringe. As we approach the end of the twentieth century we can't get away from weirdness – our TV screens are full of programmes like *Strange But True* and *Out of This World*, and fictional series like *The X-Files* have brought ghosts, UFOs and the supernatural into millions of homes across the globe. Now there are even established chairs of parapsychology at universities, and dozens of serious magazines and organizations which are investigating and discussing every kind of strange phenomenon.

This book is one step towards putting the reality of people's experiences with the inexplicable paranormal world on record. Using this book you can visit these places, speak to people who have glimpsed the unseen world, and draw your own conclusions.

As veteran instigator John A. Keel once pointed out, whether you are a believer or a sceptic, all the author is trying to do is lay the facts before you, the reader, so you can make up your own mind. Belief, or disbelief, will come to you from another direction, but *'next week, next month, or next year you may be driving along a deserted country road late at night and as you round a bend you will suddenly see . . .'*

David Clarke
Sheffield, Hallowe'en 1996

INTRODUCTION

Between 1994 and 1996 I travelled the North of England in search of haunted houses, with the aim of writing a layman's tour guide to places associated with supernatural phenomena. Since ghosts and other related phenomena are part of the fabric of British folklore, I didn't have far to look before uncovering an enthralling collection of close encounters from areas as far afield as the bleak Northumberland borderlands and the forests of Nottinghamshire. I was privileged to be able to speak to many people who had their own strange encounters to tell of, and to spend many a chilly night in a variety of places which were all rumoured to be haunted. Although I returned home on each occasion defeated, having experienced nothing out of the ordinary, I was determined to persevere.

Then, one afternoon in the summer of 1996, I visited the West Yorkshire home of a couple who had experienced a number of unusual events. They were open-minded in every sense, neither offering a 'logical explanation' for their sightings nor denouncing them out of hand. After all, they knew what they had seen and heard, and who was I to disagree? Accompanied by a friend, I took a dictaphone to record our interview, and spent a most enjoyable if rather rainy afternoon trekking around some wonderful historic parkland. The four of us eventually sat in their beautiful eighteenth-century sitting-room and chatted at length over a cup of tea, with the dictaphone left running. At some point during the conversation, our hostess excused herself saying that somebody was at the door, and left three of us still chatting. Only on her return, when she was most puzzled that there had been nobody there at all, did we three confess that we had not heard what she described as two loud clear raps at the door. We joked that the resident ghost had made a timely appearance.

I would have thought nothing more about it but for the fact that my dictaphone had been left running all the while. The following day, when I played back the tape, I distinctly heard two clear loud raps as described by our hostess just prior to her standing and leaving the room. My instant reaction was to rewind the tape and play it back over again, feeling that I had been mistaken. But the sounds were there, a clear knocking on wood, twice, just as she had described. It must be mentioned at this point that the main door to which I refer did not open into the sitting-room, but was in another part of the house. Coupled with this was the fact that, as I'd been worried about running out of tape, I'd switched the dictaphone to a slow tape-speed which actually makes the recording quality rather poor. Indeed, to hear some of the conversation I'd had to hold it close to my ear! And yet, from a significant distance away, the tape had recorded a sound unheard by three other people present as clearly as though I had been stationed next to the door itself.

A rational explanation? Well, yes, perhaps there could be. But that, I will never know. And herein lies the appeal of the supernatural, either for the armchair enthusiast, or for those who wish to take a more active role in its research. We search for proof because we simply do not know, which is the most powerful attraction of all.

Liz Linahan, 1996

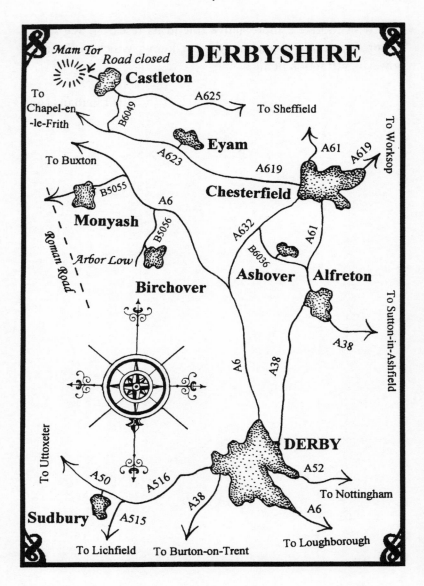

DERBYSHIRE

THE VILLAGE OF EYAM
approx. 6 miles SW of Sheffield

The picturesque village of Eyam (pronounced 'eem') attracts thousands of visitors each year, drawn not only by its scenic walks and traditional stone cottages, but also by its history as a victim of the horrific bubonic plague of 1665. The Black Death originally swept through Europe between 1347 and 1351, remaining endemic in England until 1666, when the Great Fire of London served to cleanse one of its major strongholds. It is believed that clothing taken from London to Eyam originally brought the plague to this Derbyshire village, as the consignment contained fleas whose bite spread the disease. (The Lord Mayor of London, who ordered the destruction of cats and dogs as a measure to cope with the plague outbreak in 1665, had no way of knowing that this would worsen the problem. The contaminated fleas had originally been brought to Britain by black rats, which were free to multiply further when his orders were carried out.) Eyam rector William Mompesson, who lost his wife Catherine to the plague, pioneered efforts which ensured that the outbreak was contained by persuading villagers to segregate themselves from all outside contact. Catherine Mompesson's ghost is said to still walk through the churchyard, over three hundred years after her death.

Eyam parish church published their own collection of authentic 'Plague Cures' in 1991, dating from the 1660s. It was generally believed that the horrendous black buboes (sores) which appeared on the body of a plague victim could be cured by following these directions: *'Take a Pigeon and plucke the feathers off her Taile, very bare, and set her Taile to the sore, and shee will draw out the venom till she die . . .'*

Eyam Hall is open to the public and is still the home of the Wright family several generations after its founding in 1671. The hall is rumoured to be haunted by the ghost of a girl who drowned herself in the wash-house well. Perhaps she is the White Lady who appears to foretell the death of members of the Wright family. According to the recent account of a family member, the last person to encounter the White Lady was Dorothy, shortly before her mother Charlotte's death in 1937. A phantom white horse is said to gallop across Eyam Hall's courtyard on certain nights of the year, although this spectre, along with that of an elderly man who appeared on several occasions in one of the upper rooms, has not been seen in recent years.

The Bull's Head public house, situated opposite Eyam church, was recorded as early as 1606 under the name of the Talbot, a now obsolete name for a large hunting hound. It took its current name in 1710, as the community of Eyam struggled to regain its feet in the aftermath of the Black Death. Supernatural occurrences in the building seem to be confined to an area between the bar and the first floor, the oldest part of the current structure. Several tenants and bar staff have experienced being tapped lightly on the shoulder ... and have turned to find nobody there. The door at the top of the stairs, leading to the landing, once locked itself from the inside, forcing landlord Norman Baines to dismantle the lock from the outside. Locals tell how bottles have flung themselves from the back of the bar, and tenants from the 1960s onwards have been troubled by footsteps which climb the stairs, followed by the sound of doors opening and closing, before descending again. Landlady Terry Baines has frequently experienced a feeling of 'uncanny coldness' while cashing up in the bar at the end of the evening. The Bull's Head offers bed and breakfast; in 1994 Mrs Baines remade the bed in Room 1, only to return a few minutes later to find an impression in the pillow and the bed covers, as though they had been lain on.

One of Eyam's darker secrets centres on the appearance of an unidentified figure in black, which has been seen in several locations around the village. In the early 1990s, two customers leaving the Bull's Head late at night saw a dark form loitering in a gateway opposite the row of 'plague cottages' on Church Street. The women hesitated and the figure vanished. A gentleman who lived in one of these cottages was continually perturbed by the sight of the same shady form, which appeared in front of the same gatepost in the evening, in view of his bedroom window. He eventually put his house up for sale. Norman Baines spotted a mystery figure in a dark cloak one winter morning in 1993, when walking his dog through a field behind the church, towards Water Lane. Ahead of him, next to a stone wall, he noticed a caped figure with indistinguishable features ... which vanished as he climbed over a stile.

Local man Alec Bettney was out walking his dog one winter evening in 1993 on the road between Eyam and Grindleford, when his pet began to bristle visibly at something he could not see. Mr Bettney shone a beam of torchlight ahead, and saw a dark figure and a black Labrador heading towards him. The dog's eyes briefly shone red in the torchlight before a car appeared, whereupon man and dog vanished. With high walls at either side of the road, it would have been impossible for them to have diverted on to another route. Mr Bettney also experienced the sound of phantom hoofbeats galloping past him after dark in the same area on another occasion, and three local lads walking this road one night ran back to Grindleford in fear, after hearing a creature unknown tracing their footsteps through the trees.

Eyam Hall, Church Street, can be visited between 2 April and 29 October on Wednesdays, Thursdays, Sundays and Bank Holidays. Eyam parish church is open to the public daily until 4 p.m. For bookings: The Bull's Head, Church Street, Eyam, Derbyshire.

WINGFIELD MANOR

South Wingfield, Alfreton

The substantial ruin of this medieval country mansion opened to the public for the first time in 1995. Wingfield was built in the mid-fifteenth century, and held the captive Mary Queen of Scots in 1569, a fact recalled by local legend which asserts that the ghost of Queen Mary revisits Wingfield's ballroom on certain nights of the year. Although most of the manor remained unoccupied after 1770, its remaining vaulted undercroft and tall tower go some way towards showing the former beauty of the building. It was amid great excitement that, in November 1995, the owners of the house, Mr and Mrs Butler Critchlow, opened an antiquated desk and discovered papers which indicated that Wingfield was once the site of a terrible murder. The documents had lain hidden for several generations, and detailed how a local maidservant named Mary was murdered here in 1666. According to the story, the girl had hoped to marry a local farmer, and had told the housemaid Fanny of her plans, not realising that Fanny secretly saw herself as the farmer's bride. Mary left Wingfield one afternoon to travel to her mother's house to request consent for the marriage, but never returned. The truth was only discovered when Fanny confessed on her death-bed that she had lured Mary into the manor vaults and locked the door behind her. The vaults were subsequently reopened, and Mary's remains were found lying on the vault steps.

Although research has confirmed that a certain number of people named in the papers did indeed exist, it is unclear just how authentic the account is. A friend of the Butler Critchlows commented that 'the whole thing smacks of Victoriana; it could so easily have been made up by some young lady with a fertile imagination. On the other hand, it could have been a story handed down over a pint of an evening . . . One way or the other we're never likely to find out.' However, it is interesting to note that the story claims the murder rendered Wingfield Manor 'cursed', and led to its decay. Wingfield was indeed abandoned by its resident family, and fell into ruin over a period of years, despite having once been a house of consequence.

Amid renovations prior to its public opening, a number of workmen witnessed 'phantom lights' in unoccupied areas of the manor. A contractor working in one of the smaller rooms close to the undercroft at dusk witnessed an adjacent room light up inexplicably, likening its brightness to that of an electric bulb. There is no electricity installed in any of these rooms. Several visitors have remarked on the appearance of an unusual bluish light of indefinite shape, particularly within the undercroft, and the visitors' book includes two entries recording unusual sight-ings dated December 1995 and January 1996 respectively. The former is an account written by a visiting Australian family of whom the mother and daughter noted that on 'entering the undercroft, [a] circular blue light, fuzzy white around [the] edges' appeared. They turned around to see a similar 'arch of blue light' beside them. The second account was by a local lady who noted that she found the ruin 'very atmospheric, especially in [the] undercroft,' where, she went on to add, '... several apparitions noted'.

At the foot of the hill on which Wingfield Manor is built there is a popular fishing lake. At Easter in 1996, a group of local fishermen were convinced that a person unknown was watching them from a window in the tower opposite. They continued to fish for over an hour until eventually they walked to the manor to take a closer look. The custodian pointed out that the tower in which they had seen the figure is in fact inaccessible.

Wingfield Manor is privately owned, and is administered by English Heritage. As it is part of a working farm, dogs are not allowed and the track to the manor itself may be muddy in bad weather. Visitors are advised to telephone the 24-hour infor-mation line to ascertain opening times: (01604) 730326.

THE ROYAL OAK
Market Place, Chesterfield town centre

As early as the twelfth century, a building on the site of the Royal Oak, in the medieval market town of Chesterfield, was recorded as a 'Rest House' for the Knights Templar, the infamous warrior monks. The original building was expanded over the years, being recorded in deeds and wills from the late 1600s onwards. In 1772 it was first mentioned as a public house. The Royal Oak has remained almost unchanged since, its dark-beamed interior and quirky arrangement of rooms revealing a colourful and unusual past. It is rumoured locally that the premises are revisited by the ghosts of Foreign Legion soldiers. A former resident of the Royal Oak fled her bedroom in fear one night after witnessing the appearance of a spectral pageboy. The mysterious figures of an elderly man and woman of unknown identity have also been seen here, and bar staff report 'an uncomfortable atmosphere' in some areas of the pub.

NORBURY OLD MANOR
Norbury, Ashbourne

The medieval stone-built Norbury Manor has occupied its current site since the thirteenth century, today drawing visitors interested in seeing for themselves this ancient building and its rare 'king post' roof. The legendary White Lady of Norbury Manor is believed to have been a member of the Maskery family, who lived here for a short while around the turn of the nineteenth century. She is thought to have died of pneumonia in the early 1800s while still very young. Although the current custodian remains sceptical of the supernatural himself, he notes that the ghost was most recently seen by his mother. In 1992 the family had a young friend named Kate staying with them. Early one morning they were preparing to go out when Mrs Wright thought to wake Kate, who was asleep upstairs, so that she should not be alarmed on rising to find herself alone in the house. On her way to the stairs, Mrs Wright briefly saw a young female figure walking upwards towards the landing, and decided that Kate must already be awake and dressed. When, a while later, their guest had still not come down for breakfast, Mr Wright entered her bedroom to find her still soundly asleep.

Although the appearances of the White Lady are quite rare, they have most often been known to take place around the area of the stairs, where, if supernatural tradition is to be believed, it may be no coincidence that pictures have frequently fallen from the main wall without reason, despite being firmly secured.

Norbury Old Manor can be visited by written appointment only between 30 March and 30 September, on Tuesday, Wednesday and Saturday afternoons.

THE TOWN OF CASTLETON
The High Peak, North Derbyshire

Castleton's dazzling High Peak scenery, coupled with its thriving tourist centre nestled in the bottom of the valley below Peveril Castle, make it a favourite among walkers and sightseers during summer. Winnats Pass has a particularly unpleasant reputation, since a brutal double murder in the 1750s is said to have condemned the souls of two tragic lovers to wander the ravine for eternity. The couple eloped in order to marry without parental consent, but never succeeded. They were attacked by a gang of five men and brutally murdered while travelling through the pass as darkness fell. The culprits were never caught, although the death-bed confession of a local man several years later indicated that he was the last surviving member of the gang. According to his last words, his accomplices had all died in suspicious circumstances several years previously; either suicide, madness or falling rocks in Winnats Pass had claimed them one by one. Today, ghostly cries of torment are occasionally reported to echo around Winnats Pass after sundown, and locals tell how the cave at the top of the pass, in which the robbers had stored their ill-gotten gains, is haunted. The young woman's side-saddle, from which she was dragged that fateful night, is on display in the Speedwell Cavern visitors' centre at the foot of the pass.

Peveril Castle once reigned supreme over its surrounding peak-land, being founded shortly after the Conquest by one of King William's favourite knights, William Peverel. Only after its building did a town grow up in the valley below. The castle remained in use until the early 1500s, although it had fallen into disrepair long before. Today administered by English Heritage, Peveril commands views over Castleton and Mam Tor Iron Age hill-fort. Although there are no recorded sightings of ghosts within the castle and grounds, one administrator did note that, when she was alone within the ruin, the site seemed to possess a 'certain special atmosphere'.

Peak Cavern is situated at the base of Peveril Castle, one remaining cave of a now collapsed cave-system. It has long been rumoured to be a gateway to the Otherworld, and was formerly known as the Devil's Arse! Despite time-honoured stories that certain villagers have crossed into the Otherworld on entering the cavern and then returned to tell their tales, the cavern mouth was home for many in the 1700s, hosting tiny homesteads and being known locally as Peaks Hole. The famous Blue John Mine is believed by a number of guides who operate tourist trips to be haunted by the spirits of long-dead miners. In days of old, working standards were notoriously poor and many were killed by roof collapses. Certain guides are convinced that they have heard 'disembodied voices' when underground, and one recalled feeling that he had been prodded by an invisible hand.

*

Castleton is presided over by the remains of Peveril Castle

During the reign of Charles II, the Castle Hotel, a historic stone-built public house on Castle Street in the town centre, was a popular coaching inn. It is believed that prior to its official licensing, a former owner used the upper hayloft as an illegal brewing parlour! The Castle Hotel has been believed to be haunted as far as living memory can recall, according to the accounts of senior residents of Castleton. Its beautiful wooden minstrel gallery is associated with the legend of a ghostly bride said to appear in her wedding dress. She is thought to have committed suicide when jilted on the morning of her intended marriage at some long-forgotten point in history. Although her ghost has not been seen for several years, a former member of staff described how, during an earlier tenancy, a new chambermaid had been employed to work upstairs. When the young woman disappeared without trace on the same day, leaving her coat and bag still hanging on a peg in the cloakroom, the landlord became concerned and telephoned her parents. Her mother explained that she had arrived home earlier vowing never to return to the hotel, after witnessing the ghost of a woman in white walking through a wall. The apparition appeared to walk on her knees, recalling a past period in history when the floor was on a lower level.

Another unusual sighting occurred when a party of fifteen people were leaving the hotel after a meal. They were counted back on to the coach, when one of the party asked the driver to wait for 'the man in the pin-stripe suit' who, he said, was seated next to the fireplace, with an Old English sheepdog at his feet. The landlord returned to the bar and found it empty, with no trace of the mysterious man or his dog. This particular sighting would appear to be exceptionally detailed, since other reports of the 'man in pin-stripe' refer to the upper part of his body only, the lower being invisible. Several subsequent witnesses have noted that his hands appear to be held behind his back as though he is warming them by the large fire, the only location at which he is noted to appear.

As with many 'haunted' properties, renovation work (which took place here in the summer of 1996) prompted a spate of unexplained activity. Landlady Irene Wright had taken over the tenancy of the Castle Hotel along with her husband three years previously, and noted that almost as soon as renovation work was approved, activity in the building increased. On three occasions bottles exploded in the bar, twice shattering their optics and on one occasion bursting in the hands of a member of staff. Electrical appliances began to break down, notably in the busy kitchen area, and many objects went unaccountably missing. Irene commented later that 'it got to the point where it was a good job we were closing, because nothing was working any more!'

During the Wright's tenancy, a 'sensitive' visited and felt that the building was haunted by up to four ghosts. She named one as a nurse called Agnes who had worked here in the time of Cromwell, and felt that she was located in the cellar. Pre-dating her visit, the ghost of a nurse had long been believed to haunt the premises, and a small private function bar to the right of the main entrance is known to have formerly been an early hospital morgue. The cellar became the site of frequent activity. A barman felt a hand being brushed gently down the back of his neck, although when he turned he found himself alone. In the same area, boxes of bottles are regularly moved from one particular spot to another without human aid, being discovered by the landlord and staff on numerous occasions. The unlocked cellar door was also unaccountably jammed in 1996, forcing the landlord to kick a hole in the panel, after which it swung gently open of its own accord.

Irene Wright caught sight of what she felt to be the ghost of Agnes, dressed in grey, mounting the stairs towards the gallery room during a staff meeting in the summer of 1996. Both she and other staff noted that ghostly activity at the time was seemingly accentuated when the haunting was discussed publicly. On one such occasion, furniture was heard being moved in an empty upstairs room, resembling the sound of a 'chair being scraped over bare floorboards'. Not only was there no chair in this room at the time, but the entire area was also carpeted from wall to wall. Two visiting auditors chatting about the disturbances were startled by a loud thump on the floorboards behind them, which made the floor vibrate to such an extent that they were convinced that 'somebody had jumped out' purposely to frighten them. Other inexplicable noises have been experienced by the kitchen staff; they were enjoying an after-hours drink one Sunday evening when they heard a large silver-service tray crash to the kitchen floor and vibrate loudly. Expecting to find that a shelf had fallen down, they entered the kitchen to find nothing out of place. Around the same time, a member of staff passed the dining-room and saw the chairs turned in and the fire built up ready for lighting despite the extreme heat of the day. Puzzled, he approached Irene and asked why, but when the pair returned to the dining-room the fireplace was laid with flowers and the chairs were turned out, just as Irene had left them.

A clairaudient visitor to the Castle Hotel in the summer of 1996 heard what she described as 'a gaggle of girls having a chatter and a laugh in whispers' at the entrance to the ladies' toilets. In the same area, the earlier 'sensitive' visitor, who had identified the ghost of Agnes, referred to an 'impish chattering' which she herself experienced here. Both visitors felt that the sounds ceased as soon as they entered the ladies' toilet itself. However, they were unanimous in their opinion that, despite the 'extremely haunted' feeling to the Castle Hotel, there was no truly malefic presence here.

Derbyshire psychic medium and author Wayne Anthony visited in August 1996 and toured the building, recording his impressions. He noted that 'certain rooms had a definite feeling of sadness about them. There was the strong presence of a child in the hotel, and the impressions I received suggested that the main two "haunted" rooms seemed to be the front room [the restaurant with the large fireplace] and the tunnels in the cellar. The "jilted bride" is probably just a resonant, a psychic echo. There are probably two genuine hauntings here. I thought that the "man in the pin-stripe suit" was a very angry presence. When I went into the front room the fire wasn't on but I felt that it was hot ... and there was definitely a presence which came and stood by the fire. I was aware of muffled talking and there was an awful feeling of sadness, as though this man still has unfinished business.'

Winnats Pass and Mam Tor Iron Age hill-fort are accessible for keen walkers all year round, with car-parking at the base of the Tor. Peveril Castle is administered by English Heritage and is open throughout the year. Peak Cavern, Treak Cliff and Speedwell Caverns operate guided tours throughout the season. For bookings: The Castle Hotel, Castle Street, Castleton, Derbyshire.

NINE LADIES STONE CIRCLE
Stanton Moor, Birchover

Rumours of Druidic rites and fairies dancing under the light of the full moon have been associated with this circle of tiny standing stones for centuries. Nine Ladies was once part of a burial site believed to contain over three hundred Early Bronze Age graves. Even into the 1990s, the area was reputedly avoided at night by locals who feared the spirits of the dead, said to linger here after dark. The area's Druidic connections (and hence the name of the nearby Druid Inn public house) are associated with the local Reverend Thomas Eyre, who some say practised withcraft here centuries ago. According to Derbyshire psychic medium Wayne Anthony, Nine Ladies is still 'pervaded by a sense of the supernatural', and visitors can expect to find any number of people dowsing with rods of ash for hidden water sources and ley lines which are said to run beneath the site.

Nine Ladies stone circle is managed by the Peak Park Joint Planning Board and English Heritage; entry is free.

Nine Ladies Stone Circle, Birchover

Derbyshire

RINGWOOD HALL HOTEL
Brimington, Chesterfield

Once the property of the Duke of Devonshire, this beautiful
period house, mainly dating from the early 1800s, was converted into a hotel in 1988. The hall and grounds are secluded
from public view by a range of ancient trees, and are reputedly
haunted by an unidentified Grey Lady and a phantom grey
horse. The animal is today seldom sighted, although its hoofbeats have been heard on a number of occasions. The recent
discovery of a well-concealed tunnel entrance, rumoured to lead
to Brimington church nearby, prompted a mining enthusiast to
offer a full exploration in the early 1990s. The explorer was
forced back after no more than a few yards by dangerous levels
of methane within the shaft. Ringwood Hall management today
offer any suitably trained person the opportunity to venture
into the tunnel, although they refuse to reveal the whereabouts
of its entrance to the general public. Poltergeist activity in a
local church during the mid-1990s fuelled speculation as to a
rumoured connection with the mystery tunnel.

The most commonly encountered ghost at Ringwood Hall is
that of the White Lady, who is believed to be Violet Markham,
a daughter of a former owner of the hall. Witnesses have
testified that the ghost bears a striking resemblance to a portrait
of Violet which hangs in the restaurant. Member of staff John
Ferguson regularly works in the restaurant area in which the
ghost is most frequently seen, and he has encountered her
himself a number of times, most often standing near the kitchen
door. John described how staff often point out a lone, fair-
haired woman who appears to be waiting to be seated, only to
find that she has disappeared when they take a second glance. It
is well known among hotel employees that a 'cold spot' lingers
in the area of the ghost's appearance.

The Hollingwood Room has also been the site for strange phenomena. In 1992, a lady staying in an adjoining suite complained to staff on reception that the people playing snooker next door were making far too much noise. She was horrified to be informed that the snooker table had been removed from the Hollingwood Room twenty years previously, and the room was currently empty.

For bookings: Ringwood Hall Hotel, Brimington, Chesterfield, Derbyshire S41 0DN.

SUDBURY HALL
Sudbury

The seventeenth-century Sudbury Hall, incorporating the Museum of Childhood, sits in splendour amongst traditionally landscaped gardens, close to the Staffordshire border. Its name translates as 'Southern Fort', recalling a period in history when a powerful stronghold existed at this most southern point of Derbyshire. Staff at the hall are well acquainted with rumours of two ghostly ladies said to inhabit the premises. Over the years, visitors to Sudbury have reported a woman in black who has appeared on the staircase, and an elderly lady in green velvet, who was last seen strolling into a dining-room. Neither ghost had ever been firmly identified, although it has been suggested that one could perhaps be Queen Adelaide, the widow of William IV, who once resided here. Administrator Robert Parker had his own strange experience in the early 1990s when trying to open a door which led to the boiler room. The door refused to open, although it was supposedly unlocked, so Mr Parker went to fetch a crowbar to break in. The door suddenly sprang open of its own accord. Shortly afterwards, a workman at the top of a ladder in the boiler room felt something tap him on the shoulder. He turned to find the room empty, and fled in fear. Mr Parker also has reason to suspect that a ghostly party from the past continues its revelry from time to time, after experiencing the sounds of mysterious chattering voices and music, although he has been unable to pinpoint the exact area from which they emanate.

Sudbury Hall (incorporating the Museum of Childhood) is administered by the National Trust, and opens to the public between 30 March and 30 September, Wednesday to Sunday and Bank Holiday Mondays 1 p.m. to 5.30 p.m. Picnic space is available, and there are occasional special events in the gardens.

ARBOUR LOW STONE CIRCLE AND GIB HILL BARROW
approx. 2 miles SE of Monyash

The neolithic monument of Arbour Low is known locally as the 'Stonehenge of Derbyshire', although its large limestone slabs, once believed to stand erect, now lie flat on the ground. Occupying an open field over 1000 feet above sea level, Arbour Low is believed to have been an early temple for sun worship, and the nearby Gib Hill Barrow is renowned as the largest barrow in Derbyshire. Human remains were unearthed here in the nineteenth century, and it is said that a man was once gibbeted on the earthwork, lending the site its present name. Local legend suggests that anybody hardy enough to spend the night within the stone circle will awaken spirits from the days of its construction more than four thousand years ago.

Arbour Low and Gib Hill Barrow are administered by English Heritage and the Peak Park Joint Planning Board, and are open

*at all reasonable times. Since the monument is situated on a
private working farm, dogs are not allowed and the owner of
the right of way requests a small donation.*

THE CITY OF DERBY

The historic city of Derby has more confirmed sightings of
ghosts than does its haunted counterpart York, a fact which
recently led Richard Felix, organiser of the Derby Ghostwalk,
to challenge York's self-appointed title of 'the most haunted city
in England'. As Richard explains: 'The history of Derby goes
back over two thousand years, rivalling that of York, and is just
as illustrious . . . In AD 917 the Battle of Derby was fought
between the Vikings and the Saxons, and was won by the Saxon
Princess Eathelflaeda. Mary Queen of Scots stayed in the city
shortly before she was executed, and Derby saw the last
hanging, drawing and quartering, the last pressing to death, and
the only peer of the realm to be hanged for murder. The city at
one time even had five prisons. The stories of sightings and
strange happenings which we have collected from people in
Derby total one hundred and fifty, all of which are first-hand
accounts. The city of York, by comparison, is quoted as having
only one hundred and forty *rumoured* sightings of ghosts.'

Ye Olde Dolphin Inn is situated in Queen Street, less than
200 yards from the cathedral, and is believed to be the oldest
public house in Derby. It is rumoured that, in days of old, a
particularly sinister Doctor kept practice in a building adjoining
the pub. With the help of two unscrupulous 'body snatchers'
who raided corpses from newly laid graves, he conducted
experiments on the dead, and dismembered bodies in his
basement. This basement is today the cellar of Ye Olde Dolphin,
where on a number of occasions the gas powering the beer

pumps has turned itself off without human aid. The assistant manager and bar staff regularly witness glasses which hang from hooks on a beam in the bar rocking themselves to and fro late at night, as they sit enjoying a late drink after closing. There have been several reports from customers and staff who have felt a 'strange presence' within the building, and a 'grey shape' has been spotted in a supposedly empty room, perhaps the fading ghost of a Grey Lady, a woman of unknown identity long rumoured to wander the premises.

The George Inn is the resting place for an ancient and battered skull which some believe to belong to a tenth-century warrior killed in the Battle of Derby. It was unearthed in 1993 during the digging of a new cellar foundation. Alongside the skull were scraps of leather and other bones, which proved to be animal in origin. Part of the skull has been severely damaged by what could conceivably have been an axe-blow. It is today kept safe in a niche behind the bar, although staff will gladly reveal it to the curious. The discovery of the skull hailed a number of strange happenings which have continued to the present day, including glasses exploding inexplicably into tiny pieces in the hands of female bar staff. One of the most dramatic events occurred when a guide dressed as a Viking was taking local schoolchildren on a tour of the ancient cellar. A loud crash was heard by all present, and when they returned upstairs they found that the bottle display in the bar had collapsed – despite the fact that the shelf on which it was balanced remained in its place.

Ye Olde Dolphin Inn and the George Inn are included in the Derby Ghostwalk, masterminded by Richard Felix of the Derby Heritage Centre.

THE CHESTERFIELD CANAL
Brimington, Chesterfield

Building of the historic Chesterfield Canal began in 1771, and within six years 46 miles of waterway had been completed. The canal's original purpose was to improve local goods transportation, which had previously been undertaken by packhorse trains. Today, scenic stretches of the canal provide wonderful walks, and a current restoration programme aims to return the waterway to its former functional self.

In the winter of 1993, local resident Arthur Skelhorn was walking his dog along the bank of the canal just off Cow Lane, where an outcrop of land interrupts its straight course. He noticed a very tall man, dressed in a long dark coat which trailed the floor, and a large top hat, standing several yards ahead of him. Arthur noted that his dog, who normally runs to greet strangers during her walk, would not leave his side. He also began to feel irrationally unnerved and very wary. The tall man walked on ahead, but when Arthur passed the outcrop of land he was astonished to find that the 150 yard straight towpath ahead was empty. Neither was there anybody on the embankment, and he noted that it would have been an impossibility for a person to have vanished without trace so suddenly.

Several months later Arthur Skelhorn recounted his experience to a friend who was involved with historical research into the building of the canal. He discovered that, when the canal was constructed, it was cut chiefly on a straight course through Chesterfield. However, near Cow Lane in Brimington, an outcrop of land could not be removed as it had been declared hallowed ground following the mass burial of plague victims here. Consequently the engineers excavated around the land, and the canal does not follow a straight course at this point. Over the years this became no more than a distant memory, and many locals today remain unaware of the existence of the former 'plague pit'. Arthur realised that his strange encounter with the vanishing man had occurred on this very outcrop of land.

The story, however, did not end there, for he was later told by a local resident of another sighting of 'a tall man in a long coat or cape wearing a top hat'. This had occurred twenty years previously, when the lady in question recalled how her son and a group of friends had burst into the house in terror one evening giving the same description of a mysterious figure who, she said, had instilled the same 'irrational fear' in them. This time, the unidentified man had been spotted on a lane behind King Street, close to the canal bank.

THE VILLAGE OF ASHOVER
near Chesterfield

The discovery of a Bronze Age beehive grindstone in the churchyard of All Saints at Ashover gives some idea of the antiquity of the site. Ashover was a lead and mineral mining centre from Roman times until the early twentieth century, and the nearby disused quarry is believed to be haunted. Its high crags provide a scenic walk, and locals have described how, after sundown, a powerful, inhospitable atmosphere can descend over the place. Ashover's Church of All Saints was built in the mid-1300s close to the site of an earlier religious house, and on a number of occasions local people passing the graveyard after dark have witnessed 'a robed monk' walking between the headstones. Local legend tells how Ashover farmer John Towndrow murdered his wife in 1840 by battering her to death with a hammer, and afterwards decapitated her before cutting his own throat. The ghost of a headless woman, visible only from the shoulders down, was regularly reported gliding through the

Carved chest from Ashover Church, haunted by a headless woman

church throughout the latter years of the 1800s, and was consequently assumed to be that of Towndrow's wife. Although a skull was discovered by workmen in a nearby hall towards the end of the last century, it is doubtful that this particular specimen belonged to the murdered woman.

Parts of the Crispin Inn, which is situated next to the church, are believed to date from 1350. Local records tell how several men of 'Asher' returned from the Battle of Agincourt, prompting Sir Thomas Babington to open an alehouse in honour of the survivors. Although Agincourt was fought on St Crispin's Day, it is believed that the pub took its name from the patron saint of cobblers (St Crispin), as the building formerly belonged to a shoemaker. In 1646, when Civil War divided the country, landlord Job Wall was locked out of the Crispin by rowdy Royalist soldiers whom he had tried to prevent from drinking more than their fill. When he was finally readmitted, his beer barrels were empty and not a penny was forthcoming from the lurching troops! A three-legged table (visible in old photographs of the Crispin which hang on the walls, and possibly the same item currently in the landlord's workshop) is rumoured to have been used by Cromwell to breakfast at, only hours before he beheaded a Royalist on what is now the Crispin Inn's car-park.

The phenomenal tale of the Crispin Inn's haunting was recounted by the current landlord David Spittal, who eventually enlisted the help of a spiritualist to identify the ghosts believed to haunt the premises. Sightings of a spectral monk within the building had been reported since before the 1970s, by numerous tenants and customers alike. One former landlord even testified to having seen a ghostly dog leaping from an upstairs bedroom window. When David Spittal and his wife Sue took over the Crispin in 1990, they quickly began to notice that small personal objects, such as jewellery and keys, would disappear and appear again at random. On one occasion David's soldering iron disappeared from his workshop, and after a thorough search, he bought a replacement, only to arrive home and find the original back in its place. A member of staff was alone one morning stoking the fire, when he ran out of the bar in terror insisting that 'something' had just walked past him. On another occasion, Sue Spittal heard the little handbell in the bar ringing, and, assuming that the barman was responsible, she entered the bar ... and found it empty. The Crispin Inn chief was also shocked one afternoon to see the figure of a monk materialising next to David, who, despite seeing nothing himself, simultaneously felt a 'cold shiver' run down his spine. Events were not confined to the lower area of the pub, however, as in the upstairs sitting-room the Spittals' three dogs would often wake suddenly at precisely the same time, staring at an area above the door and barking furiously. The couple were woken in the dead of night on several occasions by their three-year-old son 'talking to somebody'. Although he was alone in the room when they entered, the little boy would insist that he had been talking to 'the pirate man'.

When, in 1993, the Spittals were offered the services of a spiritualist in an attempt to lay their 'earthbound spirits' to rest, they were only too pleased to agree. A lady named Geraldine arrived from Birmingham, knowing nothing of the history of the pub or the village of Ashover, and began a tour of the many rooms in the building. Although her psychic impressions were astounding, several of them were later corroborated by certain historic truths of which she had no knowledge at the time. Geraldine detected no fewer than *seventeen* ghosts in the dining-room, the pool room, the ladies' toilet, the bottle store, the old stables, the cellar and the garage. She informed the Spittals that two Cavalier brothers from the Civil War period had been betrayed to the Parliamentarians in the inn, and had later been murdered and buried in the cellar. Unbeknown to Geraldine, forty years previously a flash flood had eroded the garden (the area of the old cellar) and had revealed two male skeletons dating from this period. In the tack room, at the rear of the Crispin, she sensed the spirit of a young girl, who had died from diphtheria in the 1700s when lodging with her family. Although her parents had moved on after her death, the family allegedly brought the plague to Ashover before dying themselves on the way to Lincoln. In the church next door, a great number of graves from the 1700s show that an epidemic did indeed sweep through the villagers of Ashover, sending a large number of them to an early grave.

When Geraldine identified the earthbound spirits of two

monks, the Spittals remembered the frequent sightings of a monk not only in the Crispin, but also in the churchyard next door. Although she alleged that one had been an unsavoury character in his lifetime, the other, named Bartholomew, had lived on the site around 800 and was not a menacing presence. Bartholomew's spirit was located near the bottle store, which is the oldest part of the building, and the Spittals opted to let him 'stay', having been assured that his only desire was to oversee the property. Geraldine also believed the Crispin to be haunted by an ex-landlord, whose illicit union with a local girl rendered him earthbound for his sins. She moved on to the stables, where she located the spirit of a horse ridden to death by a Nottingham man, who had once courted a lady of ill-repute said to live at the Crispin in former times. In the cellar she detected the ghost of an elderly lady who had fallen down a flight of steps and died shortly afterwards, being unable to get help. In the pool room, Geraldine recounted how the elder brother of the two betrayed Cavaliers had himself been executed after reporting their whereabouts to Parliamentarian troops, and that his spirit was bound to this spot.

The car-park at the rear of the Crispin is allegedly the site of another execution dating from the Civil War period. It is said that the Lord of the Manor of Eastwood Hall was tried in Ashover, before being beheaded here by Cromwell. As he had left his wife and young family to travel on alone, Geraldine felt that he could have somehow 'latched on to' the Spittals' young son . . . and, wearing a dark cape and feathered hat, may well have answered the description of a 'pirate man' in their son's eyes. Finally, in the club room, Geraldine pinpointed what she described as a 'sump of negative energy', which she believed created bad feeling amongst customers visiting the inn. Having already lit a candle, she requested help from one of the bystanders to dispel the powerful negative force which pervaded the area. Within hours of the ritual's completion, the Spittals noted that the atmosphere in the Crispin had become peaceful and warm ... and the bar area, frequently the scene of public arguments and minor brawls, suddenly became much quieter!

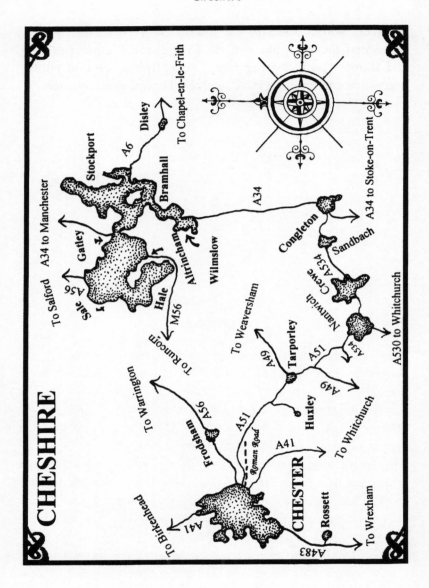

CHESHIRE

DUNHAM MASSEY HALL

Altrincham

The splendid former residence of the Earls of Stamford, the
Georgian cum Edwardian Dunham Massey Hall, sits in a
beautiful 250 acre deer park fronted by formal gardens. The
Tudor moat which surrounded an earlier manor built on the
site is still in use today, powering a Jacobean mill. Within the
house, visitors are welcomed into a great variety of rooms
displaying wonderful collections of silverware, paintings and
furniture. Several etchings of Lady Jane Grey, who was Queen
of England for nine days before her execution in 1554, indicate
her relationship to the Grey family who once resided here.
Thomas Grey, whose portrait hangs in the oldest wooden-
panelled hall, had the infamous claim to fame of signing the
death warrant of Charles I before Cromwell's signature was
added. Rather ironically, his portrait faces that of the unfortunate King himself. In 1946, Dunham Massey was visited by

George VI and Queen Elizabeth, who were entertained by the last Lord Stamford to dinner. On the way to the dining-room, the King saw Thomas Grey's portrait and proclaimed loudly, 'My God, Stamford, you've got a regicide on your wall!', at which the Earl pointed out appeasingly that, on the opposite wall, King Charles had also found his place at Dunham Massey.

One afternoon in the mid-1980s when Dunham Massey had only relatively recently opened to the public, members of staff alerted the assistant administrator Clive Alford to a small party of visitors who had rushed through the house at great speed before leaving. He managed to catch up with them in the grounds, and, concerned, enquired after their sudden departure. One lady member of the party proceeded to tell Mr Alford that as soon as she had entered the house to begin her tour, she had been assailed by 'voices from the past' which had all but deafened her. The visitor appeared to have psychic abilities which occasionally troubled her in historic buildings such as Dunham Massey. However, she had been determined to continue her tour until she approached the grand staircase, where, on reaching the first landing, she had seen a 'Victorian gentleman in a corduroy jacket with long hair'. The figure, whom nobody else in the party could see, beckoned to the lady, which prompted her decision to leave. She described to Mr Alford how on a number of occasions she had encountered similar phenomena and was always most perturbed by such events. Before the party left hurriedly, the psychic lady commented to Mr Alford that it was as though the spirit was 'asking for help' over some matter, although if this was the case, she never stayed long enough to find out.

The first-floor panelled Oak Room was used earlier this century as a guest room by the resident family, although prior to this it was believed to have been a study. No sinister secrets regarding its past are known, although this room is picked out by many visitors as the most 'atmospheric', and is also frequently felt to be 'more chilled' than any other room in the house. A former housekeeper noted that she would often smooth down the red silk bed cover on the four-poster, only to return moments later and find impressions on the material as though it had been climbed over. During the early 1990s two members of staff left cushions under tissue paper here while they went for lunch. When they returned the cushions appeared to have been trampled on. Clive Alford consequently became curious about the Oak Room's reputation, and in 1992 he prepared himself to stay overnight here. At around midnight Mr Alford awoke feeling extremely ill, and decided to leave the room as quickly as possible. Once outside he felt much better, although he declined to return. Ten years previously, a visiting member of staff staying in the Oak Room's four-poster bed was awoken in the middle of the night unable to move his limbs. At the foot of the bed three faces appeared to be looking at him, and within seconds he had been deposited roughly on the floor. On his next visit to Dunham Massey, this gentleman politely requested that he should be housed elsewhere in future.

Several members of staff have been approached by footsteps while polishing treasures in the larger show rooms, only to turn and find nobody there. Perhaps the most dramatic occurrence at Dunham Massey was witnessed by the two housekeeping assistants, who were one day preparing Lord Stamford's study for the beginning of the season, when the ornate circular ceremonial shield presented to him by a nobleman during his lifetime shot from the top of the bookcase and travelled at great speed across the room, before landing at the far side of the desk. Clive Alford points out that he himself secured the shield's handle to the wall with a cup hook to prevent it from moving.

Sightings are not restricted to the main body of the house

alone, having also occurred in the housekeeper's courtyard flat. One evening in 1990 her son was on his way out for the evening with a friend. As they made their way down the stairs, the young man in front briefly caught sight of a male figure, which he estimated to be over 6 feet in height, walking up the stairs towards him. The housekeeper's student lodger was told to 'mind the creaks' by a female voice when on her way to the bathroom in the small hours of one morning, despite the fact that the housekeeper was sound asleep at the time. Another curious encounter was described by a National Trust conservator, who stayed overnight in the top-floor flat of Dunham Massey during renovation work here in the early 1990s. The following morning she told staff that she had woken very early to find herself lying on her back, unable to move. As she breathed out, a man's laugh seemed to emanate from her mouth, lasting several seconds before she regained control of her limbs.

Dunham Massey Hall is administered by the National Trust, and is open to the public between 2 April and 30 October, Saturday to Wednesday, noon until 5 p.m.; the gardens are open daily.

THE LION AND SWAN HOTEL
Swan Bank, Congleton

A licensed building is known to have existed on the site of the Lion and Swan Hotel since 1496. Walling from the original building can today be seen exposed on the west side of the cocktail bar and is believed to date, in part, from the early 1400s. During the eighteenth century the hotel was a popular coaching inn for travellers *en route* to Manchester, and it was enlarged in the Victorian era. An interesting and antiquated feature within the hotel is the carved fireplace which sits in what is today the restaurant. Lions and abundant erotic-looking fruits are depicted along with four symbolic androgynous figures, on panels which it is believed once belonged to the ends of a traditional bridal bed. The detail possesses possible pagan overtones in its reference to fertility, and it has been suggested that a bed with such panels could once have been employed to aid the fertility of barren couples. The Lion and Swan's resident female ghost is believed to be connected in some way with the carving, being a young woman with brown hair, naked except for a pair of clogs and a broad smile, whose infrequent appearances have been noted to happen most often around the time of the new moon. Local legend claims that she died of a fever in the Middle Ages after drinking a fertility potion, and her ghost has only ever been noted in the dead of night tending to the fire underneath the beautiful carvings.

For bookings: The Lion and Swan Hotel, Swan Bank, Congleton, Cheshire CW12 1JR.

HIGHER HUXLEY HALL
Huxley, Chester

Higher Huxley Hall, a former manorial home whose lands are mentioned in Domesday, boasts a pedigree dating back to the thirteenth century. Each new generation of residents has added to and altered the building, which is still a working farm today; its current owners point out that it has been an exceptionally prosperous piece of land throughout its long history. Mr and Mrs Marks have lived at Higher Huxley for over thirty years, yet despite the great age of certain parts of their home, neither of them has any suspicions that it is haunted. Rather, it is the grounds in which the legendary phantom horse and horseman are said to appear.

Shortly after the turn of the nineteenth century, a tenant farmer named Salmon hanged himself from a beam in one of the farm buildings. The reason for his suicide has been lost with the passing of almost two hundred years, although the old oak beam from which he suspended the noose is still visible in an outbuilding to this day, carved with the name J Salmon and dated 1810, the year of his death. Following his suicide there was a spate of appearances of a ghostly man on horseback in the grounds, who was seen riding around the old horse-wash, always after midnight. The ghost was witnessed by farm labourers, and although the Marks have never encountered him themselves during many years in residence, they have been told by a local man that phantom hoofbeats can still be heard from the vicinity of the old horse-wash after dark.

Higher Huxley Hall caters for bed, breakfast and evening meal throughout the year. For bookings: Higher Huxley Hall, Huxley, Chester, Cheshire.

Phantom horseman of Higher Huxley Hall

LITTLE MORETON HALL
Congleton

Little Moreton Hall, former home of the Protestant Moreton family, dates from 1450, and is today regarded as the finest example of a moated timber-framed house in existence in the country. Extensive renovations were carried out here in the early 1990s, and visitors can enjoy a tour of the beautiful great hall and wainscoted long gallery, along with the private chapel and knot garden. There are many local stories of a secret underground tunnel attached to the building, which some say leads to Astbury church (2 miles to the north) and others, to a small copse a mile away. The fact that Little Moreton is moated would perhaps render these tales unlikely, although there are local people still living today who claim to have had first-hand knowledge of such a subterranean passage in their youth. Although the house does indeed have its own 'secret room' with sliding panelling, the Moretons and subsequent residents are believed to have used the niche as a bedroom and later a cheese store!

Little Moreton Hall was long rumoured to have been visited by Queen Elizabeth I in 1589, following Royal Doulton's use of an illustration depicting the Queen at the hall, which was reproduced on thousands of items. However, Royal Doulton seem to have been using a certain amount of artistic licence and marketing initiative, for in fact the Queen never visited Little Moreton.

Such an ancient timber-framed building as this naturally possesses more than its fair share of mysterious sounds. Although some members of staff suggest that many can be attributed to wind whistling around the eaves of the building, both they and their visitors have regularly reported the sounds of a sobbing child coming from the chapel. When they enter the chapel to trace the source of the noise, the area has always been found to be empty. The current property manager notes that this occurs regularly and has done so for a number of years. A former guide conducting a tour of the house in the early 1990s watched over the shoulder of her visitors as the figure of a woman appeared behind them and walked through the wall opposite, where there had formerly been a door. A similar mysterious female figure has been observed walking the long gallery on occasion, although there are no clues to her identity. In an attempt to discover whether Little Moreton's past would reveal anything which could lend substance to the mysterious sobbing child and the ghostly woman, members of staff undertook their own research into the history of the house. Intriguingly, they found no evidence of any legend or local folklore with which to associate the hauntings, and an all-night vigil undertaken by a local radio station in the chapel in 1994 failed to reveal any further unexplained happenings.

Little Moreton Hall is administered by the National Trust and is open between 26 March and 30 September, Wednesday to Sunday, noon until 5.30 p.m., and weekends from noon until dusk throughout October.

THE RED COW
Beam Street, Nantwich

When Libby Casson and her husband Nick took over the tenancy of the historic Red Cow public house in 1990, they were unaware that the building was believed to be haunted. The Red Cow comprises three different wings incorporating former cottages, the oldest of which dates from the fourteenth century, the fifteenth-century front wing, and the converted stable block.

Within the first few months of their tenancy, the Cassons noted small objects going missing and reappearing in unexpected places, and doors mysteriously opening and closing. When they had lived in the Red Cow for around six months, a gentleman visited one afternoon for dinner, and, just before leaving, announced to Libby, 'She won't hurt you, you know; she's part of the pub, one of the old landladies!' As the customer was leaving, Libby pursued him outside, intrigued to find out more, and discovered that he was a 'sensitive' named Stan who was receptive to psychic phenomena and had some experience in researching haunted properties. Stan told Libby that the ghost of a woman around thirty-two years of age was 'standing next to her with a baby in her arms', and said he felt that she had died in the Nantwich plague of the 1730s. He was unable to give any further impressions, including the identity of the ghost. Libby wasted no time in contacting the county archivist to find any information she could about residents of the building in the eighteenth century. Despite the fact that she was unable to give a name, the archivist quickly provided her with details of three women who could theoretically have fitted the details Stan gave of the young plague victim. The difficulty in narrowing the information down further was due to the fact that farmers and licensees buried during this century were recorded under the same section in county records, with nothing to differentiate between them. After Libby had taken up her research, both residents and staff of the Red Cow noticed that the spirit became increasingly 'lively', with more slamming doors, and objects appearing and disappearing more frequently than before.

Stan revisited the pub at Libby's invitation, and proceeded to use a method of 'dowsing' to search for the focus of the haunting. Next to the Red Cow itself is the cottage used for bed and breakfast guests, and Stan immediately approached the cottage wall through the function room and identified this area.

Libby had previously noted that on many occasions she had prepared fresh beds in the cottage only to return and find the clean duvets thrown on the floor. Libby recalled that, as Stan dowsed in the three upstairs rooms, his small ivory pendulum was spinning wildly. He then mentioned that one of the Cassons' daughters had an 'imaginary friend' named Amy. Libby was aware that her daughter talked of an invisible playmate named Amy, but was convinced that it was childish fantasy, although Stan had no previous knowledge of this. Soon afterwards she noticed that the little girl would stand in the living-room in front of the fire door and shout for Amy, and on one occasion Nick Casson watched in amazement as the heavy metal door opened itself in front of his daughter.

In 1991 two long-term guests lodged independently in the cottage, and it seemed apparent almost immediately that the young men had taken a dislike to each other. Each of them eventually confided in Libby that they were tired of being kept awake at night by the other, whose ceaseless pacing up and down and endless flushing of the toilet made it impossible for them to rest. Despite the fact that the rooms were both carpeted, the guests independently described footsteps echoing over bare floorboards. It was soon apparent that each of them was blaming the other for something which neither was responsible for. One of the young men left after six weeks, although the other stayed on for several months.

When Libby visited a medium who gave her details of the female ghost who haunted the Red Cow, she was slightly suspicious that information could easily have changed hands and that the lady may have been prepared for her visit. However, she became convinced when the medium described the Cassons' wolfhound Molly who had just died, giving an accurate and vivid picture of her habits which Libby felt she could not possibly have known. When the name Ann Salmon was attached to the ghost Libby remembered the three names which the archivist had given her earlier. One of them was indeed an Ann Salmon, who, according to records, had a young daughter named Amy.

In 1995, the Cassons were disturbed at two o'clock one morning by the downstairs interior doors of the Red Cow banging incessantly, despite the fact that the property had been securely locked for the night. Libby turned off the alarm and checked downstairs herself, convinced that an intruder had crawled in through one of the toilet windows. Although the windows were locked the activity had been so violent that she called the police, and within three minutes around ten officers had arrived. The Red Cow has been extended and altered a great deal over the centuries, and with five attics and numerous nooks in which an intruder could have hidden, the police conducted a thorough search. The present toilets are in part of the original cottage which once stood here, and when two policemen entered this area they instantly informed the Cassons that there was no intruder, it was a case of poltergeist activity, reassuring them that it was not the first time they had been called to a historic pub in Nantwich due to this type of phenomenon!

Stan had previously offered to 'calm down' the presence of the ghost believed to be Ann Salmon, although Nick Casson pointed out that she had been around for nearly three hundred years, and need not be 'removed'. Paranormal activity seemed to calm down for a while following his decision, although it was and still is noted to occur in cycles. A favourite catalyst seems to be the arrival of a new member of staff, upon which the Cassons are likely to find the kettle boiling away when the kitchen is opened first thing in the morning, and the renewed disappearance of objects and slamming of doors. During the author's research into the Red Cow in June 1996, a diary belonging to the Cassons with further information concerning the haunting had mysteriously disappeared from its shelf when Libby went to find it. They shared a joke that it would probably reappear somewhere as unlikely as the toilet, and within seconds a male member of staff, who had no knowledge of the conversation, was astounded to walk into the toilet and locate the missing diary. Within minutes of the diary being found, the chamber-maid reported the sudden appearance of a young woman with 'piercing face and eyes' who vanished quickly. It seemed that one of Ann Salmon's cycles of activity had begun again.

The Red Cow offers bed and breakfast throughout the year, and specialises in home-cooked food for which it is renowned throughout the county, featuring in several notable pub guides. For bookings: The Red Cow, Beam Street, Nantwich, Cheshire CW5 5NF.

HEATHERCLIFFE COUNTRY HOUSE
Frodsham, Warrington

Heathercliffe was built in the 1860s, its setting doubtless chosen for the caves, cliffs and natural rock gardens which pepper the surrounding land. Within its 10 acres of grounds sits the historic Beacon Hill, the highest point in the area, whose stone-carved Beacon Master's seat and steps were once used as a look-out post to scour the countryside for miles around. Nearby, an old sandstone quarry contains unusual carvings dating back to the mid-1600s. Due to the unique setting of this Victorian country house, Twentieth Century Fox used the location during January 1991 to film part of their full-length feature film *Robin Hood*, an event depicted by photographs on display inside.

Heathercliffe House showed no indication of being haunted until the 1970s. Before its transformation into a hotel, a group of students stayed here as guests and spent an evening playing with an Ouija board. They were disturbed during the night by 'something strange' and were so terrified by whatever it was they encountered that they fled the house, insisting that the local minister was woken in the dead of night to perform an 'exorcism'. It is unknown whether or not an exorcism did take place here, although numerous staff and guests, particularly the housekeeper and chamber-maids, today note a 'presence' in the rear wing of Heathercliffe, which they believe could be connected with the students' earlier misdemeanour. Objects are frequently moved around by an unseen hand in the kitchen area, and desserts have also been tipped unaccountably from the sweet trolley. Staff working upstairs often feel that they are being watched whilst in empty rooms, and the manager himself notes that a 'chilling sensation' can sometimes be felt in certain places in the rear wing. Although no definite sightings have ever occurred, the ghost is noted as rather more 'mischievous' than truly malefic.

For bookings: Heathercliffe Country House Hotel and Restaurant, Manley Road, Frodsham, Warrington, Cheshire.

LLYNDIR HALL HOTEL
Rosset, Chester

When Llyndir Hall was built in the early 1800s it was relatively modest in size, and it was not until its transformation into a hotel by the Celebrated Group in the 1980s that a further thirty bedrooms and a leisure club were added around the original building. Today, the hall, a Grade II listed building set in acres

of well-tended parkland, caters for leisure breaks and business
and training activities, and includes the highly acclaimed Garden
Restaurant.

Paranormal activity at Llyndir Hall began shortly after the
conversion, with guests and staff experiencing unaccounable
noises including hand-clapping and several sightings of the
ghost of a small, dark-haired, middle-aged woman. A former
member of staff who was staying at the hall overnight was
woken in the small hours to find a 'plump woman wearing a
white old-fashioned dress' looking down over his bed. Staff also
began to note that a number of guests asked to be moved out of
the Laurel bedroom, one of the older rooms, due to 'uneasy
feelings and unexplained noises' they experienced here. The
ghost was also seen several times in the Ash bedroom, believed
to be the oldest single room in the house.

In 1994, the restaurant manager himself caught sight of the
ghost in the Ash bedroom, and was able to identify her face as
that of an unknown woman in a portrait which today hangs in
reception. It seemed that the painting had always remained in
the house, although details of whom the subject was had been
lost with the passage of time. The identity of this lady remained
a mystery to staff, and a press release asking for anybody who
had further information on the hall's history to come forward
proved fruitless. However, in the spring of 1996, two 'sensitive'
volunteers from the Chester Psychic Centre offered to visit
Lyndir Hall to give their own opinions. Both psychics independently agreed that the spirit was that of a former resident who
seemed reluctant to leave, and that her presence was not malefic.
One psychic described the ghost as a 'plump lady with dark hair
and Victorian clothes', adding that 'she seems a bit domineering
and I suspect that this was once her house'. She located two of
the older bedrooms as the focus for the haunting, and testified
to having seen the image of the lady appear in a bedroom

mirror. As the spirit was believed to be harmless no further action was recommended, and today, both staff and guests appear to be happy living alongside their resident from former times.

Llyndir Hall Hotel offers weekend leisure breaks and a variety of theme evenings on a monthly basis. For bookings: Llyndir Hall Hotel and Restaurant, Rossett, near Chester LL12 0AY.

THE BLUE BELL INN
Northgate Street, Chester

The Blue Bell is the oldest surviving domestic building in the city of Chester and the only intact medieval inn here. It is believed that a Norman building stood on this site which, during the eleventh century, welcomed pilgrims travelling to the Abbey of St Werbergh. The first ale-licence on record is dated 1494, when the pub was known as the Bell. During this period, next-door Bell Yard was the site of the city's curfew bell, which tolled to warn strangers that the city gates were about to close. This beautiful historic building has been threatened twice in recent years with demolition in the name of 'road-widening schemes'. On both occasions it was saved by the dedicated campaigning of Chester residents.

The Blue Bell's resident ghost is known to staff as Henrietta, and is believed to be the sweetheart of a Royalist soldier who lodged here during the Civil War. On the eve of the Battle of Rowton Moor, which was fought in September 1645, Henrietta walked to the upstairs window to wave her soldier goodbye. The young man never returned from the battle, and, by nightfall Henrietta had taken her own life in the cellar. Traditionally, her ghost is to be seen climbing the cellar steps, walking through the upstairs restaurant, and peering out of the same window through which she waited for her love to return centuries before. However, Henrietta would in reality appear to be far more energetic than the legend suggests, being spotted everywhere from the kitchen to the cellar so frequently that witnesses are no longer alarmed. Staff are accustomed to her presence, and point out that even first-time visitors who are unaware of the legend have seen the ghost or felt 'something invisible' brush past them.

BRAMALL HALL
Bramhall, Stockport

Bramall Hall's name today differs slightly from that of its surrounding area, since a former owner favoured a more 'historically accurate' spelling for the estate than that used for the nearby settlement. The manor of 'Bramale' was recorded in Domesday, although the estate was only ever owned by three families over an eight-hundred-year period. Bramall Hall is built principally in the traditional Cheshire 'black and white' oak-and-plaster style; the oldest fourteenth-century parts of the building are today integrated with a collage of building styles spanning several hundred years. In 1935 the house was sold to the local district council and opened to the public for the first time the following year, since when it has welcomed tens of thousands of visitors who come to see the historic mixture of renovated medieval, Tudor and Victorian architecture. Mysterious filled-in and inaccessible doorways, 'hidden' paintings in the chapel and ballroom, and traces of earlier medieval layout make Bramall Hall a fascinating historic 'patchwork quilt' of styles and eras. Its artistic treasures include stained glass, portraits, wood-carving, furniture and beautiful plasterwork;

visitors can also see the refurbished Victorian kitchen and over 60 acres of parkland with its woodland walks, two lakes and formal gardens.

The legendary 'Red Rider of Bramall Hall' is said to have been a weary traveller who rode into the courtyard late one stormy New Year's Eve during the 1630s. He wore a bright red hood and cape which billowed out behind him in the wind. The gentleman was invited inside for rest and refreshments and was

The Ballroom, Bramall Hall, visited by the Red Rider on New Year's Eve

then promised a room for the night. However, the following morning, William Davenport, the then owner of the house, was found dead on the floor of the medieval great hall, and the mysterious traveller had vanished. The Red Rider was never found. Hundreds of years later, people local to the area of Cheshire continue the tale that a figure in a billowing red cape can be seen riding into the courtyard of Bramall Hall on each anniversary of William Davenport's murder, New Year's Eve.

In his poem 'The Maid of Bramall Hall', John Leigh recounts the story of a local girl whose lover was murdered by robbers in Macclesfield Forest, and whose ghost is reputedly the lady in white 'who appears to entertain an affection for the Plaster Room and Paradise Room' (also known as Dame Dorothy's bedroom). Although the White Lady of Bramall has not been encountered for some time, the Plaster Room would still appear to be a focus for activity within the building. In the early 1990s, a carpenter and his young asistant were working here constructing a display case for the Davenport Table Carpet, an enormous piece of embroidery. The carpenter was positioned at the top of a pair of step-ladders when he felt the jar of nails he was holding in one hand suddenly forced upwards out of his grip. His young assistant looked on as the jar was pushed from his hand and seemingly flung to the floor. A Bramall guide who spoke to the pair shortly afterwards witnessed for herself how shaken they were by the event. In 1994, a senior guide who arrived at the hall before opening one Sunday morning was asked by the caretaker to accompany him upstairs with a friend's dog. The caretaker gave no clue as to why, but the guide followed as he and the dog led the way. When they approached the Plaster Room from the Withdrawing Room the dog suddenly froze, and, to use the words of the guide, 'cowered in terror'. No amount of persuasion could entice it to enter the room. Even a trip round the house in the opposite direction, approaching the Plaster Room from the Nevills' Room, was to no avail, for the dog still refused to enter.

Charles Nevill, the late Victorian owner of Bramall Hall, planned to extend the family chapel and reopen it. Although he acquired an organ he unfortunately never achieved his aim, and the chapel remained closed. An account written by Alfred Burton, a friend of Nevill, indicates that on two occasions Nevill 'heard the most entrancing music proceed from an organ he had placed in the chapel'. He at first suspected that his wife was playing, although on trying to enter he found the doors locked.

Although there have been a number of sporadic sightings by visitors of 'an apparition' at Bramall Hall, many have been insubstantial in their detail. However, several years ago a visitor reported seeing a figure passing through a certain wall, which, when the panelling was removed more recently during renovation work, was found to conceal an early doorway.

Bramall Hall and Park are administered by Stockport Metropolitan Borough Council, and are open to the public Monday to Saturday 1 p.m. to 5 p.m. between Good Friday and 30 September; Tuesday to Saturday 1 p.m. to 4 p.m. and Sundays 11 a.m. to 4 p.m. between 1 October and 1 January; weekend afternoons only between 2 January and Good Friday. The Stables Tea Rooms are open daily throughout the year. Bramall Hall is licensed for civil marriage ceremonies and caters for wedding receptions, corporate events, education-linked events and group visits out of normal open hours. For bookings: Bramall Hall, Bramhall Park, Bramhall, Stockport SK7 3NX.

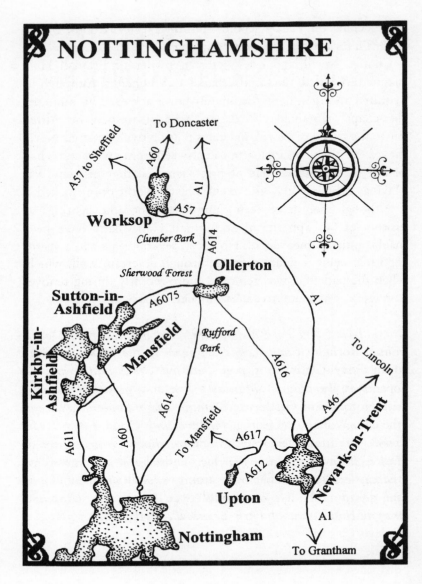

NOTTINGHAMSHIRE

NOTTINGHAM CASTLE
Nottingham City Centre

Castle Rock is riddled with a multitude of man-made subterranean tunnels dating from 1300 onwards, many of which were opened to the public for the first time in 1994. Atop the Rock sits Nottingham Castle itself, commanding superb views over the city. William the Conqueror built the original castle here in 1068, although the existing building was constructed by the Duke of Newcastle in 1679. One hundred and fifty years later, the castle was set alight by rioting townsfolk campaigning for the right to vote. It was not until 1875 that Nottingham Castle was restored to its current grandeur, preparing it to become today's City Museum.

The accounts of a Victorian architect describe locals being disturbed by ghostly singing in the castle ruins, a child's weeping spectre, and stones throwing themselves from the crumbling masonry at passers-by. It seems that the old ghosts have faded

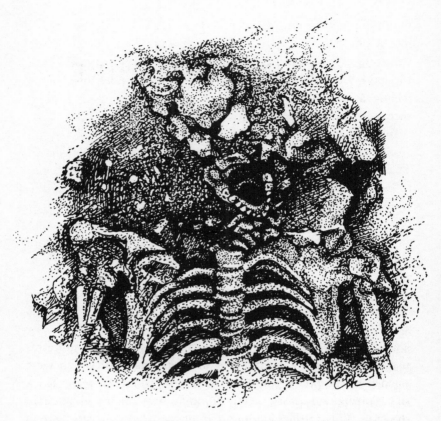

An unknown Civil War victim revealed at Nottingham Castle

from the castle with the passage of time, for modern supernatural experiences here are of an even more intriguing nature. In 1970, a security guard and his colleague were on night patrol when they witnessed a glowing white light, the size and shape of a football, appear from out of a wall at the far end of the long gallery, which today houses a fine art collection. The object began to bounce in a perfect arc, nearing them slowly, at maximum height almost touching the high ceiling. It then faded into a bluish smoky haze and formed a perfect cylinder before vanishing. The witnesses reported static crackling throughout the gallery during the whole process; one described his tongue feeling as though it had 'touched a battery', and never fully recovered sensation in it thereafter.

In 1993, a castle attendant noticed an elderly man, sitting alone in the long gallery, who appeared to be most disconcerted. The attendant approached him to enquire after his health, only to be told of an unusual encounter this man had had during the war. The man confessed to feeling extremely uncomfortable at being once more at the scene of his earlier experience, the long gallery. He had been stationed at Nottingham Castle with the air force. One night he and a colleague had approached the long gallery from the stairway and felt a strange atmosphere in the room, as though it were 'crackling with static'. The pair were forced to duck as two bright turquoise fluorescent 'hoops' of light whirled out of a wall at the far end of the gallery and skimmed towards them. The hoops, 6 feet in diameter, disappeared through the opposite wall. Again, the gentleman recounting the tale reported having felt an electric shock in his tongue, and claimed never to have had normal sensation in it since. The attendant listened in fascination to his story, and consequently undertook his own research into Nottingham Castle. Local records confirm that, when the air force was billeted in the castle, there were a number of reports of 'strange noises' being heard within the building late at night, of men's hair being pulled as they lay in bed, and of door handles rattling mysteriously.

A security guard locking up at closing time in 1992 followed a woman in black into one of the small galleries next to the long gallery, only to find that she had disappeared without trace. A similar experience was reported in the same year by an attendant who encountered a young girl in modern dress staring intensely at him from the far landing, before she vanished. The doors had only just been unlocked for the morning, and telephone calls to other staff on the site assured the attendant that nobody had, in fact, entered the castle. On telling his story to a colleague, he found that he was not the only one to have seen a mysterious teenager answering to the same description appear and disappear suddenly without trace when the area was believed to be empty.

Guided tours of Nottingham's caves are available throughout the year; Nottingham Castle Museum is open to the public daily from 10 a.m.

CLUMBER PARK AND SHERWOOD FOREST
Worksop and Edwinstowe

Clumber Park, to the north of Sherwood and formerly part of the Duke of Newcastle's estate, lays claim to possessing the longest double lime avenue in Europe, and provides forest walks and bike trails similar to those of its counterpart, Sherwood. The park features the foundations of the now demolished Clumber House, which fronted the lake until its destruction in 1938, a victim of high taxation which its proprietor could ill afford. A fine Gothic Revival chapel, dating from 1889, has fortunately remained undamaged, adjacent to the area of the former house. In the late 1980s, a local couple were picnicking at twilight close to the chapel when they became aware of a rustling sound coming from nearby bushes. Curious as to the source of the noise, as they believed themselves to be alone in the area, they waited . . . and were amazed to see a lady dressed in a floor-length, old-fashioned crinoline appear from behind the foliage before vanishing suddenly.

The mysterious woodland of Clumber Park

In the mid-1980s, a group of local picnickers were preparing to leave Clumber Park at dusk when they were pursued by 'a single, brilliant white light' along one of the more secluded roads. The driver, Phil Moore, initially suspected that a Trust warden was approaching to move them on, and accelerated away quickly. The light soundlessly matched his speed and suddenly appeared directly behind the vehicle. One of the passengers riding in the back of the van lost consciousness when it appeared frighteningly close to the window. It vanished just as suddenly as it had appeared, leaving the road empty and no other vehicle or person in sight.

In 1992, a single bright white light followed a local man's vehicle at high speed along the A616 (this road is one of several which intersect Clumber Park estate), before soundlessly veering off into an area of forestry plantation. Its glow was so intense that the driver was able to feel heat on the back of his neck as it approached. Just before the light disappeared into the forest, the driver recalls feeling that an 'object' had touched the rear of the car, jolting it slightly. On three further occasions when driving home from work, he witnessed sparks of blue light flashing over the exterior of his car on the same stretch of road. On each occasion the engine lost power, the radio began to falter and the headlights dimmed. A subsequent visit to a garage proved that there was no mechanical fault with the vehicle.

Sherwood's historic Major Oak, once known as the Queen Oak, is estimated to be around a thousand years old, and is the focus for much folklore. Legend tells how the outlaw Robin Hood and his band successfully evaded capture by the Sheriff of Nottingham, when they hid in its hollowed-out centre. Many other locations in the North Midlands are also associated with Robin and his Merry Men. Little John's grave is to be found in Hathersage, Derbyshire, from which a 29-inch thigh bone was exhumed by excavators in 1784. Although the bone was kept on display for a while, it was later reinterred. When Captain Shuttleworth re-excavated the grave in the early 1800s, once more removing the bone, he broke his leg in a hunting accident soon afterwards, and continued to suffer so much misfortune that he later reburied it on the advice of a village wise woman. Little John's yew longbow, which once hung in Hathersage church, was removed to Cannon Hall in Barnsley in the nineteenth century. Edwinstowe's Church of St Mary is rumoured to have witnessed the nuptials of Robin and Maid Marion on King Richard's return from the Crusades. St Mary's as it stands today was built in 1175, and possesses a fine collection of historic woodwork carved from the great oaks of Sherwood, and a 'Forest Measure' (thought to be an ancient ruler for measuring land) on the wall of the north aisle. The nearby historic market town of Mansfield displays a plaque on a tree to mark the legendary centre of old Sherwood.

Clumber Park and Sherwood Forest, administered by the National Trust and Nottinghamshire County Council respectively, are open to the public throughout the year. A nominal parking fee is charged in each during the tourist season. St Mary's church, in Edwinstowe, is open from April to October.

UPTON HALL
Upton, Newark

The Elizabethan manor which once stood on the estate of Upton was upgraded in 1830 under the direction of Thomas Wright, High Sheriff of Nottingham, to become the splendid Grade II listed building to be seen here today. The hall is home to the British Horological Institute, the society of watch and clock-makers, and is a registered museum as well as a training ground for those interested in the craft.

During World War II, Upton Hall was occupied by a school

for the blind which had been evacuated from the London area. In 1945 St Joseph's Roman Catholic Theological College transformed the house into a training centre. An elderly gentleman who worked here during this time recalled that the premises were haunted by a White Lady who was initially seen in a room which is today the library. When the order of the Holy Ghost Fathers took over the house, she was seen again, but this time in the college chapel. The ghost appeared to remain dormant for a while with no more sightings being reported for a number of years. Then, in the summer of 1996, a member of the Horological Institute staff visited the library alone to deposit some papers. She suddenly felt that somebody was close behind her, and turned around quickly, noting a strange swishing sensation as she did so, as though whatever was present attempted to avoid her gaze. Only a month earlier the caretaker's wife had been descending the rear staircase alone when she had encountered a dark-clothed man passing her in the same direction. The man never reached the bottom of the stairs, and on investigation the corridor proved to be empty, and the doors were still locked.

Upton Hall, the British Horological Institute, is open to the public every afternoon except Saturday between Easter and 31 August from 2 p.m. to 6 p.m. Group visits may be booked on other occasions. Special open days occur at the start and end of British Summer Time, during which the public are invited to bring in clocks and watches to discuss with the resident panel of experts.

WORKSOP PRIORY GATEHOUSE
Worksop

In the early twelfth century, William de Lovetot, owner of Worksop Castle, founded an Augustinian priory whose gatehouse today remains intact, close to the market place in Worksop town centre. Much of the priory was pulled down during the Dissolution in the late 1530s, although the gatehouse remained and the ruined Lady Chapel was restored in 1922.

At the turn of the century it was well known among locals that a 'figure in white' could be seen to walk through the perimeter fence of the gatehouse on certain nights of the year. The phenomenon became so popular that a sketch of the ghost was reproduced on pre-war postcards of Worksop. The original perimeter fence was removed many years ago, and as the town expanded, sightings of the ghost seemed to decline. However, in 1970, when the gatehouse formed part of the Abbey girls' school, there was a popular belief among the students that the ghosts of a Blue Lady and a monk were in residence. On one occasion a youngster passed out in the toilets after witnessing what she described as 'a white feather floating past her'.

Reported sightings of the ghost began again in 1988, when a local teenager claimed to have seen the 'blue' figure of an elderly lady with an unhappy expression on her face walking in the priory gardens behind the gatehouse. Another local witness reported feeling a 'presence' in the grounds and saw 'something sitting in a tree'. He was unaware that, according to tales which were being told by the girls of the Abbey school around twenty years earlier, the ghost of the Blue Lady was indeed reputed to sit in the branches of a crooked tree in the grounds.

Worksop Priory Gatehouse contains an art gallery which is open to the public at selected times throughout the week (further information is available from Worksop Tourist Information Centre, based in the town library).

THE SALUTATION INN
Houndsgate, Nottingham

The thirteenth-century Salutation Inn was built above a cave system of eighteenth-century origin, which was formerly an ancient dwelling. Parts of the public house itself date back to 1240, making it one of the oldest surviving buildings in the city of Nottingham. Accounts from staff and customers indicate that at least four different ghosts have been encountered here over a period spanning many years. Regulars drinking in the main bar claim to have been startled by the figure of a 'highwayman' wearing a black tricorn hat, who is to be seen rushing out of a wall before stopping close behind the nearest unsuspecting drinker and vanishing. The ghost of a Civil War soldier carrying a dated firearm through the cellar caves once paused to offer a young boy on a tour a bite from his apple. The most mysterious spectre in residence is that of an unidentified man dressed in white, whose legs appear to be 'bound'. However, the Salutation's best-known ghost is that of a little girl nicknamed Rosie, who is believed to have been tragically mown down by a horse and cart outside the inn in the seventeenth century. Rosie's ghost is blamed for playing tricks in the premises, such as throwing stones down the stairs and stealing small items. Danny and Linda Shaw-Andrews took over the tenancy of the Salutation in 1996, and noted that within weeks personal belongings, particularly vital keys, were vanishing and reappearing at random. The couple on one occasion even changed all the locks before discovering their missing keys on top of the bar. Another set of keys, which had been missing for eleven weeks, reappeared in the bath on the day that renovation work was approved for the pub.

Today, the Shaw-Andrews allow any interested visitors to tour their cellar caves, and the courageous may even volunteer to spend the night locked in! According to recent witnesses, the caves are the focus for regular sightings. A woman visitor saw the ghost of Rosie sitting on the steps leading up into the pub during a tour in the summer of 1996. That autumn, a group of four young people overnighting here encountered the phantom soldier. They had no previous knowledge of this ghost as its appearance had not been noted for some twenty years.

Of the rooms above the haunted cellar, cleaning staff feel that the top bar has a peculiar atmosphere, and the landlord notes that after locking up on certain evenings he often experiences the feeling that he is not alone. His young niece also regularly speaks of seeing 'a man' in one of the bars when it is supposedly empty. In the private flat upstairs, a member of the family once saw a pair of legs disappearing round a corner. She followed and found the area empty, the only sign that somebody had passed through being a cup of coffee which had been knocked over on to the floor.

THE BEESTON-MANSFIELD ROAD

British ghostlore is peppered with stories of 'ghostly re-enactments' of events which happened long ago. Civil War battles, infamous shipwrecks and funeral processions, to name but a few, have been reported in various parts of the country, long after they originally happened. Witnesses often note that such re-enactments appear to be solid and very real, such as the bedraggled legion of Roman soldiers returning from a campaign described by Harry Martindale in York (see the section on

North Yorkshire). Such hauntings are often cyclic, since many recur either on or close to the anniversary of the original event.

Just as mysterious are occasions when witnesses believe themselves to have seen an episode not from the past but from the future. Precognition of this kind often foretells a natural or man-made disaster. Some theorists have put forward the suggestion that, for a reason unknown, a 'window in time' can sometimes appear which allows an unsuspecting witness to glimpse in brief either the past or the future. Herein lies a possible explanation for the following story, which is recounted by Mansfield resident Kerry Barnett:

'It was November 1994, and I'd been working late. I was working in Beeston [Nottingham] at the time. We'd been doing some fridge cleans and I was the person who was looking after the store. I'd locked up when we finished, and I'd taken four of the women home. Afterwards I was driving home in the dead of night at around 2.30 or 3 a.m. It was a very cold misty night, not properly foggy, but you couldn't see very well ahead. I was travelling along my normal route on the road I usually go on, driving through the mist, when I saw ahead that there was something happening. I could see shadows and people. I slowed down and as I drew closer I could see that an accident had happened. I came to a standstill, because I could see a police-woman in front of me, although she didn't have a yellow coat on. She was just dressed in a black uniform even though it was the middle of the night. She was standing inches away from my windscreen, waving me on with her hand. In front of me was a car which had hit the iron railings by the side of the road. It was smashed up, and I could see where another car had hit it, although it had obviously been towed away. There was no ambulance and I didn't see either of the drivers around, so I presumed an ambulance had already left the scene and had taken them away. There was no police car, either, just another policeman, and he was at the other side facing the other way towards the oncoming traffic. There were four cars coming in the opposite direction, and he was waving them on. They were passing me and yet the policewoman on my side was waving me on as well. If I'd actually done what she said and carried on, I would have crashed into the other motorists coming in the opposite direction. I didn't. I sat there shaking my head saying, "No, no!" because if I had moved I would have hit another car. She carried on waving me on! I waited till the other cars had gone and then I did go round. I carried on past the accident and I looked back in my mirror, but I couldn't see anything there, although at the time I put it down to the mist. So I drove home.

'The next morning I had to be at work for 9 a.m. I was on the same stretch of road again no more than five hours at the most later, and I decided to look and see if there was anything of the accident still there. I knew where the exact spot was because I had sat and waited there for a couple of minutes for the other cars to pass. I looked, but I saw nothing there at all. The railings were straight, not bent. They hadn't been replaced overnight because they still looked old – the paint was chipped off them, and they looked just like they always had done. There was no broken glass, there was nothing on the road, and there was no sign that there had been an accident there the night before. Of course, I had thought nothing of it at the time, but when I thought back I realised that the police present had not been wearing yellow coats despite the fact that it was pitch black and misty – and they were just standing there in their black uniforms. And there had been no police car.

'I can still remember the policewoman's face – she had short bobbed hair and olive skin. The policeman had short hair and a beard. I wish now that I could remember more details about her uniform, but I can't. The four cars coming the other way which were waved on by the policeman had been going fairly slowly anyway because of the mist, but I realised afterwards that I hadn't seen them brake further when they saw the accident. They just carried on at the same speed, almost as though they had seen nothing at all. Thinking back, at the time there had been no car behind me. I realised afterwards that perhaps if another driver had been behind me and hadn't seen anything, he would have pipped the horn when I stopped. When I later told the story, it was suggested that perhaps I had "witnessed" an accident which happened in the past or even in the future.'

Witnesses to ghosts and other phenomena are often in a 'receptive' state of mind at the time, perhaps being relaxed or tired; they may describe themselves as 'having nothing on their minds'. Kerry Barnett concluded by adding that 'at the time I had been extremely tired and my mind was nowhere in particular – I hadn't really been thinking about anything at all.'

NEWSTEAD ABBEY
Kirkby-in-Ashfield

The medieval priory of Newstead was founded by the Black Canons in 1170, being converted into an expansive family home following the Dissolution in the sixteenth century. Despite being home to the Byron family for many generations, Newstead still retains many of its original monastic features. Visitors can see the interior of the house and also its grounds, which cover over 300 acres and include waterfalls, lakes and ornamental gardens. Newstead is today best remembered as a former home of the poet Lord Byron, whose famous monument to his old dog Boatswain is situated within the grounds. Inside the house itself, Lord Byron's personal quarters, along with larger family rooms such as the salon and the great hall, depict a life of wealth and splendour which was the privilege of former occupants.

Tales of the spectral 'black friar' are still recounted by staff, although no recent sightings have been reported. A doctor is said to have once lost his way in Newstead's grounds when visiting a resident who was shortly to give birth. He was directed through the park by a black friar whom he came across unexpectedly, although when he arrived safely at the house he discovered that there was no religious order in the area, and Newstead's black friars had not been in residence for several hundred years. Superstitious belief also tells that the sighting of the black friar is a warning of impending doom, since the ghost is believed to have been seen by Byron shortly before his unhappy marriage to Anne Milbanke. The ghost of 'little Sir John' was encountered by numerous servants in the last century, most often sitting underneath his own portrait, reading. New-stead Abbey's White Lady is believed to be Sophia Hyett, a bookseller's daughter who was a tenant of Byron's. The deaf spinster, who was unable to speak, fell in love with her landlord. She was forced to leave her home on the estate in the early 1800s when she became too poor to pay the rent, but she only got as far as Nottingham when she was killed by a coach and horses. The coachman who mowed her down was unaware that her deafness prevented her from hearing his approach.

The poet's beloved dog Boatswain has also reputedly made an appearance from time to time, having been spotted darting across the roads around Newstead before vanishing. Matthew Lovett, who was a child when his father worked as a night security guard in the house in the early 1980s, witnessed a shadowy figure passing through the corridor outside the guards' office late one night when he had accompanied his father to work. He recalls watching the drapery hanging on either side of the corridor billowing although there seemed to be no draught; this was followed by the sensation of an icy chill as the figure walked out of one wall and through another. More recently, in

1995, a member of staff described how a heavy garden roller resting unattended on one of the lawns 'moved itself' a considerable distance overnight!

Newstead Abbey is administered by Nottinghamshire County Council, and is open to the public from April until October, from noon onwards. The grounds and restaurant are open throughout the year.

YE OLDE TRIP TO JERUSALEM
Brewhouse Yard, Nottingham

The Trip to Jerusalem, one of the oldest public houses in the country, with a pedigree dating back to the eleventh century, nestles at the foot of Nottingham Castle. It reputedly took its name after pilgrims *en route* to the Holy Land frequented a brewing-house on the site, situated in the original Norman castle stores. Secret passages from the pub's cellar bury deep into its sandstone surrounds, along with others which link up with the castle above. A former security guard reputedly encountered the spectre of a knight on horseback in one such cave, which was later discovered to have been used during Norman occupation as a stabling area. The ghost of the traitor Roger Mortimer is said to haunt a cave known as Mortimer's Hole, named after Edward III used it to enter Nottingham Castle secretly in 1330, to secure the arrest of his mother Isabella's lover. The entrance to the Hole is reputedly within the Trip to Jerusalem itself. Thoroton's seventeenth-century history of the town of Nottingham states that '*the rock-yard into which the last and lowest gate of Mortimer's Hole opens is called in old writings the brewhouse of the castle...*' It has long been rumoured that Queen Isabella haunts the top bar, close to

Mortimer's Room, a small niche in the pub, although her ghost has not been seen in living memory.

Cellarman Dave Clark vouches for the fact that the pub does indeed have a mysterious presence, although he believes it to be benign. Gas taps are turned off in the cellar, and small items are moved around (including sums of money which have been rediscovered later in locked drawers). The most common experience is that of phantom perfume which permeates the back room, and pipe-smoke which hangs thickly in the top bar when nobody has actually been smoking. The landlady experienced 'something cold' pushing past her in the 'condemned cell' of the cellar, although the presence itself can often be quite helpful, turning on lights in the flat before the person entering has had time to reach the light switch.

The 'cursed galleon' (a small metal ship hanging in an upstairs room) came to public attention in 1995, when alterations meant that it had to be removed. According to local legend, the last two people to clean the ship, one of whom did so in the 1960s, died shortly afterwards. When an architect touched it in 1989, he suffered a broken femur within days. Two psychics visited the pub in 1995 to form their own impressions, although only one believed the galleon to be genuinely cursed. Workmen involved in the renovations refused to touch the ship, forcing the tenants to look for an eager volunteer . . .

RUFFORD COUNTRY PARK AND ABBEY
Ollerton

The Cistercian abbey at Rufford was founded by Gilbert de Gant in the mid-twelfth century, becoming a prosperous establishment which owned a number of large farms in the area. Rather at odds with the assumed wealth of the brethren are

Rufford Abbey is haunted by a skull-faced monk

records which tell that two monks were charged with highway robbery in 1317, less than forty years after one of the brotherhood here was arrested for murder. The abbey and its lands were granted to the 4th Earl of Shrewsbury by the King shortly after the Dissolution. The estate passed into the hands of the Savile family by marriage, and a new house was built, incorporating the remains of the ancient monastic structure, in the late seventeenth century. It remained a family home until financial hardship forced its sale during the war, and as the house was deemed unsafe, most of it was pulled down in the 1950s. After extensive archaeological exploration to reveal the original layout of the site, the lay brothers' frater is now open to the public. The beautifully landscaped grounds including a lake and woodland were designated a country park in 1969, and a craft shop and restaurant have been incorporated into the former working buildings on the estate.

Rufford Abbey's most infamous ghost is that of a huge monk with a grinning skull under his cowl, traditionally seen descending a staircase or roaming the grounds. This omen of doom reputedly caused the death of a local man many years ago; according to the parish register of nearby Edwinstowe, he 'died from fright' after encountering the terrifying spectre. The unfortunate man's final resting place is Ollerton churchyard. During the time Rufford was requisitioned for the war effort, a warrant officer encountered the monk and is said to have gone 'mad with fear'. A separate incident occurred when a member of the Coldstream Guards watched a ghostly figure appear, from the knees up, on the main staircase, causing him to topple backwards and injure himself quite seriously. Later investigation revealed that the original staircase had indeed been at a lower level.

Many gruesome stories are attached to Rufford, although how many began in truth can only be guessed at. The ancient well which still exists in the old kitchen (formerly private accommodation) supposedly holds a terror so great that one investigator, who braved its depths during the nineteenth century, is said to have returned to the surface raving mad. A slab of flooring in the chapel which always seemed to be damp was removed for repair around the turn of the twentieth century, to reveal the remains of an unknown victim who appeared to have been shot. Certainly, a great number of human bones have been unearthed here during excavation work. The excavation of the cloister walk during the 1960s revealed that part of the old house had been constructed on top of the monks' burial area. Eight skulls were later found at another location during the digging of the sewerage system.

Domestic staff working at Rufford during its time as a family home regularly spoke of a black-robed apparition resembling a monk, which would tap them on the shoulder, or could be seen behind them reflected in mirrors. Interestingly, the Cistercian order who once resided here wore white robes! A number of lady visitors staying at the abbey recalled being woken during the night to feel a 'cold and clammy' baby nestling beside them in bed. Among the many other spectres reputed to walk the house and estate are a little old lady in black (last encountered in 1956), a White Lady, a Grey Lady associated with the second floor of the old house and a sobbing boy-child. Their identities are open to dispute, and their stories have been long since forgotten, except for the age-old tale that a child was chased through the abbey sobbing before meeting his untimely end at the hands of his murderer. The White Lady's appearances traditionally occur in the vicinity of the lime tree avenue, although the most recent sighting of the ghost, reported to a park ranger in the mid-1990s, occurred on the ornamental folly on the lake. A visiting couple were convinced that they saw a woman in white on the bridge. Another reputed haunting is that of a phantom stage coach with no driver, said to rattle along the old road which runs parallel to the Nottingham A614 through the Rufford estate. The former manager of the park was acquainted with somebody who had witnessed the spectral coach and four first-hand.

During the demolition of the house in the 1950s, a local ghost-hunter stayed overnight in the remaining portion of the building. Shortly after midnight he watched astonished as a snowy white owl flew soundlessly past him along a landing and into a room. The bird appeared to have vanished without trace, although the windows were tightly shut and there was nowhere for it to remain concealed. The only unusual feature in the empty room was a hollow-sounding panel in one of the walls, indicating a secret niche. The following day this was exposed, to reveal the long-hidden carving of a huge white stone owl. Its origin remained as much a mystery as the event which led to its discovery, and it was removed to safety before the last of the bulldozers moved in.

The old stable block and mill buildings today incorporate a craft centre, gallery and restaurant. Part of the building was formerly used as lodgings by volunteers who were involved in work on the estate. There were regular reports of the sounds of 'distant voices', of sighs and of furniture being moved after dark. The former manageress of the restaurant was working alone in the kitchen one afternoon when she heard somebody enter and walk across the room. She began to chat to the customer and on receiving no reply came into the dining area, to find herself alone. In 1996 a park ranger who was passing the mill buildings one evening was surprised to hear voices within, and assumed that a colleague was working late. The following day he found that the office in question had been closed at the time, and was supposedly empty. The ranger later commented that a visiting psychic had felt part of the block to be haunted, and noted that a colleague had also seen a mysterious face at the upstairs window of a locked and empty room in the same block. This occurred one weekend, despite the fact that this area was only opened on weekdays, and the keys were not kept on site. In the adjoining stable block courtyard, another member of staff working late one night was convinced that she saw two men in 'period' costume swordfighting, accompanied by two ladies in the same dated dress. The area was closed to the public at the time.

During November 1994, two visitors were enjoying a walk along the Abbey Meadow path when they were most surprised to hear a child's sobbing coming from the nearby woodland. Curious, they followed the noise and could soon hear the sound of a woman's voice comforting the fractious child. They drew close to the area of the old family mausoleum (from which all remains had been removed and reinterred in the 1930s), but encountered nobody. On their return, the puzzled visitors reported their experience to a park ranger.

No visit to Rufford Abbey is complete without an inspection of the beautiful atmospheric brick and stone undercroft, which has seen centuries pass by with very little change. During the 1990s, a visiting psychic declared that 'something bad' had occurred in one particular corner of the undercroft, and described how he saw a 'face appear in the wall'. It is here that a volunteer worker encountered an icy chill spreading over the back of his neck for no apparent reason. He turned, half expecting to encounter somebody or something, but found himself alone.

The remains of the house and abbey are administered by English Heritage. Rufford Country Park is maintained by Nottinghamshire County Council and is open throughout the year.

LINCOLNSHIRE

THE SUN INN
Bridge Street, Saxilby

The terrible tale of Tom Otter the wife-murderer is well known to frequenters of the Sun Inn, not least because the hedge stake Otter used to batter his pregnant wife in the early 1800s was kept behind the bar here for many years. The couple had been married for only hours when Mrs Otter was murdered; her husband left the scene (today known as Tom Otter's Lane) and escaped unchallenged. Otter was unaware that there had been a witness to his crime, a local man named John Dunkerley, who had picked up the murder implement and taken it secretly to the Sun Inn, leaving it outside. When Otter eventually reappeared in Saxilby over a year later, his clothing allegedly showing evidence of old bloodstains, Dunkerley's eyewitness account was used to send him to the gallows. Otter was gibbeted close to the scene of his crime. Thereafter, on the eve of Mrs Otter's death, the hedge stake used to kill her would disappear

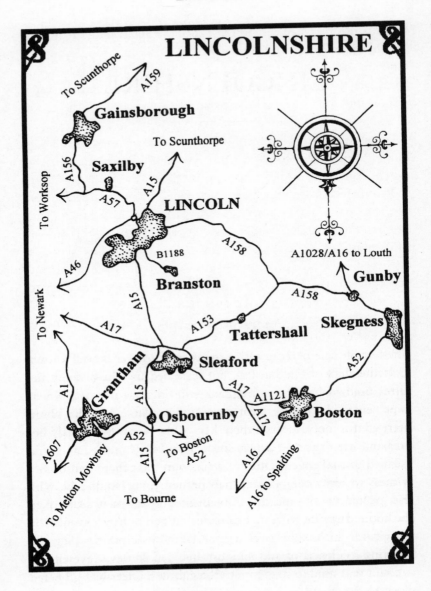

from its resting place behind the bar of the Sun Inn and reappear by the roadside on Tom Otter's Lane. Although the Bishop of Lincoln eventually 'exorcised' and burned the stake, John Dunkerley made a death-bed confession that he had been responsible for its annual disappearances, saying that the ghost of Tom Otter had commanded him to move it.

David and Kate Thompson took over the tenancy of the Sun Inn in April 1993. One of the upstairs rooms situated under the roof is rumoured to have been formerly rented by Tom Otter, shortly before his fateful marriage. The Thompsons decided to use this particular room for storage. Kate had hidden the children's Christmas presents here in December 1993, and on Christmas Eve she was busily wrapping them when she was disturbed by feet stamping violently on the floor close behind her. Kate turned around, but the room was empty; needless to say, she fled in terror!

On several occasions, Kate sensed that a certain area in the main bar was host to a female presence which seemed to 'visit' in the small hours of the morning. A wineglass once lifted itself from the shelf at the back of the bar, and moved through air before landing upright and unbroken on the bar top over 6 feet away, to the amazement of several witnesses. A short while later, a customer observed three heavy bar stools tip themselves over, one after the other, in the same area of the pub.

The Thompsons' experiences were soon to become the subject of a television documentary, when they accepted the help of ghost-hunter and psychic Eddie Burkes in a bid to lay their earthbound spirits to rest. Eddie visited the Sun Inn in March 1995 with a Swiss camera crew, although on arrival in the Thompsons' upstairs storage room, the camera unexpectedly cut out, and filming had to recommence the following day. He was able to give details of two ghosts he believed to be behind the paranormal activity, although, surprisingly, the ghost of

Tom Otter was not among them. Eddie declared one spirit to be that of a young man who had died in the Napoleonic Wars, and the other to be a woman who had lived at the Sun Inn in the 1920s, and had died shortly after giving birth. Following Eddie's visit, Dave and Kate Thompson are pleased to report that the Sun Inn is fairly peaceful at present, although the tale of Tom Otter will doubtless be told for many years to come.

The A57 road from Lincoln to Saxilby is also believed to be haunted, by the ghost of a hitch-hiker dressed in black. In November 1994, local man Mark Stoneham was driving home from work after eleven o'clock at night when he noticed a dark figure by a bend in the road, near a small copse. He made no comment to the companion travelling with him at the time, although when he saw the same sight the following night at the same time, it occurred to him that it was an unusual place for a hitch-hiker to wait. The figure's face was impossible to see, being swathed in darkness. On driving the same route for the third night in a row, Mark asked his companion to look out for a person unknown standing by the bend in the road. He saw the dark figure once again, waiting in the same place ... although his companion could see nobody there at all.

CHURCH FARM MUSEUM
Skegness

Church Farm, whose oldest parts date from 1750, was formerly a working family farm until its transformation into a museum which today holds regular seasonal events related to 'traditional' farming. The assistant curator gave her own account of working in this historic building, which both she and fellow staff independently concluded to be haunted: 'During the winter the museum is closed to the public. However, as my office is upstairs in the farmhouse I open it up five days a week and always lock the front and back doors behind me when I come and go to prevent anybody entering without my knowledge. As part of the locking-up procedure, before I leave the museum I walk through the farmhouse to check that everything is safe and secure, and on several occasions during the winter of 1995, which was my first here, I was certain that somebody else was in the farmhouse with me, either in the parlour or in the kitchen. At first it alarmed me and I spent some time checking for intruders but after a while I became quite used to it . . .

'After the museum opened this season [1996] I was talking over a cup of coffee with the museum assistant and mentioned that I had a feeling of not being alone in the farmhouse. I expected her to laugh at me but she told me that over the years she has been working here she too has had a definite feeling that somebody is either in the kitchen or in the parlour. However, she did not tell me about our invisible resident when the museum closed last autumn because she knew that I would be working from November to April alone in the farmhouse and she did not want to worry me.

'On a separate occasion a visitor remarked to staff in the shop that he liked the costume of the man he had met at the back door of the farmhouse. The visitor had apparently seen a man dressed in a farmer's smock and thought this person was a demonstrator at the museum. However, on this particular day there were no demonstrators working in the museum! Whether or not the unseen person in the farmhouse is the same farmer or somebody else I really don't know. And because we have regular events throughout the season with demonstrators in costume and the farmer appeared in broad daylight, many other visitors may have seen him and not been aware of who he really is . . .'

Lincolnshire

Church Farm Museum, on Church Road South, Skegness, is open to the public daily between 1 April and 31 October (except for Good Friday) between 10.30 a.m. and 5.30 p.m.

BLACKFRIARS ARTS CENTRE

Boston

When the people of Boston welcomed a new and revolutionary Dominican order into their home town in the mid-1200s, they had little idea that, seven hundred years later, the Black Friars' medieval homestead would still be welcoming visitors from all over Lincolnshire, in its capacity as a theatre and arts centre. The friary was rescued from dereliction in the 1960s, following the campaign of a local drama group to find a suitable site for a theatre. Visible remains of the early friary refectory and private chambers can be seen in the front and first floor of the building, as well as in the beautiful chamfered windows and fourteenth-century doorways.

Blackfriars is believed to be haunted by the spectre of a monk dressed in black, the common habit of the Dominicans. Margaret Doughty has worked on the site for many years, and describes certain areas of the building in which she has encountered a 'strange' atmosphere, noting that on many occasions she does not feel 'alone'. Margaret was in the theatre during renovation work in the 1960s, when she witnessed first-hand the spectre of a monk walking across the back of the stage. She felt at the time an underlying message in the ghost's appearance, as though she was being told to leave until renovations were complete. In 1994, another member of staff was surprised early one morning by the figure of a monk stooping over something in the kitchen. Before the apparition vanished, the witness was able to note that its dark habit was made of a coarse woven cloth.

Gainsborough Old Hall

Blackfriars Arts Centre, on Spain Lane, includes the Boston Tourist Information Centre, and is open to the public throughout the week.

GAINSBOROUGH OLD HALL
Gainsborough

The site on which Gainsborough Old Hall stands today was once home to a castle, besieged by King Sweyne of Denmark and his men on the second Danish invasion of England in 1014. Legend states that King Sweyne was killed by a spear-wielding spectre within the castle itself – none other than the ghost of St Edmund, who had been martyred by the Danes one hundred and forty years earlier. Sweyne's son Canute was later proclaimed King, and the River Trent, running close to the castle, is believed to be the legendary water whose tide refused to 'turn back' when Canute commanded it. Sweyne's ghostly moaning can reputedly be heard echoing through the great hall of Gainsborough, under whose foundations lie the remains of the earlier castle.

Gainsborough Old Hall is believed to be haunted by the ghost of a Grey Lady, the daughter of a former owner. During the Wars of the Roses, the young woman is said to have fallen in love with a knight from Newark Castle. Unfortunately, the lovers' families supported opposing sides during the conflict. The girl's father believed the liaison to be unsuitable, and locked her in the tower. Whether she died here or was later released is unknown, although it appears that all records of the girl disappeared from the hall's books at the time she was believed to have been held prisoner. In the 1970s, a caretaker reported seeing the spectre of a woman in grey follow him along a corridor, before disappearing through a wall. Later renovations at Gainsborough Old Hall uncovered a secret doorway, previously plastered over, at the very spot at which the caretaker had seen the ghost disappear.

Gainsborough Old Hall is maintained by Lincolnshire City Council and English Heritage, and is open throughout the year, Monday to Saturday 10 a.m. to 5 p.m., and, between Easter Sunday and 31 October, Sunday 2 p.m. to 5.30 p.m.

The great hall of Gainsborough Old Hall

TATTERSHALL CASTLE
Tattershall

Tattershall castle is a rare example of a red-brick fortification, constructed around 1440 by Ralph, Lord Cromwell, Treasurer of England during the reign of Henry VI. The ruins of an earlier castle built by Robert de Tateshale in 1230 occupy the same site, although it is the later building which is believed to be haunted. The legendary walk of the White Lady is said to take place after dark on certain nights of the year, as she drifts around the battlements of Tattershall Castle looking for her lost love. The current custodian has never encountered the spectre, and neither did his predecessor, but in 1995 a new member of staff, Ann Tick, saw what she described as 'a woman in a white gown and a Norman head-dress' standing by her side in the office one afternoon.

Ann today works in a turret room in the castle where information leaflets are displayed; on numerous occasions both she and fellow staff have unlocked in the morning to find the leaflets scattered all over the floor. She believes that the legendary White Lady is not the only unquiet spirit at Tattershall Castle. Ann described how, whilst working alone in the turret room, she often found the name 'Maude' entering her mind for no apparent reason. Despite knowing little of the castle's history at this time, she began to find that she was drawn to one particular window continually. She soon noticed an antiquated coat of arms above the window, and discovered that this belonged to an early family who had resided at the castle – and that a woman named Maude had indeed been one of their number. Ann recalled feeling that the presence in the turret room was decidedly different from the spectral White Lady whom she had encountered in the office previously. When her car keys were hurled off a table as she was locking the turret room one afternoon, she felt that the presence had possibly become hostile – and pointed out firmly that she had no intention of leaving. Following this, activity in the turret room seemed to quieten down.

Tattershall Castle is administered by the National Trust, and is open to the public between 30 March and 31 October, Saturday to Wednesday 10.30 a.m. to 5.30 p.m., and between 1 November and 18 December, weekends only, noon to 4 p.m.

THE WHITE HART HOTEL
Bailgate, Lincoln

The White Hart is an imposing hotel with a pedigree dating back to 1460. It is believed that an inn was built on the site as early as 1387, following a visit to Lincoln by King Richard II (whose emblem was a white hart). Having been expanded and added to over the years, the oldest part of the building is today the east wing, which dates back to 1710. Hauntings within the hotel have been documented by BBC radio and television over a period of several years. A ghostly child wearing a mob-cap, who was allegedly murdered by the hotel rat-catcher in the 1700s, has been spotted in a corner on the first floor. A small, plump gentleman wearing a 1920s smoking jacket has disturbed a number of guests in a suite on the third floor, reputedly wringing his hands in distress and asking if anybody has seen his 'ginger-jar'. Several guests have also encountered the mysterious figure of a man in the old courtyard area, now spanned by the 'orangery' dome of the hotel. Dressed in a long dark cape, the man hides his face, revealing only a pair of dark, vengeful eyes. As Lincoln was once a favoured stop-off point for travellers *en route* to York, the area was renowned for its highwaymen, who would lie in wait for the unwary. Local legend suggests that one such highwayman was horrifically burned when a Lincoln coachman thrust a blazing torch into his face ... and that his soul has been condemned to haunt the courtyard, forever seeking vengeance on the coachman responsible.

For accommodation: The White Hart Hotel, Bailgate, Lincoln LN1 3AR.

GUNBY HALL
Gunby, Skegness

Reputedly Tennyson's 'haunt of ancient peace', the magnificent red-brick Gunby Hall was constructed in 1700 under the direction of Sir William Massingbird, and was extended in 1870 to its current proportions. A fine collection of Reynolds paintings is on display here, alongside traditional English furniture and beautiful gardens. Gunby Hall's most famous legend concerns an earlier Massingbird property, Bratoft Castle, situated close by. Sir William Massingbird allegedly hired an assassin to kill his daughter Margaret's rumoured paramour, the hall's postilion rider, nicknamed Button Cap. The grounds do indeed have a Button Cap Lane and Button Cap Halt (a small wood), and numerous locals testify to having seen a spectral couple walking the footpath between the nearby villages of Candlesby and Bratoft. Following the death of her lover, Margaret supposedly cursed the family line, vowing that no man would follow successfully to inherit his father's estate. For his part in the murder, Sir William was forced to visit the College of Arms in London each year, where his coat of arms was ceremonially smeared with blood.

A path known as the Ghost Walk, leading to the church, was

the site of a ghostly encounter in the 1980s, when a local man on his way to church came face to face with a lady in a bonnet and crinoline who faded slowly before his eyes. Having been known as the Ghost Walk for many years previously, this path has probably been the site of many a supernatural encounter, although details of how it originally took its name are unknown. Within the house itself, the Red Room, a former bedroom, is believed to be haunted by a lady in evening dress. An Air Force Captain visiting during the war saw her looking out of the bedroom window, and, believing her to be a fellow guest, apologised for the fact that he had not brought evening attire with him. Needless to say, when he described the reason for his concern, the family could not account for the beautifully dressed woman. In more recent years, the daughter of a member of staff who stayed overnight in the Red Room recalled feeling distinctly uncomfortable. A small dressing-room door leading from the bedroom had the habit of opening and closing itself during the night.

Gunby Hall is administered by the National Trust. The hall and garden open Wednesdays only between 30 March and 31 September, 2 p.m. to 6 p.m. The garden is additionally open on Thursdays 2 p.m. to 6 p.m.

ST WULFRAM'S CHURCH
Church Street, Grantham

St Wulfram's parish church is claimed to possess one of the finest and most picturesque silhouettes in the entire country, rivalling even cathedrals for the honour. Although a church is believed to have occupied the site since Saxon times, the current building, with its wonderfully graphic gargoyles and carved stone heads, is largely Norman incorporating many later additions.

During World War I, two local bell-ringers were changing a rope on one of the bells between services. They had finished their task and were closing the door at the foot of the tower, when both heard a young man's voice calling out. One of the gentlemen recognised the voice as that of his nephew, who had joined the army and had recently been posted to France. Despite the voice, neither of the bell-ringers saw any other person present at that time. The following day, a telegram containing news of the young man's death was received by his family.

St Wulfram's is believed to be haunted by the spirit of a schoolboy, who was spotted several years ago by the chief bell-ringer, wandering into the choir vestry. When the child vanished, the witness reported the incident to the then verger, who had been playing the organ at the east end of the church throughout. The verger was not in the least surprised by the tale, although it is not known whether he himself had ever encountered the ghost; certainly, there have been no recent sightings of the mystery child. However, in 1996, the current parish clerk noted an unusual experience he himself had shortly after Midnight Mass on Christmas Eve some years previously: 'It was the Midnight Mass service, Christmas 1983 or '84. The chancel of the church is lit with some fifty to sixty candles for this service including the four large candles at the High Altar. During the service I noticed that one of the large candles had gone out and it remained out for the rest of the service. The servers extinguished all the candles after the service and I prepared the church for Christmas morning services. It was now 1.30 a.m. and I turned out all the lights (as I thought), locked up the church and prepared to go home but then realised that there was a light still on inside the church. I went back in, found

Carved effigy, St Wulfram's Church

the offending light, switched it off and in total darkness looked round the church. There were no more lights on anywhere and I went home. I returned at about 7.15 a.m. on Christmas morning and entered the church, and my first task was to switch on the lights of the Christmas tree. I reached the chancel step and I stopped dead in my tracks when I saw that the candle at the High Altar that had not been lit during the Midnight Mass was now burning brightly. I stood looking at it in disbelief for about a minute before gathering my thoughts, and went to switch on the lights on the Christmas tree.'

LINCOLN CASTLE
Lincoln City Centre

The site of Lincoln Castle, overlooking the city from a vantage point at the top of Steep Hill, was once occupied by a Roman fortress. Following the downfall of Roman supremacy, many Saxon townsfolk moved into its remains to build homesteads. William the Conqueror had other ideas for the site, however, and promptly evicted all Saxon families on his claim to the English throne, to make way for the building of the castle. The medieval Lucy Tower provided unhallowed ground for the burial of execution victims and convicts, who had formerly been housed in the strict prison at its foot. Reputedly the most haunted place within the castle walls is the Victorian prison chapel. According to castle staff, reports of the supernatural here are confined to the occasional sensing of an unseen 'presence' in the small tiered pews. The castle still hosts a sitting court within its fortified walls, a stone's throw from which the splendid cathedral can be seen. Lincoln Cathedral is famed for its unusual stone-carved demon, visible on top of a pillar in the 'angel choir' and known as the Lincoln Imp. Its origin remains a mystery, although local legend suggests that it was turned to stone by angels after flying into the cathedral to cause mischief. The Imp is today the official emblem for this historic city.

Lincoln Castle is open throughout the year, with guided tours operated periodically each day.

Lincoln Castle with its tiny prison chapel

STRAGGLETHORPE HALL
Loveden, Lincoln

Stragglethorpe Hall was formerly attached to the monastery of Sempringham, having been bequeathed to the Gilbertine order by John of Gaunt in the fourteenth century. Roman finds around the site indicate that a homestead existed here centuries before the Gilbertines tended to the care and education of disadvantaged women, a purpose for which Stragglethorpe Hall was originally intended. In common with a great number of such properties, the hall fell into the hands of Henry VIII's Exchequer during the Dissolution. Today, Stragglethorpe provides handsome accommodation for visitors under the management of Michael Rook, whose family have resided here for many years.

A private road once ran from Stragglethorpe to Stubton Hall, which was regularly used by inhabitants of both houses. Local legend tells that Lady Brierlands, a one-time resident of Stragglethorpe, was travelling home late one night in her carriage after a dinner party at Stubton, when she was accosted and murdered for her fine jewellery. Although the course of the original road has now been lost, several of the older villagers claim to have seen a spectral coach rattling through two fields, still known today as The Brierlands, on the anniversary of the murder.

Close to the time of major renovation work at Stragglethorpe Hall in 1914, a Mrs Jack Leslie noted in a letter to Major Alan Rook – the uncle of the current owner – that several strange occurrences had taken place. The hall's attics were frequently beset by loud hammering noises, which often continued for two to three hours at a time. Their source was unknown. Chains could be heard dragging over cemented floors in other areas of the building, and a bell was known to ring occasionally without human aid – this bell still hangs at the top of the house today, although the current residents have not been disturbed by any such ghostly ringing. However, the Rook family have reason to believe that something unexplained still manifests itself here from time to time. Michael's daughter sleeps in a small four-poster bed which has a hanging light on the headboard canopy. Shortly after the family moved into Stragglethorpe in 1990, she had settled herself down to read one evening when the light began to swing to and fro from its flex, rapping against the woodwork; although she held out a hand to stop it, it soon began to move again. Rather than leave the room in terror, the courageous girl turned off the switch during one of its passes and settled down to sleep.

In February 1991, Michael was disturbed in the dead of night by a loud rattling from the brass fittings on an antique chest of drawers, which stood in the main bedroom. He flicked on the light and the noise ceased instantly. It occurred to Michael that his much-loved grandmother, affectionately known as 'Granny Peacock', who had died in this room several years previously, could well have been paying a visit to the site of her old bureau, and be showing her frustration at unsuccessfully searching out old correspondence! Indeed, shortly after this incident, Michael recalls passing through the garden hall into the library (once his grandmother's living quarters) when he became aware of the most beautiful perfume. This he recognised instantly as Granny Peacock's favourite fragrance, which she had worn frequently during her lifetime.

For bookings: Stragglethorpe Hall, Loveden, Lincoln LN5 0QZ.

THE BARN GALLERY
Osbournby, Sleaford

In 1993, Lizzie Neville and her husband bought an old farm cottage and an adjoining barn in Osbournby, near Sleaford, with the aim of converting the barn into an art gallery. Before their purchase, a local friend had commented that, when passing the empty cottage, she had the inexplicable feeling that 'somebody extremely sad' was staring out of one particular window. As the Nevilles were moving in, the same friend visited, and, being rather 'sensitive' to certain atmospheres, noted what she described as a 'horrid feeling' attached to the place, for which she could give no explanation. Within weeks the Nevilles became aware of the old-fashioned door latches clicking regularly despite the fact that nobody was moving around in the house. Their daughter caught sight of a 'shadowy' woman in long, dated clothing standing at the top of the stairs, which is the oldest part of the house and dates from the sixteenth century. After living here for a year, the family decided to have their rooms blessed by a priest. Although their daughter was the only person to have clearly seen an apparition, they began to feel that the blessing was somehow the 'right thing to do'. Following this, no further sightings of the ghostly woman have occurred, and the friend who previously described an unpleasant atmosphere herself noted an immediate change for the better. Today, the Barn Gallery shows work from local and international artists, and the Nevilles are planning to open up their cottage as bed and breakfast accommodation . . . although Lizzie notes that she still occasionally hears the old door latches mysteriously clicking in and out of place.

The Barn Gallery, 18 West Street, Osbournby, Sleaford, is open to the public throughout the year from 10 a.m. to 5 p.m., Tuesday to Saturday.

BRANSTON HALL HOTEL
Branston, Lincoln

On New Year's Day in 1903, Branston Old Hall burned to the ground, eventually deteriorating into foundations which are still partially visible today on the far side of the park's ornamental lake. The house had been built by the son of the 1st Duke of Ancaster in 1735, although it was later relegated to staff quarters when the Hon. Leslie-Melville founded the current hall in the nineteenth century. This beautiful Victorian pale stone building, set in acres of wooded parkland on the opposite side of the lake to its predecessor, is today run as a country hotel. Branston Hall's lakeside walks are reputedly haunted by a Grey Lady, a former member of the resident family who is said to have died in a boathouse fire, while engaging in a clandestine meeting with a stable lad. According to local legend, her ghost is traditionally seen gliding across the lake in the early hours of the morning.

Although the Grey Lady has not been encountered for some time, within the house itself a number of unusual phenomena have been recorded over a period spanning more than twenty years. The hall was formerly used as a TB sanatorium, during which time all infected corpses were incinerated to prevent the spread of disease. A building adjoining the cobbled courtyard was used as a morgue, and housed the incinerator. These rooms are today redecorated and once more in use, although, after dark, certain members of staff entering the courtyard through its pair of stone pillars have described an 'uncanny chill' in the vicinity. In the case of house manager Michelle Forest, this proved to be so strong that she was physically unable to enter the courtyard on one occasion when she experienced what she described as an invisible 'wall of fear' there. Branston Hall continued as a hospital during the 1970s, during which time nursing staff were plagued by the constant sound of running water, often traced to unaccountably running taps. This happened so frequently that they eventually banded together to conduct their own all-night vigil in the hope of catching what they assumed to be a trickster ... only to find yet another running tap in an empty area of the building.

In the 1980s, a small spiral stairway (today only used by staff) was the site of mysterious sobbing, resembling that of a child, which seemed to be triggered when a certain step was walked over. One gentleman was so convinced by what he heard that he returned to the stairwell armed with a tape recorder, and successfully recorded the sound of crying. Whether there is any truth in the story that a child once fell to his death on these stairs is unknown, and today, as the steps have been altered somewhat, there have been no further incidences of this phenomenon.

In 1993, general manager Julian Atkin and a colleague decided to list a number of tasks which needed to be completed throughout the building during a quiet period. They checked the store room and returned minutes later intending to sweep a build-up of old packaging into the centre. When they opened the door they were amazed to find that the job had already been done, despite only the two of them being present in the house. On another occasion, Julian unlocked the store room, leaving the pass key on its chain in the door, and went in to fetch something. When he turned to leave he stumbled into a stack of chairs which had suddenly and soundlessly appeared in the middle of the room. On attempting to relock the door, he found that the key which had previously been left in the lock was now a different one, which would not fit. A similar experience was recounted by another member of staff, who, some time later, had removed every piece of furniture to the centre of the store room to sweep the floor. He returned a couple of minutes later to find everything back in its original position. Today, this room has been converted into a conference room for business visitors, which appears to have ended the activity.

In January 1994, three members of staff were sitting in the lounge late one night, when Michelle commented on the 'awful old-fashioned jazz music' playing over the speakers, and suggested a change of CD. The CD machine was found to be empty, and the source of the mysterious, dated music could not be accounted for, despite the fact that everybody present had clearly heard it coming from the main speakers. A member of staff later commented that, on reflection, the music sounded as though it was playing from an old scratched record, something which Branston Hall does not possess. Other unexplained sounds heard in various places around the hall include two chatting female voices in empty rooms and corridors, and the sound of running water which perhaps recalls the experience of the nurses in the 1970s. A building team were recently called in to check for leakages, and they themselves were amazed to hear running water in an area from which they had removed every water pipe.

Branston Hall's cellar, a stone-flagged undercroft which runs the entire length of the building, and its stairwell entrance have also been the location of unaccountable phenomena. The stairwell is used to store decorating equipment which regularly rearranges itself despite remaining unused, and a number of staff are convinced that they have been touched on the shoulder here by an invisible hand. House manager Michelle once opened the cellar door to witness the lights turning themselves on before she had time to reach for the switch.

In April 1996, a visiting clergyman cheerfully mentioned to reception on his departure that he had seen two ghostly 'Victorian children' playing together late the previous night, running along the first-floor corridor. Although staff were inclined not to take his story seriously, earlier in the same year Branston's receptionist Ali had heard footsteps running up and down the main staircase when she was alone in the bar one evening. Rather perturbed as nobody was in sight, she turned up the volume on the CD player, noting that, as she did so, the footsteps became gradually louder also.

Branston Hall caters for leisure breaks, private functions and business events. For bookings: Branston Hall Hotel, Branston, Lincoln LN4 1PD.

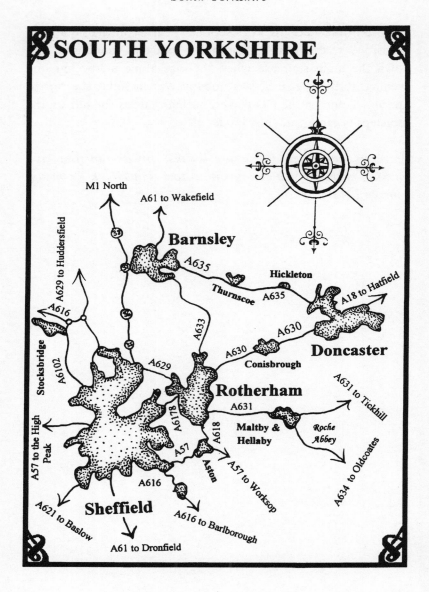

SOUTH YORKSHIRE

M1 North

A61 to Wakefield

A629 to Huddersfield

Barnsley

A635

Hickleton

Thurnscoe   A635

A18 to Hatfield

A616

A633

A630

A630

Doncaster

Stocksbridge

A6102

A629

Conisbrough

A57 to the High Peak

A6178

Rotherham

A631 to Tickhill

A631

A619

Maltby & Hellaby

Roche Abbey

A57

Aston

A57 to Worksop

A634 to Oldcoates

A616

Sheffield

A621 to Baslow

A616 to Barlborough

A61 to Dronfield

SOUTH YORKSHIRE

CONISBROUGH CASTLE
Conisbrough, Doncaster

The surviving tower, or donjon, of Conisbrough Castle is believed to be one of the finest examples of its kind in the whole of Europe. Built by Earl Hamelin Plantagenet after the Conquest, this twelfth-century structure over 90 feet in height was restored to its former glory after renovation work during the mid-1990s. Conisbrough Castle remained in the de Warenne family for several generations, until Earl John de Warenne was evicted in 1371 for kidnapping Alice de Lacey, the wife of Thomas of Lancaster. Although Earl John's role in the plot was merely to help the lady elope with his lovesick squire, rumours spread quickly that he had taken her as his mistress due to the fact that his own wife could not bear children. When Lancaster laid siege to the castle in a bid to recapture his wife, the King intervened. Conisbrough and its lands were awarded to Lancaster, much to Earl John's disgust. However, the ultimate chance for revenge came soon afterwards, when Earl John sat in judgement over Lancaster at a political trial. Naturally, he found him guilty, and Lancaster was beheaded.

A mound of earth close to the visitors' centre is known locally as the Grave of Hengist, supposedly being the burial-place of this Saxon warrior. Hengist was reputedly captured by Aurelius Ambrosius, King of the Britons, while trying to make his escape into the safety of a fortified structure which existed here before the Norman castle was built. On his capture, Ambrosius beheaded Hengist, but promised a pagan burial as befitted his victim's beliefs. Accordingly, a burial mound was constructed where Hengist fell. Unfortunately, current regulations have vetoed the possibility of excavating the mound.

A building with such a history as Conisbrough is not surprisingly suspected to have several ghosts. The spectre of a grey monk has been recorded here over the centuries, first being noted in 1778 by the Yorkshireman Richard of Glafsby, who wrote, after an uneasy stay at the Castle: '*On the night before today, in Castle built of Cunisbro' stone myne eyes have seen Phantom of Abbot Monk alowne. In the castle with a candel lyt, he wos only in castel chapel wore he dyd not syt.*' In the 1840s two Conisbrough locals again saw the 'spectre of a grey monk', although whether this was in the chapel spoken of by Richard of Glafsby or elsewhere is not known. In 1940 it was the turn of a local clergyman, who reported the same ghostly figure wandering the grounds.

The small chapel is reputedly the most haunted room in the castle, and is situated just off the Earl's bedchamber. Many modern Conisbrough folk have seen a mysterious light shining in its tiny window after dark. After an attempted break-in within the castle grounds in the winter of 1994, local police who were called to the scene witnessed the phantom chapel light for themselves. At the time, renovation work meant that the power supply to the castle had been cut off, leaving general development manager Ian Thompson just as mystified as the police were as to the origin of the light.

The ghost of an unknown White Lady is rumoured to wander the lonely battlements of the donjon, re-enacting the scene of her death, where she was reputedly pushed over the edge as a punishment for being unfaithful to her husband. Only one recent sighting of this ghost is known to have occurred, by a local man who visited the castle in the early 1990s with a historical re-enactment society. A castle employee had a vision of a woman in blue standing by the window seats in the Earl's Room in 1994, whom she believed to be the beautiful Countess of Cambridge (who died a mysterious death in the mid-1400s). The vision made the sign of three loud raps on the woodwork before fading from sight ... and later the same day, another member of staff reported three loud raps emanating from an empty area of the donjon, although he knew nothing of his colleague's earlier experience.

An all-night vigil undertaken at Conisbrough in the spring of 1996 by the Sheffield Paranormal Research Group and the Aphelion Ghost Research Society provided interesting results when two members of the party saw a bright light flash twice out of a small recess leading from the second floor. They assumed that a colleague was taking photographs, but found the area to be empty, and, being solid stone without a window, sealed from all outside light. More intriguing still, the groups on the ground and first floors were frustrated to hear constant banging, shuffling and pacing footsteps which they each attributed to the floor directly above. These noises continued throughout the night. All the investigators present were experienced in attaining the conditions required for a vigil, and knew that any movement should be avoided unless absolutely necessary. Each group denied responsibility for the noises and blamed the party above, who in turn felt that the noises actually came from the party above them, although all present testified to having remained silent throughout. The mystery was never satisfactorily explained. When the vigil was repeated a number of weeks later by the Aphelion Ghost Research Society, the same disruptive noises were noted once again.

Conisbrough Castle is administered by English Heritage and the Ivanhoe Trust, and is open to visitors all year round, daily between 10 a.m. and 5 p.m.

MOSBOROUGH HALL HOTEL
Mosborough, Sheffield

The town of Mosborough is mentioned in Domesday, and was once the site of a fortified building, recalled in its name, which stems from 'fort on the moor'. Although no trace of this building remains today, the current Mosborough Hall is believed to have been constructed over the foundations of a much earlier building whose history has been lost with the passage of time. The oldest parts of the present hall, which is chiefly seventeenth-century, date back to the fourteenth century, and despite the building's former dereliction, much of the interior panelling was successfully retained. During renovation work prior to Mosborough Hall becoming a hotel, several subterranean passages were unearthed which were found to lead to a nearby private house and various locations around the estate.

The ghost of Mosborough's White Lady is legendary in the area, and has been encountered throughout this and the last century. She is supposedly the spectre of a young maidservant stabbed to death by her lover in the seventeenth century, after confronting him with her pregnancy. Her ghost is traditionally

116

to be seen running across Hollow Lane and through a wall around the first week in September. Legend asserts that the ghost is re-enacting her final flight from her knife-wielding pursuer. During the 1980s there was a spate of sightings, including the figure of a woman darting in front of motorists before vanishing, and a young girl in white walking down Hollow Lane several inches above ground level.

In 1994, a local woman recounted how her grandmother, who had worked as a cook in the hall in the late 1890s, had spoken of terrible poltergeist activity which seemed to centre on the former library. The squire at the time was most disturbed to find this room in regular disarray, and at first accused his servants of trickery. Objects were tossed around and smashed on a regular basis, and eventually the staff were fearful of entering the room. The squire held an overnight vigil outside the locked and secured door in an attempt to rule out human interference. The following morning he unlocked the door to find that an unseen hand had repeated its actions and ransacked the room. What further action he took, if any, is unknown. Mild poltergeist activity has been prompted in more recent years by structural alterations.

An unidentified Grey Lady has been noted by numerous staff and visitors, as she 'glides' across the dining area before vanishing at the far end where there was formerly a corridor. In 1994 the hotel receptionist was able to give a vivid description of a dark-haired woman in a grey Georgian dress with white cuffs and collar, following her own sighting during which she had been seated in the bar area. A matter of days later, a visitor announced that he too had seen a ghostly woman in a grey dress walking the same route. However, the most haunted room in Mosborough Hall Hotel is firmly believed to be Room 22, where guests' experiences range from sensing 'a strange atmosphere' and hearing disembodied voices, to witnessing a beautiful spectral woman and even a ghostly black hound. The manager of the hotel maintains a dossier of paranormal encounters, which are reported on average once a fortnight, by guests and staff alike.

For bookings: Mosborough Hall Hotel, High Street, Mosborough, Sheffield S19 5AE.

THE STOCKSBRIDGE BYPASS
Stocksbridge, Sheffield

This stretch of South Yorkshire roadway has hosted so many strange events that its reputation today rivals that of some of the most haunted locations in the country. In the mid-1980s, the local council planned a four-lane bypass near Stocksbridge, and enlisted a huge team of workmen to complete the task. When the planned number of lanes for the bypass was reduced, the workforce began to speculate about the discovery of an 'ancient burial ground'. Site worker Donald Nutbrown spotted the figure of what appeared to be a 'huge black monk' watching him from a pine plantation as he worked one afternoon. Two Sheffield security guards saw a similar figure late one night, and also observed a 'luminous form' approaching them from the far side of the then incomplete bridge. Thoroughly frightened, they visited a local clergyman the following morning, to enlist his help in the form of an 'exorcism' . . . and later resigned their posts. A resulting investigation by local police served to convince them of the truth of the sightings. While on late patrol duty one night, two officers were startled by a hooded figure whom their car headlights shone through. Within seconds, a phantom gentleman in a dark jacket and white cravat had appeared by the side of their panda car . . . and vanished just as suddenly.

When the Stocksbridge bypass was eventually opened in 1988, a spate of serious accidents took place. Donald Nutbrown points out that most of these occurred in the area in which the 'black monk' had been spotted during building operations. Motorists travelling this route have noted a 'hooded figure' which walks slightly above the current ground level along the roadside. There have also been reports of vehicles filling with

The infamous Stocksbridge bypass

the 'phantom' smell of pipe-smoke, and car engines failing inexplicably. One Sheffield lorry driver who broke down on the bypass checked his engine and found that the fan belt had been completely removed, and yet was unbroken.

In the winter of 1993, a young woman travelling to Sheffield on a family visit was on the bypass when she became aware that her windscreen wipers had seemingly crossed themselves over the windscreen. She visited a garage the following day and was told by a mechanic that, for the wipers to have been crossed in such a fashion, they would have had to be taken apart by hand and reassembled the way they were found. Since the car showed no other evidence of vandalism, both the mechanic and the motorist were at a loss to explain the nature of the damage. The motorist thereafter refused to use the bypass when travelling into Sheffield.

Also of interest are the high number of reported sightings of UFOs in the same area, which one local noted are so common that they no longer cause a stir. UFO's have been witnessed here by local police, residents and security guards attached to the industrial site at Stocksbridge, as well as passing motorists who have reported their sightings to UFO research groups. When public curiosity about paranormal encounters in the area was aroused, local people came forward to discuss their own strange experiences on and around the bypass. It was discovered that sightings of the 'black monk' dated back at least to the late 1800s. No proof of a disturbed burial ground in the vicinity has been discovered, and the reason for the unusual activity around the Stocksbridge bypass remains a mystery.

HICKLETON CHURCHYARD
Hickleton, Doncaster

The small porch of Hickleton churchyard contains an inbuilt stone case in which three aged skulls were interred behind glass many years ago for all to see. The skulls were believed to be those of three condemned highwaymen, and were set here in the early 1800s as a public reminder of their untimely fate. Underneath the display cabinet, an inscription in stone reads, '*Today For Me, Tomorrow For Thee*'; this is believed to be a curse against their removal. Local legend tells how superstition had such a firm hold in the area that people would often run past them in fear when passing the churchyard late at night. In the summer of 1996, an unknown vandal smashed the glass display panel, which had held the skulls for over a hundred years, and stole one of them. Father Tony Delves immediately issued a public warning that 'the skulls were never buried because they were cursed', adding that the inscription implied that 'the curse will be transferred to anyone who interferes with them'. He advised the perpetrator of the deed to return the skull to the church, and meanwhile removed the remaining two from the display cabinet to a safer location.

CARBROOK HALL HOTEL
Attercliffe Common, Sheffield

Carbrook Hall proudly proclaims itself to be 'Sheffield's most haunted public house', and has indeed been visited on more than one occasion by specialists from the Society for Psychical Research. The hall, whose foundations date back to the twelfth century, still features beautifully intact moulded plasterwork ceilings and panelled walls of seventeenth-century origin. Subterranean tunnels are said to lead from Carbrook to Manor Lodge (in whose surviving Turret House Mary Queen of Scots was imprisoned prior to her execution), and other nearby sites of consequence. The hall as it stands today was built by Steven Bright, whose son John became one of Cromwell's most distinguished soldiers during the Civil War. Cromwell himself visited Carbrook frequently, using the building as a stronghold for anti-Royalist plots and military organisation. There have been several sightings of a ghostly gentleman in Puritan dress, said to be John Bright, still wandering the premises over three hundred years after his death.

A former landlady looked on as a man wearing 'a black cap and high white collar' appeared next to paranormal investigators, on a tour of the building in the early 1980s. Both she and customers had encountered the same mysterious figure appear-

Carbrook Hall Hotel, Sheffield's 'most haunted public house'

ing in various areas of the bar from time to time. A local band practising in an upstairs function room also encountered a man in Civil War uniform who appeared and vanished just as suddenly. In 1994, the current landlord, Phil Skelton, was ascending the stairs one evening when the stocky figure of a man wearing 'heavily draped clothing' suddenly appeared ahead of him. Phil moved aside in astonishment for the stranger to pass, and felt his arm gently brushed; at this his hair stood on end. The ghost, which he noted was rather more of 'an impression' than a solid object, vanished when it reached the foot of the stairs.

Locals tell of many apparitions traditionally attached to the premises, including an old lady in 1920s clothing who sits in a rocking chair in an upstairs room, an old man wearing a flat cap, and even a 'hooded monk'. However, the last known detailed reported sightings of any of these ghosts occurred in the 1980s. Throughout the 1990s a 'dark shadow' has been encountered passing through the bar area, and bottles have been regularly seen to propel themselves from the back of the bar at high speed. In the early days of the Skeltons' tenancy this proved to be rather alarming, although by 1996 it was such a common occurrence as to be considered quite mundane! The Black Oak Room (resplendent with its original panelling) has been heard to echo with the sound of unexplained footsteps, and in the Skeltons' private living quarters, small objects have moved around of their own accord. Phil has known the outside lighting to turn itself on and off at will late at night, despite the control cupboard being locked. A number of complaints have also been received from customers unwittingly trapped in the toilets when the doors mysteriously jam for no apparent reason.

One of the most unusual experiences at Carbrook Hall, seemingly unconnected with the building's historic past, occurred in the early 1990s. Phil was awoken at around two thirty one morning by the sounds of children playing outside. The area was dark and empty, and he could offer no logical explanation for the 'playground' noises he had clearly heard. Several months later, Phil was telling a regular customer of his experience when the gentleman pointed out that, in the 1920s, the land adjoining the hall had been a children's recreation ground. This had been removed many years before.

ROCHE ABBEY

Maltby, Rotherham

Nestled in the bottom of a small valley, its remaining arches standing over 70 feet tall, sits the once magnificent but now ruined twelfth-century Abbey of Santa Maria de Rupe. Legend states that its colloquial name of Roche (rock) stemmed from the finding of a sacred stone, said to bear the sign of a cross, which had originally inspired the monks to build here. The abbey was founded in 1147 by a group of Cistercian monks who had travelled from Northumberland, and remained prosperous until the Dissolution. In 1538, its brethren were turned out into the surrounding woodland. Local records describe how the monks hid religious relics in their habits and tried frantically to bury them under the trees, to no avail, since local peasants were already raiding abbey stone, and taking wooden pews to repair their carts and wagons!

Roche Abbey belonged to the private estate of the Lords Scarborough for many years. It had become so overgrown that, in 1772, one visitor noted that 'Lord Scarborough, to whom it belongs, neglects it as much as if he was afraid of ghosts...' Two years later, the 4th Earl employed the famous landscape gardener Lancelot 'Capability' Brown to 'make the abbey scenic' once again. Only when the Ministry of Works took over custodianship in 1921 was much of the unnatural 'landscaping' removed, revealing previously buried stonework.

The spectre of a monk, dressed in white Cistercian robes, has been seen flitting at great speed through the ruins of the abbey after dark. In 1991, local teenagers Caroline Abrahams and Liz Baker witnessed a robed figure, 'shining with an unearthly greyish light', crossing the lawn in the direction of the public footpath which runs around the abbey. Local people maintain that on certain evenings, strange unearthly noises can be heard coming from the secluded car-park.

Abbey House was built as a hunting lodge in the middle of the seventeenth century. English Heritage custodian Les Hallford has been told on several occasions by visitors that they have seen a phantom Grey Lady appear at one of the upstairs windows. One of the upper rooms is rumoured to have been the place of a maidservant's suicide in the eighteenth century, and several have heard the mysterious crying of the illegitimate child she is supposed to have murdered here. Several years ago, one visitor saw the spectre of a maidservant dressed in a black and white uniform disappearing up the stairs. In the summer of 1995, a visiting party from a local historical society regretted staying the night when they were disturbed by heavy footsteps on the empty staircase.

Staff and visitors have on occasion caught sight of an unidentified black shadow flitting through the old walkways which once gave entrance to the now demolished kitchen. In May 1996, a keen photographer who visited the abbey alone one Sunday afternoon was startled to hear asthmatic breathing and coughing behind him as he took photographs in the grounds. Believing a visitor to be in trouble, he turned to find himself alone, and felt an icy cold blast 'rush past' him. The mystery was compounded when the gentleman noted that he could hear distant bells ringing throughout – the abbey's situation renders this impossible, and its own bells were removed at the Dissolution several hundred years previously. When his photographs were developed, they featured a mysterious white haze.

Roche Abbey is administered by English Heritage, and can be visited between 1 April and 31 October from 10 a.m. until dusk. The surrounding woodland public footpaths are accessible all year round.

PACKMAN LANE
Kiveton Park, Rotherham

Packman Lane is an ancient and relatively isolated former trade route which runs for around 2½ miles from Kiveton Park station, Rotherham, to the village of Whitwell, on the Derbyshire border. Until the 1800s it had been known as Rykenild Street and later the Street, and its partially straight course, coupled with the fact that Rykenild was the name given to many Roman roads, suggests that, barring the modern tarmac, in parts Packman Lane is well over a thousand years old. It connects with a network of similar lanes which cut through the arable fields and woodland in the area, which have long been believed by locals to be haunted. A ghostly Roman legion has been seen marching here by moonlight, on a ground level significantly lower than that of today. Although no recent sightings have been recorded, it is interesting that Packman Lane's Roman connections are not necessarily common knowledge in the area.

There are, however, regular sightings of another ghost on both Packman Lane and its surrounding roads. A phantom highwayman, on a dark-coloured horse and resplendent in a tricorn hat and a cape, materialises in front of approaching

An archaic carved stone in Thorpe Salvin churchyard

cars. Witnesses note that his appearance seems to be triggered by car headlights. The figure quickly darts from left to right across the road, one silver stirrup flashing briefly, before vanishing into the fields and foliage. Sightings of the highwayman have only been noted in areas without street lighting, and after dark. In the early 1990s a party of local ghost-hunters successfully 'triggered' the apparition a number of times by driving repeatedly over a certain section of the road.

Local legend records that a highwayman was once gibbeted by a boundary wall near the village of Thorpe Salvin as a public warning. Perhaps connected to this haunting are further sightings of a ghostly highwayman who appears on Dinnington Lane, just off the Red Lion Hotel crossroads. The last known sighting occurred in the late 1980s when a local woman driving home after dark was startled by the appearance of a dark shape in front of her car. She described it as 'the figure of a man sitting on a horse, wearing a hat of the old-fashioned tricorn type, with a long flowing cape spread out over the horse's rump'. The horse and rider darted in front of the car and vanished over a hedge into the adjoining field. The motorist, curious as to whether a natural feature in the landscape had possibly misled her, investigated by revisiting the site in daylight. She found nothing which could possibly have been mistaken for a figure on horseback.

CROMWELL'S EATING HOUSE
Conisbrough, Doncaster

Cromwell's Eating House, beautifully restored and converted into a public house and licensed restaurant in the 1980s, was originally a farmhouse built in the seventeenth century. The building passed through many hands and was the subject of constant alteration, becoming a school, a post office, and then a community centre prior to its current transformation. Local legend tells how a former owner of the farm prompted his wife's suicide by confronting her about an alleged affair. Too afraid to live with the consequences of her actions, the woman hanged herself above the stairs. Before recent alterations, the stairs were in the old coffee lounge in which an icy 'cold spot' was noted to make a regular appearance. However, ghostly sightings at

Cromwell's are varied and seemingly unconnected with this particular legend. During renovation work in the early 1980s, an electrician was working upstairs in near-darkness when he was 'brushed past' by a man wearing what he later described as dated farm labourer's clothing. In the early 1990s, a member of the kitchen staff was startled by the sight of a cloaked gentleman in a feathered hat, reminiscent of a Cavalier, who was walking down the stairs. The figure vanished in an instant before his eyes. Shortly afterwards, the landlord and several customers remaining after last orders heard what they described as 'a huge gust of air screeching past' them as they sat in the downstairs bar. The invisible force 'banged' into one of the downstairs walls violently, and the remaining customers left in a hurry. A spate of accidents also occurred in the kitchen area, when an unseen hand seemed to slam the kitchen door in the faces of staff as they carried piles of plates to and fro.

HELLABY HALL HOTEL
Hellaby, Rotherham

When Ralph Fretwell returned from business in Barbados in 1692, he began to build Hellaby Hall in the style of the Dutch colonial homes he had seen abroad. Unfortunately his stay on English land was to be brief. Ralph and his wife did not see eye to eye, and this prompted him to return to Barbados where he remained until his death. Following the Fretwells, Hellaby Hall passed through the hands of a small number of families during which it was let to tenant farmers and even rented out in part. A renowned resident during the earlier part of the nineteenth century was Samuel Clarke, remembered for introducing Methodism to the adjacent parish of Maltby.

Hellaby's estate includes a deserted medieval village which is now registered with English Heritage, its history of occupation stretching back as far as the tenth century. The remains of a well, an enclosure, examples of medieval ridge and furrow ploughing, a corn-drying oven and a post-medieval 'long house' have been found. Research has indicated that the village could have been abandoned during the 1400s, possibly after an economic catastrophe such as the outbreak of an epidemic, perhaps even the Black Death.

Hellaby Hall remained empty from 1976 until 1989. In 1980 the building was gutted by fire, and, over the next ten years, the house and its approaching lane became a site of local intrigue as many Hellaby and Maltby villagers reported sighting an apparition which was never successfully identified. Several witnesses testified to having seen figures moving behind its darkened and empty windows late at night. In 1989 a redevelopment programme began which transformed the hall into a hotel. Despite three years' work on the building, it traded for only three months before going into receivership. Tomorrows Leisure plc acquired the hotel in May 1995, and within weeks it was open for trade.

Previous tenants of the building were able to give only vague descriptions of the hauntings which occurred here. They noted a 'little male ghost' who is said to occupy a corner of the drawing-room, and an 'unknown presence' in the old barn. Current staff have nicknamed their third ghost 'Granny Fretwell', and note that, although no firm sightings have ever occurred, lights operate themselves and furniture sometimes moves of its own accord within the oldest part of the building, the old hall. Curiosity prompted staff to publicise their unseen ghost in 1996 in an attempt to coax a public response and ascertain further details. Unfortunately no information was forthcoming, and since the atmosphere in this remnant of the original building is decidedly warm and friendly, staff and visitors are happy to observe the occasional example of inexplicable phenomena with curiosity.

For bookings: Hellaby Hall Hotel, Old Hellaby Lane, Rother-ham S66 8SN.

JUNCTION 31, M1
Aston, Sheffield

The county of South Yorkshire has a long tradition of random appearances of large, mysterious black cat-type creatures. Such encounters have been recorded over several centuries, beginning in 1456 with the 'Barmboro Wildcat'. This huge beast is said to have pounced on local man Percival Cresacre in the porch of Barnburgh church, which still features a dark 'bloodstain' on its stone floor. Cresacre struggled so valiantly for his life that his feline attacker died with him, and thereafter, a wildcat was incorporated into the Cresacre family coat of arms.

Over five hundred years on, the legend of the mysterious wildcat was resurrected when a well-documented spate of sightings of an unusually large black feline occurred in the Aston/Todwick area. In 1993, a local out walking his dog encountered what he described as a 'huge black wildcat', which slunk into foliage on arable land in Todwick. The following summer, Karen Baker was leaving the M1 northbound at Junction 31 in Aston one night, when she was startled by a dark shape on the island. Out of the thin mist which lay at ground level ran a large black animal with an extremely long tail, too large to be a domestic cat but certainly not a dog. It vanished at the opposite side of the road. Within months, local man Steve Moore noted the brief appearance of the same creature when walking one dawn along the same stretch of road close to

Junction 31. Comparable sightings occurred in other areas of Sheffield and Rotherham, but no witness ever captured the reclusive creature(s) on camera, and no physical evidence of its existence was found.

The mystery seemed closer to being solved when two walkers stumbled across the grisly remains of a large rotting carcass of seemingly feline origin in the summer of 1996. Scottish wildlife experts showed an interest in examining the remains, which were of an animal considerably larger than a domestic cat. Intriguingly, the badly decayed carcass had been discovered 100 yards from the River Dearne, close to a place known as Cat Hill.

THE LINDHOLME AREA
Doncaster

The site of the World War II aerodrome at Lindholme is now occupied by Lindholme prison, although those fortunate enough to take a glider flight from the local air club will still be able to see the line of the old runway scarring the land below. This area of South Yorkshire is particularly boggy, its peat being used by a local fertiliser company who inadvertently unearthed a lost Polish fighter plane while digging here in the early 1980s. The pilot's corpse had been preserved well in the peaty conditions, although the only means by which he could be identified was by his style of dress. This unknown war casualty was soon after accorded a full military burial.

Over the years there have been many sightings of the shadowy figure of a spectral airman appearing around Lindholme. Local workers and residents alike tell tales of hearing voices and being approached by a stranger wearing antiquated flying uniform, who disappears in an instant. It was assumed that the rediscovery and consequent burial of the airman at Lindholme would finally lay to rest any 'presence'. However, certain discoveries and reported hauntings in the Lindholme area indicate that more than one casualty of war occurred here. Local man Aidan Caddick remembers a British World War II Lancaster bomber crashing into a field close to his Lindholme home, following an error during take-off. All four of the crew were killed instantly. Although the authorities took responsibility for removing the bodies and sifting the wreckage, the impact of the crash meant that human remains were in evidence in the field for long afterwards. When, in the early 1980s, a farmer friend of Mr Caddick discovered the long-forgotten remains of the aeroplane during ploughing, the pair began to investigate further. They unearthed the back of a human skull and immediately contacted a local RAF base with their story. Having been informed that the area was not a designated war grave and that digging was therefore perfectly legal, the pair visited the site once again. Although they found parts of the fuselage and took away bullets as souvenirs, the earth had very quickly swallowed up most of the remains and neither Mr Caddick nor his colleague ever successfully relocated their grisly discovery. Soon after he took the Lancaster's fuselage home, Mr Caddick's daughter (who knew nothing of the discovery) was startled one night by the appearance of a young man in World War II flying gear, who appeared at the end of her bed before vanishing suddenly. Mr Caddick's wife also began to experience chills when walking past the wreckage souvenirs which her husband had left in the kitchen. She insisted that they were removed to an outhouse, where they still remain today.

Another unusual experience from the Lindholme area perhaps indicates the existence of yet another ghost. Local man John Parsons was walking to the works department close to the hangars where trainee pilots were based long after the end of the war. A bad fog had risen off the marsh surrounding Lindholme, and, in the middle of winter, it was already dark at 4 p.m. Mr Parsons heard a 'well-educated officer's accent' call out to him, 'Have any planes made it back tonight?' Immediately he answered that he did not know, and turned to see who had asked such an unusual question. A man wearing an old-fashioned flying suit was disappearing into the mist towards the old equipment store. Mr Parsons was aware that modern trainee pilots still wore dated regulation issue, although on arriving at his destination he realised that nobody could possibly be flying on such a night. His colleagues were not surprised by his encounter, and attributed it to the ghost of 'Lindholme Billy'. Soon afterwards, Mr Parsons learned that other members of staff had also heard myterious Polish voices around the old airfield, indicating that 'Lindholme Billy' was not merely one ghost, but a name used for at least two, possibly more, phantoms believed to haunt the area. More intriguing still, local records indicate that Lindholme was once believed to be haunted by the ghost of a medieval hermit named William de Lindholme, whose grave was discovered in the early 1700s, long after his death, close to the old Lindholme Hall. William de Lindholme could well be the original prototype for the legendary local ghost today known as 'Lindholme Billy'.

EAST YORKSHIRE

BURTON AGNES MANOR
Driffield

Burton Agnes Manor is a rare example of a Norman manor house, expanded and encased in brick during the seventeenth century. Sir Henry Griffith undertook alteration of the building in the early 1600s, and the manor has remained within his line of descendants to the present day. The legendary 'screaming skull' of Burton Agnes is today bricked up in a secret cupboard, although its associated tale of murder and intrigue continues to draw visitors from throughout the country.

The screaming skull is reputed to be that of Anne (Catherine) Griffith, who was attacked by vagabonds whilst returning from a visit to Lady St Quentin at nearby Harpham Hall. Although Anne managed to raise the alarm, and was taken home to Burton Agnes, she died within days from injuries sustained during the attack. Her death-bed request was that her skull should always be kept within the house she had loved. Unfor-

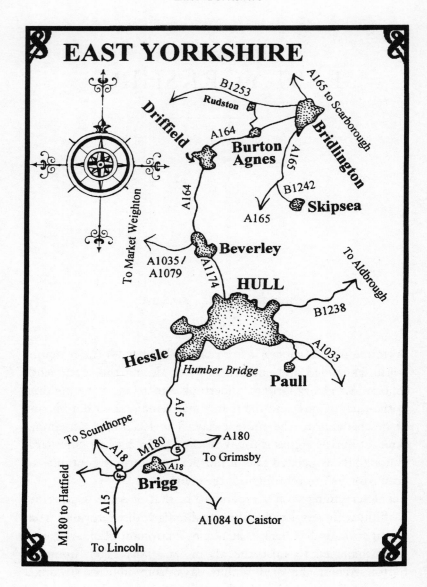

EAST YORKSHIRE

B1253
Rudston
A165 to Scarborough
Driffield
A164
Burton Agnes
Bridlington
A165
B1242
Skipsea
A165
A164
To Market Weighton
Beverley
A1035 / A1079
A1174
HULL
To Aldbrough
B1238
A1033
Hessle
Humber Bridge
Paull
A15
To Scunthorpe
A18
M180
A180
To Grimsby
M180 to Hatfield
A18
Brigg
A15
A1084 to Caistor
To Lincoln

tunately, Anne's sisters Margaret and Frances did not honour her dying wish, burying her instead in the local churchyard. The manor was soon plagued by poltergeist activity, namely terrifying wailing, slamming doors, and unaccountable hammering noises from within the wooden panelled walls. Accounts of the story vary from here onwards, some suggesting that Anne's body was exhumed within weeks to reveal a bare skull decapitated from the body, others stating that two years elapsed before her head was finally removed and taken back to the manor. All accounts seem to agree that this gesture finally quelled the ghostly disturbances, and the skull was kept on display, in a casket on the table of the great hall. Two further attempts were made to remove it, once when it was buried in the garden (resulting in renewed wailing and banging within the manor), and finally when a servant tossed the skull into a passing cart. The donkey harnessed to the cart became transfixed, and refused to move until the skull was taken back into the house. Thereafter, it was bricked into a secret niche to avoid a repeat performance at some point in the future.

The identity of Anne Griffith remains something of a mystery, as there is no firm record of her birth or death. Although the local church possesses a memorial tablet which records the deaths of Sir Henry's three sons and two daughters, Anne is not among them. Further records also indicate that only two of the Griffith children reached adulthood – again, Anne being neither of these. More intriguing still, the large and beautiful painting by Geeraerts on display at Burton Agnes (depicting Frances, Margaret and Anne resplendent in fine costume) shows Anne in mourning dress, suggesting a posthumous reproduction.

Custodian Keith Hawkins has worked at Burton Agnes for over fifty years, the latest in a line of his forebears to do so. He noted that as long as the manor is 'kept right', staff are rarely bothered by supernatural phenomena ... although when occasional alterations have taken place, unaccountable noises have echoed once more throughout the building. The mother of the late owner was convinced that Burton Agnes was haunted, having seen for herself a spectral lady in a long gown wandering into a bedroom, and seating herself on a chair by the fireplace. In 1992, a young boy visiting Burton Agnes with his grandmother swore that he had seen the spectre of a headless woman in the old Norman undercroft. The boy talked at length to staff working in the café at the time, and all who listened to his account were convinced of his sincerity.

Cleaning staff at Burton Agnes regularly encounter a 'beautiful phantom perfume' on unlocking certain state rooms in the morning. Keith Hawkins has accompanied the cleaners in the hope of experiencing this for himself, but has so far been unsuccessful! Mr Hawkins' sister-in-law once lived in Burton Agnes' gatehouse, and recounted how she regularly saw a ghostly lady (with head intact) peering over the side wall before vanishing. Fortunately she remained unperturbed by these encounters, although canine visitors to Burton Agnes today do not appear to accept its haunted history quite so calmly, often refusing to venture past the manor door.

Burton Agnes Manor is adminstered by English Heritage, and is open to the public throughout the year, at any reasonable time. The adjoining Burton Agnes Hall and gardens are privately owned and closed to the public.

THE TOWN OF HESSLE
Hull

'The Ancient Town of Hessle', as its road signs points out, is a place with a great deal of history. Until the early 1900s Hessle was renowned as a smugglers' haven, its foreshore on the banks of the River Humber being the point of delivery for consignments of contraband. Several smugglers' tunnels are rumoured to run from the foreshore to various locations around the town, although they are no longer used and their entrances are forgotten. During the building of the health centre in The Square in the 1980s, an ancient tunnel was discovered which did indeed run in the direction of the foreshore; this was later sealed off for safety reasons. The foreshore itself is rumoured by locals to be regularly in use by a local coven of witches, who were stumbled across by one unwary local gentleman out for a night-time stroll in 1994.

The Square is a remnant of Hessle's historic past, its beautiful church and historic buildings successfully integrating modern additions. Many of the staff and locals who frequent The Square's old taverns are willing to discuss Hessle's supernatural history with the curious, including the rumour that 'angels' have been known to manifest themselves in Hessle church from time to time. Jenny Brough Lane took its name from a young girl murdered here on a moonlit night in the last century. Her decapitated body was found lying in a ditch, although the head was never recovered. Several unwary travellers are said to have encountered the phantom of the poor girl wandering the lane on moonlit nights, and during the 1980s there was a spate of reports of 'phantom screams' in the area whose source was never traced.

Tranby House, a former family home later converted into Hessle High School, is renowned by locals for having once been owned by a gentleman who had the misfortune to book a ticket on the *Titanic*'s ill-fated maiden voyage. As the great ship began to sink, and the captain ordered that women and children must be evacuated on to the scant lifeboats before their menfolk, the cunning man dressed himself hurriedly in women's attire . . .

and lived to tell the tale. Whether it is his guilty spirit which currently haunts the school is unknown, for an atmosphere of supernatural coldness pervades the main staircase and the stage, and is still experienced by pupils to this day. Several former pupils suggest that the staircase is haunted by the spirit of a young girl who once resided here, committing suicide after being forbidden to marry her lover, others have heard rumours concerning the alleged murder of a young girl by a former caretaker in days long since past.

The Admiral Hawke, as it stands today, incorporates an earlier, smaller pub, which was used in the last century as a boarding house for Customs and Excise men hoping to capture local smugglers. The oldest part of the building is now listed, ensuring that no major alterations can remove its historic timbers. Annie Melhuish, landlady of the Admiral since 1991, has become accustomed to the regular visits of a restless spirit of unknown origin. Although the ghost has never materialised, Annie and her staff have the distinct impression that the presence is female, and have nicknamed her Mary. Barman Nick Stubbs was unfortunate enough to be standing with his back to a large bottle display when it was tipped off the back bar in 1995, although miraculously nothing was broken. Glasses and paperwork stored at the back of the bar have regularly been thrown at certain members of staff, particularly on Sundays! Annie's office, situated upstairs, is frequently visited by a 'presence' which causes the lighting to flicker and dim; it is often accompanied by a 'cold draught' which rustles paperwork pinned to the walls and which Annie points out has nothing to do with an open window. The ghost has also been known to lock the unwary in the cellar, on one occasion forcing Annie to turn all the beer pumps off so that staff at the bar would be alerted as to her whereabouts. Despite frequent ghostly tampering with the electricity and glasses whizzing through the air,

Annie Melhuish feels in some way comforted to know that she is not alone as she locks the doors of the Admiral Hawke at night, preferring to think of her resident ghost as a protective spirit.

The Marquis of Granby, a former coaching inn, is next door to the Admiral. Perhaps ghostly activity between the two public houses can be linked, for here also bar staff report unusual phenomena. In 1995 a member of staff was accompanied to the ladies' toilet by an invisible visitor. She clearly heard the main door open and close, after which a cubicle door was opened and then locked, although on investigation the cubicle was empty, and the door appeared to have locked itself.

FORT PAULL
Paull, Hull

At first glance, the antiquated building which nestles on the north bank of the River Humber appears to be no more than a World War II fortification. The history of the former Paull Point Battery goes back much further, however, the first artillery strong-point being recorded here in the time of Henry VIII. Much of the building of Fort Paull as it stands today was begun in the 1860s, as part of England's coastline defence against the threat from Louis Napoleon Bonaparte, Emperor of France. Consequently, the fort is a listed building and a scheduled ancient monument which, despite never having suffered a wartime attack, was designed to be utterly impenetrable and extremely well hidden. Fort Paull's survival was recently threatened, prompting its current owners to suggest a restoration plan including the creation of a military museum and heritage centre here. In 1996 English Heritage and the Holderness Borough Council approved the proposals, and it is hoped that the fort will be opened to the public for the first time during 1997.

Fort Paull is associated with the ghostly presence of a Victorian lady known locally as Rabbit Nanny, who paraded the streets towards the end of the last century, earning her living from selling rabbits. Rabbit Nanny was born in Leeds but plied her trade in and around Hull, where her selling call was said to be so loud that it carried clearly across the banks of the River Humber. Being very poor, the lady took the decision to bequeath her body to medical research, duly receiving a sum of money whilst still alive. After her death, her body was used by a Hull medical school, where her skeleton was then kept for several years. When the establishment closed, a local man purchased the bones, eventually selling them on to forces billeted at Fort Paull. For many years the skeleton of Rabbit Nanny was used to frighten new recruits, being hidden for pranks in one of the sentry boxes or hung in a window with a glowing lantern behind it to frighten passers-by. Finally its disposal was ordered by an officer who had become tired of his comrades' mischief-making. Rabbit Nanny's bones were buried in the grounds of the fort. Brian Rushworth, the administrator of the site, is aware that a number of local people have reported hearing the selling call of Rabbit Nanny echoing through the area, particularly on dark and misty nights, and others have testified to witnessing a spectral form assumed to be Rabbit Nanny close to Fort Paull.

THE CITY OF HULL

During the early 1990s, a number of eyewitnesses reported seeing the ghost of a man walking across the Humber Bridge. The apparition appeared on several occasions and startled motorists with its unnerving habit of stepping suddenly into the road. On each occasion vehicles were forced to brake hard to avoid the figure, who was then seen to vanish suddenly into the night. A local woman who encountered the ghost described how she saw a 'misty shadow', which she somehow recognised as the figure of a man, appear in front of her moving vehicle. She performed an emergency stop and the apparition vanished into thin air.

According to a Hull-based psychic study group with an interest in local hauntings, Albion Street is the focus for a number of sightings of another, different male ghost. In years gone by, Albion Street was considered one of the more fashionable areas of the city, perhaps explaining the spectre of an elderly Victorian man in topcoat and tails who, leaving behind him the strong smell of cigar smoke, has been encountered here. Dr Les Sallis, the society's founder member, undertook an overnight vigil in January 1989 at a former private house on Albion Street to which the ghost was believed to be attached. Both he and a research assistant were stationed in the old wine cellar of the building when they witnessed the materialisation of a male figure. Recording their impressions separately in notes, both observers were able to agree that the figure was that of 'a tall man, [with] silk top hat, [a] long face, long straight grey hair hanging below [his] hat, [and a] white silk cravat with a stud in [the] centre'. Dr Sallis made an attempt to speak to the apparition before it disappeared but received no reply. Its appearance was both preceded and accompanied by the strong smell of cigar smoke, which was noted independently by both researchers.

Visitors to the oldest part of the city of Hull, with its network of cobbled streets and fine historic buildings, may well find themselves at a public house known as the George Inn, on a tiny street eloquently named The Land of Green Ginger. This pub lays claim to having 'the smallest window in England', and was until relatively recently renowned as one of the most haunted pubs in the city. Tales of ghostly happenings here seem to have quietened down since earlier in the century, when the dumb waiter supposedly had a life of its own. Although this Victorian serving device is still visible in the main bar, current staff are no longer troubled by the unseen hand which once operated it. The George Inn ghost had a reputation for ensuring that dirty crockery put into the dumb waiter arrived at the kitchens mysteriously clean. These days, everything has to be done by hand.

SKIPSEA CASTLE

Skipsea, near Bridlington

The surviving earthworks of this once splendid Norman motte and bailey castle, located in a farmer's field with public access, are all that now remain of Flemish soldier Drogo de Bevere's estate. De Bevere was awarded lands throughout the region for his services to William the Conqueror. He was also lucky enough to be offered the hand of one of William's nubile relatives, although legend tells how this nuptial entanglement proved to be his downfall. De Bevere treated his wife brutally, and is said to have poisoned a goblet of wine with which he plied her soon after their marriage. After her agonising death, he disposed of the body in a well (or at another site both unsavoury and unknown). Realising that his wife's mysterious disappearance would not please William, de Bevere borrowed funds to escape abroad, and was never traced again. His castle was destroyed in the thirteenth century.

The ghost of a young woman dressed in a long white gown has been witnessed wandering the lane close to the castle by local people throughout this and the last century. Early recorded accounts tell how she was seen walking next to the lane which runs alongside Albermarle Hill, before vanishing without trace. Today, however, according to locals of the area who indicate that the legend is very much alive, the White Lady is to be seen riding a white horse along the bottom of the dike at Skipsea Brough, close to the castle earthworks. While some associate the spectre with the legend of the Lady de Bevere, others suggest that the White Lady of Skipsea is in fact the ghost of a woman murdered during the time of Henry VIII, several hundred years after the castle was demolished. It is said that her murderer was an assassin paid for his part in the deed. It seems likely that two separate 'hauntings' from two different points in history have been combined in local folklore.

Skipsea is also associated with at least one more unidentified female ghost, this time that of a woman wearing a tatty shawl and rags who has been seen walking across the road fronted by the Bound Inn, not far from the castle earthworks. The last recorded sighting took place in the late 1980s when a regular customer, who watched her from the roadside, initially assumed the ghost to be a poverty-stricken traveller.

Skipsea Castle earthworks are situated in a private field through which there is a public right of way, and are accessible at all reasonable times. The castle is administered by English Heritage.

ELSHAM HALL COUNTRY AND WILDLIFE PARK
Elsham, Brigg

Elsham was first recorded in Domesday, later becoming the site for an Augustinian monastery where errant and lazy canons were sent, as a penance, to 'fast' on bread, fish and beer. Consequently, at the Dissolution of their monastery under the orders of Henry VIII, the brethren fled to Belgium and went on to found a brewery! In 1931 the Elsham estate was purchased by the Elwes family, whose careful restoration has transformed it into a fascinating craft and conservation centre which opened to the public for the first time in 1970. Alongside attractions such as craft workshops, a trout lake, tropical aviaries, a nature trail and a falconry school, Elsham's award-winning Barn Theatre offers regular entertainment . . . and is believed to be haunted. Staff and members of visiting theatre companies alike have noted doors closing themselves without human aid, and a variety of objects which had been unaccountably 'moved'. Staff consequently nicknamed their unseen presence Mrs Jackson, and the strange phenomena which often occur prior to performances at the Barn Theatre are generally regarded as a 'lucky omen' for productions.

Elsham Hall Country and Wildlife Park is open daily from early April to mid-September (weather permitting) 11 a.m. to 5 p.m.; it is also open at weekends only from mid-March and up until late September. The Barn Theatre, Granary Restaurant and Conference Complex are open throughout the year subject to reservation. The hall itself is not open to the public.

THE TOWN OF BEVERLEY

The pretty market town of Beverley comprises medieval, Gothic, Elizabethan and Georgian architecture patched together around two traditional market squares and the red-brick North Bar, the last remaining medieval gateway into old Beverley. The historic minster was built on the foundations of an early Saxon church, and still holds one of the only two 'frithstools' left in the country. This is a sanctuary seat of Saxon origin which once earned fugitives thirty days' protection from the authorities. A baron of William the Conqueror, known as Toustain, violated the sanctuary of Beverley Minster when he led a band of soldiers here in pursuit of innocent townsfolk during a raid. It is said that as Toustain crossed the threshold a flash of light engulfed his body, deforming him into a hideous mass of tangled limbs. William ordered that the sanctuary privileges of Beverley Minster were never to be abused again. (St Mary's Church, Beverley, is also famed for its quirky medieval carving of the 'Pilgrim Rabbit', on which Lewis Carroll is believed to have based the character of the White Rabbit in *Alice's Adventures in Wonderland*.)

The tormented ghost of Sir Josceline Percy, a son of the 4th Earl of Northumberland, is legendarily to be encountered driving a coach and headless horses through the centre of town on stormy nights. Sir Josceline was poisoned in the sixteenth century shortly after he willed his estate to his servants. On his death, the servants took their employer's money and belongings and left the house. Although an investigation into Sir Josceline's death was staged, the jury were friends of the servants involved. Shortly after their acquittal, Sir Josceline's frustrated spirit began its nocturnal appearances.

The restored part-stone, part-brick buildings of Beverley Friary are set inside a traditional walled garden along with the remains of several ancient wells once used by its brethren. Inside the main building medieval paintings and murals have survived, and the friary is the only remaining example of a Dominican establishment in the county. Today, Beverley Friary incorporates a youth hostel, and over the years there have been sporadic sightings of a phantom monk in the vicinity. One local man was horrified to see a robed figure step out in front of his car one

The Pilgrim Rabbit, St Mary's Church, in haunted Beverley

night on Chantry Lane. He braked hard and the apparition vanished. The Beverley Ghost Walk includes the friary. In 1995 the tour guide was approached by a woman in her mid-twenties who had grown up in the area and who told him how, as a child many years before, she regularly took a short cut home through the walled grounds. On two separate occasions she recalled being 'silently watched' by a hooded friar in a long habit who was standing with his back against the perimeter wall as she passed by.

THE RUDSTON MONOLITH
Rudston

The breathtaking Rudston monolith, reputedly the tallest standing stone in Britain and most likely a pagan symbol marking an early sacred site, towers 26 feet above ground level in the graveyard of All Saints church in the village of Rudston. It is estimated that the monolith may be embedded up to 25 feet below ground level to prevent it from toppling over, and it is thought to have been hewn from the grey rock of the Cleveland Hills by people of the Bronze Age. This enormous stone is today capped with lead to prevent further corrosion, and certain faint scoring on its surface could suggest that it was once patterned with a linear design. The monolith is the focus for many superstitions which have grown up around it over the centuries, including an alleged link with black magic at an earlier point in history.

The Rudston monolith is situated behind the Church of All Saints, Rudston, and may be visited at all reasonable times.

Rudston Church and Monolith, perhaps the largest standing stone in Britain

BURTON CONSTABLE HALL
near Hull

The Constable family were landowners in East Yorkshire's Holderness region in medieval times. Although it is not known at what date the original foundations of the medieval manor were laid here, in 1570 John Constable enlarged an existing 'tower house' which was once used in the defence of a long-gone market town. Parts of the medieval manor today survive in the north wing of Burton Constable. Throughout the following centuries, the house was expanded and enlarged several times, with both its exterior and interior becoming more grand and lavish with each step. Today, members of the Chichester-Constable family still live here, as they have done for over four hundred years, amid the finery, *objets d'art* and 'curiosities' collected by previous generations of the Constable family and now on display to the public.

Burton Constable's surrounding parkland is reputed to be haunted by a phantom Roman legion which still marches along a long-lost Roman road here. Although the legion does not appear to have been active in recent years, the hall itself has several ghosts attached. In 1987, Burton Constable was featured on the TV programme *Bellamy's Bugle*, during which the renowned scientist and self-confessed sceptic David Bellamy stayed overnight here. Although paranormal occurrences at the hall do not happen to order, and Bellamy encountered nothing out of the ordinary during his stay, current staff note that both they and visitors have observed a series of inexplicable events. The most commonly witnessed apparition at Burton Constable is that of a woman wearing dark, dated clothing who has been identified as Nurse Dowdall, a companion-housekeeper who lived in the house around the turn of the nineteenth century. Tradition suggests that the ghost appears as a gesture of welcome to certain visitors, and her appearance has been taken as a sign of approval. When the mother of John Chichester-Constable arrived at the hall during her son's incumbency, Nurse Dowdall appeared to her on her first night here. More recently, in 1994, a child of around ten years old who was visiting with her parents approached a guide and asked whether she was 'a servant at the hall'. The guide replied that she supposed she was, and the child asked why she was not dressed 'like the lady in the ballroom'. The description she gave was of a woman in a long dark skirt with a shawl over her shoulders, which staff consequently felt to be yet another sighting of Nurse Dowdall. A male apparition which was identified as William Constable, who owned the hall in the eighteenth century, was witnessed on one occasion by John Chichester-Constable's grandmother. There have also been several reports of the spectre of a nun who seems to 'glide' along the landings and through the ballroom, having some link with the Nun's Room from which the ghost has been seen to appear. However, a previous member of staff commented on the wonderfully 'peaceful' atmosphere of this room, and regularly used to rest here!

Another resident ghost is that of a black Labrador, of which there have been numerous sightings over the years. On two separate occasions in 1996, a guide felt what she took to be a dog brushing up against her legs and gently 'shaking itself' in the State Bedroom.

Burton Constable Hall, administered by the Burton Constable Foundation, is open to the public between Easter Sunday and 30 September, Sunday to Thursday, and additionally on Saturdays in July and August. The house opens from 1 p.m. to 5 p.m., the grounds and tea room from noon.

WEST YORKSHIRE

TEMPLE NEWSAM HOUSE
Leeds

Originally owned by the mysterious Knights Templar, the secretive and wealthy order of warrior monks, the grand Temple Newsam House has been called 'The Hampton Court of the North'. It passed into the hands of the Hospitaller Knights of St John, an early form of the Red Cross, before becoming a palatial family residence. Today, Temple Newsam is an art gallery and museum with a haunted history stretching back more than two centuries.

The house was known to be haunted as early as 1751, when the Georgian ghost-hunter James Earnshaw visited and subsequently included Temple Newsam in his book of regional ghostlore. At this time the house was the seat of Viscount Irwin, and Earnshaw took details from the Viscount and his staff concerning the legend of the White Lady of Temple Newsam. This ghost was believed to be that of Lady Jane Dudley, a ward

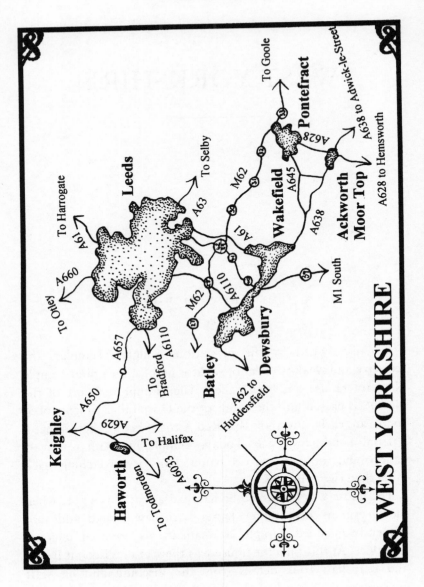

of the Countess of Lennox, who resided at the house during the 1560s. She reputedly fell in love with Lord Darnley, who was born at Temple Newsam. When Lady Jane heard of Darnley's marriage to Mary Queen of Scots in July 1565, she made a noose out of her girdle and hanged herself within the house at a location today forgotten. Her spirit, wearing a white robe, lace cap and small ruff, was known to appear in the sixteenth-century part of the building. According to Earnshaw's accounts, a maidservant who had witnessed the apparition in 1735 fell into severe convulsions brought on by shock, from which it took her some time to recover. Throughout the eighteenth century the ghost of Lady Jane continued to cause consternation amongst staff and residents, and as late as 1891 an elderly maid gave a description of an apparition dressed in white which tallied exactly with Earnshaw's earlier account of the White Lady.

Temple Newsam's Blue Lady is thought to be a member of the Ingram family who resided at the house in the late 1600s, during the reign of Charles II; if so, it is her portrait, resplendent in a blue gown, which still hangs in the house today. Her ghost has been seen by a number of people, including former resident Lord Halifax, who watched intrigued as a spectral young woman dressed in blue walked across his firelit bedroom and through a wall into the adjoining dressing-room, one evening in 1908. When Miss Ingram was young she was the victim of an attack which scarred her for life. She was returning from a visit to local friends when her coach was attacked by three robbers, who pulled her from it and ripped rings and other jewels from her person. It was said that Miss Ingram never fully recovered. She became obsessive about hiding her valuables in and around the house, and was in constant fear of being robbed. Even towards the end of her life she remained the same, and it was said that she could never rest for long periods. In 1926 Temple

Newsam was visited by a psychic gentleman who knew nothing of the hauntings associated with the house. He gave a detailed description of a lady in a Carolean costume whom he could see standing by a doorway inside the house. Both he and other witnesses to this ghost have noted a scar over the woman's right eye. This scar is not apparent on the portrait of Miss Ingram, and whether it was due to the robbers' brutal attack will never be known.

In 1704, on the victory of Marlborough at the Battle of Blenheim, Temple Newsam was in uproar with celebration, and an enormous bonfire was set ablaze in the grounds to mark the occasion. Servants and estate workers were invited to partake of food and ale alongside the resident Irwin family, and a sizeable crowd gathered to feast and make merry. A manservant named William Collinson had developed an obsession with a fellow employee, a maid named Phoebe Gray. When Phoebe disappeared briefly into her room to retrieve something, Collinson followed. It will never be known what passed between them, except that he strangled her and removed the corpse to the old well in the house, dumping it unceremoniously while the party continued in the grounds. For several days his secret remained undiscovered, until at last the fully clothed body of Phoebe Gray was recovered. Unbeknown to Collinson, another servant had witnessed him near the maid's room on the night of her disappearance. He finally confessed to the murder and was hanged at York. His ghost was reported over the following century, with at least two recorded accounts in the 1930s. All accounts described how the manservant wore curious, 'old-fashioned dress', which tallied exactly with clothing detailed in an eighteenth-century household account, today kept at Leeds Reference Library. According to local writer Grace Gladwin, who researched Temple Newsam's haunted history in 1949, visitors who spent the night next to the room in which the murder was committed heard strange tapping and dragging noises which they likened to the sounds of a woman wearing high heels being dragged backwards across the room. These sounds were always accompanied by shuffling footsteps.

In 1996, Leeds resident Deborah Singleton recounted an experience she herself had when visiting Temple Newsam in the early 1980s with her father. It was early evening and the pair had arrived rather too late to enter the house, as it was just being locked, so they decided to enjoy a walk around the grounds with their dog. Deborah related: 'As we approached the house from the field, my dad stopped to wait for our dog and I carried on up to the house. The house is built along three sides of a square, the cut-out side which overlooks the large field having windows facing on to it from all three storeys, and a paved area with benches around, dedicated to people who have died. Along the top of the building there is a carved inscription, which can be read along, from one side to the other, just under the eaves and above the third-storey window. As I followed the writing round, dusk was beginning to fall, the house was in complete darkness and it was starting to get a little chilly. I got to the middle of the building and as I looked at the very middle window, I saw a woman, dressed entirely in grey, almost as if she was made up of smoke. She looked sadly down at me for around half a minute, and then disintegrated into nothing. Rumour has it, apparently, that the house is supposed to be haunted by a Grey Lady, although I was not aware of this at the time, being quite young.'

Also shrouded in mystery are a number of reports of sinister screams coming from the Red Room, along with a 'ghostly mist' in the long gallery. Visitors have occasionally witnessed the spectre of a Knight Templar, and a monk in a brown cowl and a robe who could possibly be connected with the early St John order who once resided at Temple Newsam.

Temple Newsam House is administered by Leeds Leisure Services, a department of Leeds City Council, and is open daily throughout the week and from 1 p.m. on Sundays.

THE ACKWORTH–PONTEFRACT ROAD

During 1991, Deborah Singleton travelled to Ackworth to spend the weekend with a friend. On the first evening it was decided that they would go to nearby Pontefract, and Deborah's friend agreed to drive. Late that night they returned to Ackworth via the long, unlit Ackworth–Pontefract road. As they reached an avenue of curiously leaning trees which grow by the roadside at one particular point, Deborah suddenly saw the back of a stagecoach appear directly in front of the bonnet of the car. It seemed to be travelling at exactly the same speed as the car itself, at around 50 miles per hour. Deborah was briefly aware of seeing the 'billowing coat-tails' of a coachman before she shielded her head with her hands instinctively, expecting an impact. However, the stagecoach, which she later recalled as having been surrounded in mist, vanished in a second, and her companion had seen nothing at all.

Long Lane in Ackworth is also the site at which at least two locals have independently heard the sounds of a large crowd marching close to the houses, on each occasion at around three in the morning. Despite the fact that one described the sound as seeming to belong to a 'Roman legion', local history suggests that the area is likely to have once been on a Crusaders' route, since the remains of a Crusaders' hospice exist in the foundations of what is today a private cottage in a nearby village.

THE TOWN OF HAWORTH

The beautiful moorland town of Haworth attracts visitors from far afield with its rugged open countryside and traditional Yorkshire stone dwellings, not to mention its connection with the renowned literary family the Brontës, whose clergyman father settled at the parsonage here in their childhood. Visitors to Haworth who look carefully at the architecture of certain houses and shops will notice a number of antiquated carved stone heads set into the masonry and brickwork. It is no coincidence that this area was once a Celtic stronghold, being inhabited by the Brigantes, who revered the human head as the symbolic font of all knowledge and power. Carved heads such as the examples to be seen in Haworth today were used protectively, being believed to ward off evil and bring prosperity to the household they adorned. The practice has never been totally forgotten. Visitors who drink at the Old Sun Hotel on the ancient packhorse route of West Lane will notice a stone head set above the door. The Old Sun was once a coaching inn and was extensively renovated before the turn of the last century. However, far from this head having been set into the masonry in the distant past, its carving was commissioned by landlord Ian Hollings in 1980! Previous tenants had complained of ghostly activity within the building. The figure of a man had been known to appear in a corner of one of the upstairs rooms. Local folklore attributed the haunting to the spirit of a workman killed tragically during the building's early renovations. Despite the fact that Mr Hollings considered himself a disbeliever in such supernatural matters, he adhered to tradition in the hope of banishing any unwanted presence, and noted that the Old Sun was at peace thereafter.

The Black Bull public house at the top of Main Street has changed minimally since Branwell Brontë, brother of Emily,

Charlotte and Anne, came here to drink and game with dice and cards. Branwell's favourite haunt was the little back parlour, from where, if rumours are true, he often had to flee through an open window from creditors to whom he had lost small fortunes. Haworth Parsonage, today the Brontë Museum, contains many personal belongings of the Brontës, and possesses one of the most atmospheric and photographed graveyards in the region. Keen walkers can visit the Brontë Seat (a large gritstone boulder which has been engraved with the words C. Brontë), The Brontë waterfalls, and Top Withens, the derelict farmhouse which is generally felt to be the setting for Emily Brontë's *Wuthering Heights*.

An ancient packhorse trail once wound its way downwards from the old village of Stanbury towards Top Withens farmhouse, and it is along here that the spectre of a young woman huddled in a cloak has been seen battling against the elements on particularly stormy nights. The figure vanishes on approaching Top Withens. Although there is little to link this spectre to any of the Brontë women, there are those who feel that the ghost is that of Emily, still wandering her adored moors over a century after her death. Emily's ghost also reputedly appeared dressed in black at the funeral of her sister Charlotte, when mourners claimed to have seen her watching the proceedings from a distance. Anne Brontë's ghost is remarkably attached to a wooden staircase which once graced Blake Hall, the model for the house in her novel *The Tenant of Wildfell Hall*. When this historic property was demolished after World War II, an American woman purchased the staircase, and after its installation in her New York home, encountered the phantom figure of a long-skirted lady gliding up the stairs.

The Brontë Parsonage Museum, administered by the Brontë Society, is open to the public from 10 a.m. to 5 p.m. between

Top Withens farmhouse, inspiration for Wuthering Heights

April and October, and from 10 a.m. to 4.30 p.m. throughout March and November.

THE THREE HOUSES INN
Sandal, Wakefield

The original Three Houses Inn formerly stood at the opposite side of Barnsley Road to the current Three Houses, and was once the favourite haunt of seventeenth-century highwayman Ben (John) Nevinson. Nevinson's ride from London to York in fifteen hours (a distance of over 200 miles) was later mistakenly attributed to Dick Turpin. The highwayman allegedly robbed a wealthy man in Chatham at four o'clock one May morning in 1676, and, realising that only an alibi would save him, rode at breakneck speed across country (doubtless changing horses at a number of inns along the way), arriving in York in time to play bowls before eight the same evening. A witness to his presence was none other than the Lord Mayor of York himself, a factor which served to acquit Nevinson of any connection with the crime. The infamous highwayman was captured and escaped many times, until he was finally seized in the Three Houses Inn in March 1684, asleep in a large oak chair which can be seen today in the local church. Nevinson was hanged in York in May of the same year. A number of visitors to the Three Houses in recent years have told vague stories of 'strange sightings' and 'atmospheres' here, and although details have been scant, popular superstition claims the assumed ghost to be that of Nevinson. Joanne Worth and her husband Roger, current tenants of the inn, remain sceptical, however, feeling that the influence of strong ale probably has more to do with any such stories!

Visitors to the Three Houses will find themselves only a stone's throw away from Sandal Castle, of which all that remains today are scattered stone walls and arches, and a mountainous earthwork which can be climbed to reveal mile upon mile of beautiful West Yorkshire scenery. Originally built in the early 1300s by John de Warenne (for his mistress, Maud), Sandal Castle passed into fable when the Duke of York was killed in battle here in 1460. Queen Margaret ordered that the Duke's head be cut off, and it was subsequently fixed to a pike and displayed on one of York's city gates.

Sandal Castle may be visited at any reasonable time throughout the year and includes free car-parking facilities.

OAKWELL HALL AND COUNTRY PARK
Birstall, near Batley

'*The old latticed windows, the stone porch, the walls, the roof, the chimney stacks ... rich in crayon touches and sepia lights and shades*' are the words in which Charlotte Brontë immortalised Oakwell Hall, renaming it Fieldhead and using it as the home of the heroine in her novel *Shirley*. This Elizabethan manor house, surrounded by over 100 acres of parkland including a traditional medicinal and culinary herb garden, is kept for visitors in the style of the Batt family home of the late seventeeth century. The story of Oakwell Hall's ghost has remained a source of fascination for hundreds of years. Although the spectre is best documented in its first appearance, the writer Mrs Gaskell saw fit to include the tale in her book *The Life of Charlotte Brontë* many years after the legend was born. In 1995, the administrators of Oakwell Hall approached *Schofield's Quest*, a TV research programme, in a bid to find out more about the supernatural tale.

The ghost was reputed to be that of William Batt, a twenty-five-year-old bachelor who owned Oakwell Hall in the late 1600s. On 9 December 1684 William was away from Oakwell on business, while his widowed mother Elizabeth remained at home awaiting his return. Mrs Gaskell recounted how, that very night, William, '*in the dusk ... came stalking along the lane, through the Hall and up the stairs, into his own room, where he vanished...*' William Batt had been killed in a duel in London that same afternoon. He reputedly left a bloody footprint in his bedroom. There are no recorded accounts of his ghost ever being seen again, although Mrs Gaskell noted that the short lane which approached Oakwell Hall through pastureland in her lifetime was known as Bloody Lane, and was reputedly still haunted by Batt's ghost.

Subsequent research undertaken by Oakwell Hall staff uncovered a bond surviving in the archives which stated that William was indeed in London on 9 December 1684, at the Black Swan in Holborn, where he had borrowed a sum of money. The local diarist Oliver Heywood noted two entries regarding William's death, firstly that he had died 'in sport', and secondly that he had been 'slain by Mr Gream at Barne near London'. William Batt was buried in Birstall on 30 December 1684. The initial approach to *Schofield's Quest* was to request further information regarding William, his death, or his ghost. Although the publicity was unsuccessful in prompting any further information about William, a number of first-hand accounts from former Oakwell employees and visitors revealed a multitude of paranormal encounters which had taken place here.

During the 1960s it was well known that the gardener refused to set foot inside the house, preferring to spend his tea-breaks in the garden shed. The curator eventually persuaded him to look round the hall before it opened. After they had visited the clock room to see the collection of long-case clocks, the curator explained that the door had to be closed and locked to help maintain an even temperature. This done, they were on their way downstairs when the door was 'flung open and slammed'. Unperturbed, they continued their tour, and ended downstairs in the ancient timber-framed corner room at the left-hand side of the house. One of the back doors was unaccountably flung open, and although the day was still and calm outside, a wind blew a flurry of leaves into the house. At this point the gardener admitted to having encountered this very 'ghost' on a regular basis, and explained that this was why he generally refused to enter the house. In the 1970s, a child of one of the staff helping with renovation work at Oakwell visited along with her father. The caretaker told them to make sure that they locked the door to the clock room when they left, which they duly did, and checked.

However, as they began to walk downstairs, they heard a click and turned to see the latch on the door lift up, and the door open and close by itself. Nobody had entered or left the room. The curator himself also noted ghostly activity in the vicinity of the lane outside the hall, where he had heard 'running footsteps and horses' hooves' on several occasions after dark. Local legend maintains that these sounds date back to the Roman occupation!

A senior resident of Birstall who often visited Oakwell as a child recalled an occasion when she saw a 'man in a tricorn hat' standing at the bottom of the stairs, to the left of the entrance, who suddenly 'disappeared in a cloud of fog'. This lady noticed that both her dog and that of a friend showed extreme reluctance to approach the cellar for some unknown reason; on one occasion one of the animals bolted from the house and ran home alone, where it was later found cowering. The former educational officer at the hall was involved in renovation work during which the building was closed to the public. He arrived to lock up one night and heard the sound of 'voices raised in anger' echoing through the house, although on checking, the building was empty. This gentleman also noted that his 'hair stood on end' when he passed the great parlour that evening. During renovation work there were a number of call-outs due to the alarm system being activated. On one occasion the educational officer arrived to find the police desperately trying to coax their dog into the house. The animal, which was whimpering, refused steadfastly to go any further.

Oakwell Hall and Country Park, on Nutter Lane, are administered by Kirklees Metropolitan Council, and are open to the public daily all year round, Monday to Friday between 11 a.m. and 5 p.m., and weekends noon until 5 p.m. A variety of special events are held here throughout the year. The hall is also licensed for civil marriage ceremonies.

ABBEY HOUSE MUSEUM
Kirkstall, Leeds

Kirkstall Abbey was built in 1152 by monks of the Cistercian order, eventually falling into disrepair after the Dissolution. Today its expansive ruins can be visited, along with the former gatehouse which houses Abbey House Museum. The gatehouse is believed to be haunted by the spectre of a former abbot, and it is here that poltergeist activity has been observed in the past. The current curator, despite being sceptical of the legend, notes that there is no explanation for the fact that certain displays in the museum often fall over inexplicably during the night, to be discovered by staff on opening up the following morning. An underground passage is rumoured to lead from the abbey to the City Varieties Theatre on the Headrow in Leeds, which, until the 1860s, was a public house known as the White Swan. (The theatre itself has numerous ghosts attached, including that of a sad-faced woman thought to be a former actress.) The most infamous legend associated with the abbey concerns a gruesome murder which took place here in the last century. A young local girl went missing during an evening stroll around the ruins, and her family eventually sent her dog, Rover, to look for her. Rover's howls are said to have shattered the peace for miles around, for when the dog was eventually located, he was found to be crouching over his young mistress's corpse. A public house close to the museum later took its name from the tale, becoming the Hark to Rover.

Kirkstall Abbey House Museum is administered by Leeds City Council, and is open Tuesday to Saturday 10 a.m. to 5 p.m., and 1 p.m. to 5 p.m. on Sundays.

THE LEEDS–FARSLEY ROAD

Occasionally the casual observer can be witness to a phenomena which seems to fall into no known category of paranormal experience. Tales such as the following are possibly the most intriguing of all, and only serve to remind the curious that sometimes paranormal experience knows no bounds, and refuses to sit comfortably within any 'accepted' category. The following encounter, which took place in 1994, is related by a resident of Farsley in Leeds.

'My husband and I had been visiting some friends between York and Hull and we left to return home at around 12.30 a.m. I drove as my husband slept in the passenger seat. The A64 is a dual carriageway which connects Leeds to the east coast, via York. As we came on to it, there were no other cars going in our direction and it was unlit and pitch black. It is a boring road even in the daylight, banked by high grass hills at either side. Eventually, we got to Leeds and I joined our ring road, which leads to within a mile of Farsley and home. The last 2 mile stretch goes down into a small valley, before climbing towards the last roundabout before my turn-off. My husband was still asleep as I started on the hill down into the valley. On each side are grass banks with trees and a wide verge and path. As you pass into the valley, the road dips and crosses the railway track from Leeds to Guiseley, the River Aire and the Leeds–Liverpool Canal, all next to each other. As I approached to cross the railway, something caught the corner of my eye and although I did not get a direct look at whatever it was, I was filled with sheer and utter terror. The hairs on the back of my neck stood on end and I went so cold I started to shake. At the side of the road, there was a cut-out for a bus stop and standing back from this, from what I could make out, without daring to look directly, was a shape around 8 feet tall, completely covered in dark shaggy hair. It began to shuffle forwards towards the kerb and I could feel its eyes boring straight into me, although I was so gripped with terror, I couldn't look. I accelerated to get away and as I looked in my rear view mirror it had stepped off the kerb and on to the road. It was around 2.45 a.m. and there was no other traffic on the road at all. Whatever it was, it was certainly not human and as far as I could make out, not animal either. When I told a friend the next day, she came up with the "logical" explanation that it was someone in fancy dress waiting for a bus! But no buses run up there at that time of night, and there are only a couple of houses in the valley. Besides which, I had felt terrified and unnerved before I even saw the thing. As soon as we got home, I woke my husband and ran into the house, nearly breaking my neck to get the door locked! Needless to say, I didn't sleep too well that night. I don't like going down that stretch of the ring road at all after midnight. I went to investigate the following day, to try and convince myself that it was only a tree, but it wasn't. The mystery remains unsolved.'

ROGERTHORPE MANOR
Badsworth, Pontefract

On the edge of the legendary Barnsdale Forest, famously associated with Robin Hood, sits the Domesday estate of Rogerthorpe whose manor house dates from the early 1600s. Rogerthorpe Manor was built under the direction of Samuel Saltonstal, whose family resided here for several generations. The Saltonstals held the estate throughout the Civil War period, during which time it is said that a little girl living at Rogerthorpe was tragically killed by her Royalist father's horse when she ran out to greet him as he rode home. A different version of the tale suggests that the little girl ran in front of a local huntsman and was ridden down. In this version, her grandmother is said to have witnessed the accident from an upstairs window, falling to her death down a flight of stairs as she ran to her aid.

The ghost of an unidentified, pale-faced child wearing Victorian clothes was encountered at Rogerthorpe during the last century, its favourite pastime being rattling doorknobs throughout the manor. Additionally, a superstition among local children (which continued into the twentieth century) suggested that the spirit of a former Rogerthorpe boy-servant could be summoned by circling his tombstone, in Badsworth churchyard, seven times. The child had accompanied Colonel Edward Rawstorne back from India in the late eighteenth century when the Rawstorne family lived at Rogerthorpe. On the boy's untimely death, the Colonel erected the pyramid-shaped memorial stone which later became the focus for local superstition.

Rogerthorpe Manor is today owned and run as a hotel by Charles Birdsall's Parkside Inne and Leisure company. Before Mr Birdsall took over the premises in 1992, a visiting Frenchman is said to have encountered the ghost of a Cavalier here. Although there have been no recent sightings of this ghost, a number of staff have seen an unidentified male figure in various locations around the building. He has been spotted walking into the restaurant (from which he had vanished when a member of staff followed him in) and past the doorway to the bar. General manager Brian Watson was sitting in the bar with an assistant after closing time one night in 1996 when he saw what he described as 'the outline and shadow of a person' entering the bar before 'scampering out again quickly'. Brian leapt over a bar stool and attempted to follow the figure, which had vanished without trace, leaving every available exit door, including the fire door, unopened. Another member of staff saw an old lady sitting in the bar alone one evening. He has assumed her to be a customer until she disappeared without passing any of the staff on duty. A check on the guests present showed that nobody answering her description was booked in at that time.

Staff also note that a number of courtesy trays left in unoccupied rooms have been thrown to the floor with some violence, their contents often being shattered. Until recently Rogerthorpe had a baby grand piano downstairs; in 1995, two residents from separate rooms independently arrived downstairs at three in the morning to find out who was playing it . . . and found nobody there. A former manageress was preparing to open the manor one morning when she found that a number of silver service 'flats' (serving trays) had been laid out 'like stepping stones' to the back door. Since she had locked up the previous night, and all had been well, she could offer no explanation.

Rogerthorpe Manor caters for accommodation, functions, conferences and banquets, and is licensed for civil wedding ceremonies. The hotel runs Murder Mystery dinners and a Ghosts and Ghoulies dinner at which ghost stories of the manor are told and some of the 'ghosts' make an appearance! For bookings: Rogerthorpe Manor, Thorpe Lane, Badsworth, Pontefract WF9 1AB.

NOSTELL PRIORY
Nostell

Nostell was the place chosen by an early Augustinian order for the founding of a religious house in the seventh century. Bede's Chronicles mention a certain 'James of Nostell' who, as early as the Whitby Synod of AD 635, resided here. During the reign of King John, the wealthy Nostell priors were known as the Lords Prior, entitling them to a seat in the House of Lords. The earliest priory probably consisted of individual dwellings favoured by the Augustinians. A later monastic building is thought to have been situated next to where the current house was built by the Winn family many centuries later. This sprawling eighteenth-century mansion is today open to the public, and only its name recalls the previous purpose of the site. The priory refectory, a low-roofed building opposite Wragby church on the border of the estate, is the oldest surviving intact building at Nostell and dates back over a thousand years. The priory's grounds have never been excavated in order to reconstruct the layout of the early monastery, and today its former importance has been all but lost with the passage of time.

The Reverend Hugh Gallagher lives with his wife Janis in the Little House, private accommodation which fronts the stable-block courtyard. At one time Lord and Lady St Oswald, descendants of the founding Winn family, lived in the Little House, although it remained empty for several years before the Gallaghers' arrival in the winter of 1991. Janis recalled their first night here: '. . . it was really foggy and cold and we went to bed reasonably early; we got into bed and all hell broke loose. There were footsteps and doors banging. We knew that people had been getting in here, because it had been empty for so long, and we thought that perhaps somebody had broken in. The noises stopped, and started again. We got up. We had a couple of dogs at that time, and yet they didn't bother at all, which I thought was strange, and made me convinced that nobody had got in. For two or three days we continued to hear the same thing, then it all settled down, and the house then "felt" a lot better.' Two years before moving into Nostell Priory, Janis had lost a gold chain whilst living at the vicarage at Fitzwilliam, and believed that it had possibly been stolen. In the early days of living in the Little House the couple returned from the super-market one afternoon to find the previously missing gold chain lying on the kitchen floor. A number of other 'lost' objects reappeared in a similar manner in equally unexpected places.

A 'sensitive' friend of the Gallaghers described sensations she picked up whilst standing in their living-room, commenting on a 'terrible noise' here, as though the area had formerly been 'some kind of busy market place full of people who seemed to be greeting each other, chatting and then leaving'. The Reverend Gallagher himself feels that the site of the Little House could very well be that of the original monks' hospice, which, as a pilgrim centre, would have seen many thousands of visitors at a much earlier period in history.

The back door of the Little House is shared with the residents of the neighbouring flat. One afternoon in the summer of 1992, Janis entered the house by this door and caught sight of a woman in a grey dress who was standing on the stairs. Expecting it to be her neighbour she called out a greeting, but the woman had vanished. The priory gardener also saw a female figure upstairs in the Little House as he passed by one weekend afternoon. Expecting it to be Janis, he waved as she looked down, and thought it unusual that the woman did not acknowledge him. During the following week he discovered that the Gallaghers had spent the weekend away and the house had been empty. Janis also notes that her two dogs have on occasion followed something seemingly invisible across the living-room with their eyes before settling down again, unperturbed.

Lady St Oswald herself witnessed what she described as 'a group of people dressed in grey, painting' in the grounds of the Little House on a number of occasions, adding that the figures were 'like an image – not exactly transparent, and they seemed very real'. The small party always vanished after a second or so. Lady St Oswald supposed them to be daughters of the house from a former period in time.

During a visit to the Little House in the summer of 1996, the author used a dictaphone to record accounts being given by the Gallaghers regarding the haunting. During the taped conversation Janis stood up suddenly and excused herself to answer the back door. She re-entered the room rather puzzled as nobody was there. During this time the dictaphone was left running, and despite the fact that three other people present in the room besides Janis had not heard the knock at the door, when the tape was played back the following day it had clearly recorded two loud raps prior to her standing and leaving the room.

Wragby Church of St Michael and Our Lady, situated in the grounds of Nostell Priory, is built on the foundations of the original priory church, although its renovation in 1533 altered and restored much of the architecture, and the church today bears this date. The beautiful Swiss stained glass windows, made up of many tiny brightly painted segments bearing both sacred and secular scenes, were recently refitted here after many years in exile. Visitors can also see the beautiful marble tomb effigies to the right of the west window which depict the grandchildren of Sabina Winn.

The Reverend Gallagher and the church caretaker were approached one afternoon in 1990 by a gentleman who was convinced that his wife was suffering from an over-vivid imagination. He described how, a week earlier, she had witnessed a hooded figure walk behind the altar from left to right before it vanished through the wall. The Reverend Gallagher was aware that there had formerly been a door to the left of the altar, which would once have been the prior's entrance, and, across at the other side, was another door for him to leave through. The visitor who reported the apparition had no knowledge of this at the time.

The church organ was formerly a chamber organ, probably moved from the house at some point during the 1700s. The organ was renovated during the 1970s, and the church warden arrived around three o'clock one afternoon intending to watch the team at work. She was rather distressed on her arrival to find the organ pipes laid out over the floor, with not a person in sight and half-eaten sandwiches, flasks and cups littering the porch. The warden immediately telephoned the contractors and demanded to know where the team had gone. She was informed that they were not prepared to return as the church was 'haunted'. The team had heard the organ begin to play itself during their lunch-break. Since it was totally stripped and its pipes had been removed, this was an impossibility. The late organist of Wragby church himself informed the Reverend Gallagher that he too had heard the organ play itself on a number of occasions, although he seemed to be far less affected by the experience.

Nostell Priory, situated on Doncaster Road, is managed by the St Oswald family and is still in parts a private home. Public visiting is administered by the National Trust between 26 March and 30 October, weekends, between noon and 5 p.m. Between 1 July and 8 September the priory is open daily, noon until 5 p.m., except for Fridays.

NORTH YORKSHIRE

THE THEATRE ROYAL
St Leonard's Place, York

Structural remains of the medieval hospital of St Leonard, including an ancient crypt, were incorporated into York's Theatre Royal during its building in the late 1730s. The hospital was originally staffed by an order of nuns, to whom a particularly sinister story is attached. Local legend tells how an errant novice was bricked up alive in a wall, as a punishment for her earthly sins. A spectral form known as the Grey Lady is popularly believed to be the ghost of the nun, of which sightings have been recorded since Edwardian times. Witnesses most often report a rather formless grey mist which appears in the dress circle, although a small number of more detailed sightings have been noted.

In 1967 a workman clearly described a woman wearing grey whom he had taken to be the theatre 'housekeeper', although he was assured by staff that nobody answering her description

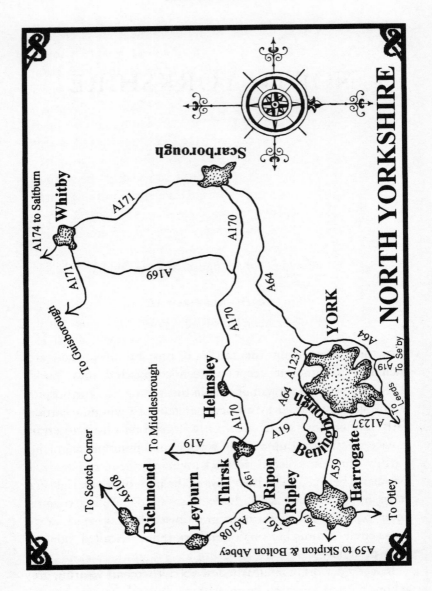

was employed there. An actress standing in the dress circle also saw the figure of 'a small nun in a grey habit and white wimple' leaning over the edge of the stage box. In 1975, the production company rehearsing *Dear Octopus* were astonished to see a greyish-white mist appear at one end of the dress circle which proceeded to drift in front of them. As the leading lady stopped singing, the mist appeared to 'contract' into a ball and disappear. The director called for a rerun, and to the cast's amazement, when the leading lady reached the same song, the strange mist appeared again and only vanished when the music eventually stopped. The following year, an actress involved in a seasonal Victorian show was rehearsing vocal harmonies with her colleagues in the theatre's green-room, when she caught sight of a 'shimmering' robed figure outside, which she felt instinctively to be female.

Other less dramatic experiences were recorded by visiting actors and theatre staff throughout the 1980s and '90s. Most commonly reported is the feeling of 'being watched' whilst in empty rooms, and being touched or nudged by unseen hands. Sightings still occur to this day, such as the mystery figure spotted on a supposedly empty stage during the 1994 production of *Dracula*. The Grey Lady appeared once again during the dress rehearsal of *Moll Flanders* in 1995, which then went on to win the Regional Best Musical Award, continuing the popular belief that her appearances are a lucky omen for productions.

The theatre was visited by a psychic in the early 1960s who 'contacted' the spirit of what she described as a black-robed nun, whom she felt to have been formerly bricked up alive into a wall here. Previous sightings of a 'black shape' had been noted emanating from one wall and drifting into another, although for some reason the nun attached to the well-known story was assumed to have been dressed in grey. The psychic herself noted that an old building with such a history would probably harbour several entities. At her intervention the nun's spirit was believed to have been released, although the fabled Grey Lady remains in residence.

RIPLEY CASTLE

Ripley, Harrogate

The Ingilby family can trace their pedigree back to the eleventh century, and the traditional family seat of Ripley Castle remains under the wing of the twenty-fourth generation of the Ingilby family today, being home to Sir Thomas Ingilby, his wife Lady Emma, and their five children. The castle is a pastiche of various building styles spanning many generations, which can be seen in the medieval gatehouse, the sixteenth-century crenellated Old Tower, and the late eighteenth-century additions masterminded by Sir John Ingilby. The Ingilbys' rise to knighthood came in 1355, when King Edward III was saved from the charge of an injured wild boar by Thomas Ingilby, whilst out hunting in the Forest of Knaresborough. The King knighted Thomas and granted the family the emblem of a boar's head, which still tops the family crest today. A decade later Sir Thomas was awarded the right of Free Warren, the honoured seal of royal approval enabling him to hunt freely in the Forest of Knaresborough. Centuries later, in 1644, another member of the Ingilby family earned herself a place in history when she dressed as a man and rode into battle at Marston Moor in full armour alongside her Royalist brother Sir William. Trooper Jane, as Jane Ingilby later became known, returned to Ripley Castle after the battle and showed Cromwell a clean pair of pistols on his request for entry. Cromwell eventually persuaded the lady to admit him into the gatehouse on the promise that she could retain her firearms. The following morning he left the castle and Jane unharmed, but not before shooting a number of Royalist prisoners against the gatehouse wall, leaving musket-shot holes which can still be seen today.

The current Sir Thomas Ingilby notes that according to family legend, when a particularly pale fallow deer is seen in the castle deer-park, the birth of a son and heir is imminent in the Ingilby family. A pale fallow deer appeared in the park shortly before his own birth in 1955, and the same thing happened again shortly before the birth of his and Lady Emma's eldest son James, in 1985.

Ripley Castle's tower was completed by Sir William Ingilby in 1555, and at some point before 1583 was allegedly the site of a strange experience involving his son Francis. Records of this survive in a paper dating from *c.* 1590, which was written by a member of the Society of Jesus, to whom the story had been recounted by one of Francis's brothers. Francis had apparently been sleeping soundly wben he was disturbed one dawn by his bed 'shaking with such violence' that he was soon wide awake. The phenomenon continued, and it seemed to him 'that not only the bed but the tower itself and the whole room in which he was' were quaking. Afraid, Francis made the sign of the cross and commended himself to God, and heard a voice calling him to 'rise and set forth'. This experience was repeated a number of times and was reputedly accompanied by 'visions', most likely of a religious nature although Francis is said never to have discussed them in detail. The experience culminated in his journey to the Continent where he was ordained as a priest in 1583. Francis was persecuted by the Protestant authorities, and was condemned to be hung, drawn and quartered three years later. The sentence was meted out on what is now York racecourse (formerly Knavesmire), and it is said that within hours of Francis' execution, Henry Cheke, a renowned opponent, died after falling down a flight of stairs. Within days,

Ralph Huddlestone, a member of the Northern Council, collapsed suddenly, his body reputedly 'entering a condition of instant putrefaction'.

Two ghosts are associated with Ripley Castle, both having made their presence felt in the twentieth century. Before World War II, a phantom nun was regularly reported to wander around the building. Although her identity is unknown, the Ingilby family were formerly staunch Catholics and Ripley Castle is known to have harboured champions of the old religion during times of dissent, including priests. At least two female members of the family took holy vows, Elizabeth Ingilby in the latter part of the sixteenth century, and Lucy Ingilby, who became a Benedictine nun during the early part of the seventeenth century. It is likely that many more unrecorded persecuted Catholics found temporary sanctuary here, and therefore the nun's identity remains a mystery. Alongside the phantom nun, a disruptive poltergeist manifested itself in the tower during the early 1940s. Renovation work was taking place in the tower at the time, and a team of contractors had uncovered a fireplace which had been formerly panelled over. Poltergeist activity ensued shortly after the area had been disturbed, with tower furnishings being tossed around and regular supernatural 'disruption' being noted. An exorcism was never performed, however, and the strange activity ceased of its own accord almost as soon as it had begun.

Ripley Castle is open to the public at weekends, 11.30 a.m. to 4.30 p.m., throughout April, May and October (also Good Friday and Bank Holidays); Thursday to Sunday throughout June and September; and daily during July and August. Groups of more than fifteen people can arrange to visit the castle and gardens on days other than those specified. Ripley Castle caters for wedding receptions and functions, with medieval banquets

and *Murder Mystery weekends arranged on request; the estate
also hosts a variety of events throughout the summer. For
nearby accommodation: The Boar's Head Hotel, Ripley village,
near Harrogate.*

BENINGBROUGH HALL
Shipton-by-Beningbrough, York

Beningbrough Hall was built in 1716 by John Bourchier,
although the site of this grand Georgian mansion, set in several
hundred acres of parkland, was originally occupied by an earlier
Elizabethan building. It is the earlier Beningbrough Hall to which
the following tale of murder and supernatural legend is attached.
In 1670, Marian, the housekeeper of the old hall, was drowned
in the river Ouse by a local poacher, who had been paid for his
part in the evil deed by the hall's steward. When the poacher was
later caught breaking into a building on Beningbrough estate to
appropriate a hoard of valuables whose whereabouts had been
secretly known to Marian, he confessed to her murder and was
subsequently hanged at York. Contemporary records document
that the lady of the hall, having discovered the involvement of
her steward in the affair, attempted to dismiss him, only to find
herself caught in a gunpoint struggle at which she narrowly
escaped with her life. The steward ran, but, aware that the
authorities were closing in, shot himself at his lodgings within
the hour. The ghost of the murdered Marian is reputed to walk
the banks of the River Ouse, near the hall, at the spot at which
she met her watery grave.

Local folklore also recalls a different version of the tale, in
which the housekeeper's beau was press-ganged and taken to
York, upon which she threw herself into the River Ouse, and
drowned, being condemned to walk the banks in spirit ever

after. It seems likely that two different legends, each concerning the death of a woman in the river, could have become confused over the passage of many years. House steward Rob Turpin notes that local legend tells how a disembodied voice is sometimes to be heard calling out from the river bank, said to be that of the drowned woman calling to her absent love.

In 1988, the former housekeeper was alone in Beningbrough Hall one morning when she heard mysterious laughter echoing from the floor above. Its source was never accounted for. In 1995, a guide arrived for work early in the day to find the front door locked. On glancing inside the house, she saw a smartly dressed man staring at her through a window . . . and identified him from a family portrait as one of the long-dead Dawney family who had once resided at Beningbrough.

Beningbrough Hall is administered by the National Trust, and is open between 30 March and 30 October, daily except Thursday and Friday, between 11 a.m. and 5 p.m. Throughout July and August the hall is additionally open on Fridays. The National Trust advise that visitors wishing to examine the portraits on loan from the National Portrait Gallery should visit on bright days, as some rooms have no electric lighting. Croquet is available for hire in the grounds, and guided garden walks take place most weekends.

DUNCOMBE PARK

Helmsley

'*The place in the country by far most worth the attention of the curious traveller, it cannot be viewed without the most exquisite enjoyment*': thus the traveller Arthur Young recorded his impressions of the palatial Duncombe Park in 1770. The house had then only been standing for around fifty years, in splendid medieval parkland formerly used as Helmsley Castle's hunting-ground, much of which still remains unaltered today. Duncombe Park was let as a school for girls following the death of the 2nd Earl of Feversham in World War I, although in 1985 the present Lord Feversham (a direct descendant of its founder), along with his wife, once again took over the house and began extensive restoration before opening to the public.

Duncombe Park was seriously damaged by fire in 1879, afterwards being extensively rebuilt, for the most part to its original design. The ghost of an unidentified woman has been seen in the estate office, who is rumoured to have been a victim of the fire. Intriguingly, she is only visible from the knees up from the floor, suggesting that her existence predates the alteration of the (now higher) floor level here today. According to Lord Feversham, this detail would date the spectre as certainly pre-1894 and possibly even pre-1844, structural alterations having taken place in these years. John Dale encountered the ghost in 1993 whilst working in a room off the estate office corridor. He described his experience: 'I'd been photocopying when I turned to straighten the papers and then turned back to leave the room, and I saw a lady walk past the door. I could only see her from the knees up. She had a bluey-grey dress on. I looked out into the corridor but there was nobody there!' John checked the vicinity and also explored the possibility that natural 'shadows' cast in the corridor were to blame, although he noted that the weather outside was fine and clear at the time. A colleague standing with him in the photocopying room at the time had her back turned to the doorway and saw nothing.

Lord Feversham also notes that, in the private part of the house, 'a ghost which has never been seen, to my knowledge, has been heard by a number of people, including myself. It seems to inhabit the top floor of the main block and can make a lot of noise, sounding as though it is dragging trunks or coffins around the attics.' The mischievous spirit has also been known to turn electric lights on in the middle of the night (particularly in Lord Feversham's son's room), and to change programmes on the radio (most recently experienced by the caretaker whilst he was decorating an attic room by the lift shaft).

Duncombe Park and its grounds are open to the public between April and October inclusive between 11 a.m. and 6 p.m., although days vary and visitors should contact the estate beforehand. Duncombe caters for private and business functions, and is licensed for civil wedding ceremonies. For bookings: Duncombe Park, Helmsley, York Yo6 5EB.

RICHMOND CASTLE
Richmond

On the banks of the River Swale at the entrance to Swaledale, Richmond Castle still presides over the small town which grew up around it shortly after the Conquest. Originally built for Alan of Brittany, a favoured knight of William the Conqueror's, Richmond's battered walls have withstood more than nine hundred years of exposure to battle, siege and the elements. Richmond began to fall into disrepair during the sixteenth century, although rebuilding was undertaken to ensure that it never deteriorated into total ruin; later, the castle was used as a military base during both World Wars. The extensive keep, which was added a century after Richmond's founding by Earl Conan 'the Little', is particularly impressive. A small tower at the far end of the Great Court, known as the Gold Hole Tower, is reputedly the source of secret buried treasure unearthed here by an unknown adventurer.

An archaic carved stone found near Easby Abbey

It has long been rumoured that a secret tunnel exists which runs from the nearby Easby Abbey to Richmond Castle. Legend tells how soldiers discovering its entrance sent a young drummer boy to explore, hoping for a chance to sneak into the castle and break its defences. For half a mile they followed the beat of the boy's drum above ground, until it ceased a short distance from the castle. The drummer boy never reappeared, although at certain times of year ever since, the beating of a phantom drum has been heard in the vicinity. Richmond Castle is also attributed with an Arthurian connection, local legend stating that a secret underground cavern contains a hunting horn which, when blown, will rouse King Arthur and his knights from their perpetual slumber within. Many years ago a local potter named Thompson supposedly stumbled across this chamber quite inadvertently, and, impressed by the hoard of jewellery he found littered on the floor, neglected to blow the horn. A thunderous disembodied voice pointed out the error of his ways, and the potter was evicted without further ado, the cavern sealing behind him.

Richmond's keep is divided into two rooms, one of which has a wooden floor – and the current custodian has noted to her surprise that several visitors have expressed discomfort at the threshold of this room and refused to venture any further, often leaving the keep in a hurry. There are no current reports of any unusual phenomena in this area, and neither can visitors who do not wish to enter the keep give a detailed account of why they should feel so disturbed.

Richmond Castle is administered by English Heritage, and is open to the public between 1 April and 30 October 10 a.m. to 6 p.m., and between 1 November and 31 March 10 a.m. to 4 p.m.

BOLTON ABBEY
near Skipton

Founded by the Augustinians in the twelfth century, Bolton Abbey flourished until the Dissolution. Its expansive ruin is still the site of a worshipping church today. The abbey boasts several well-documented sightings of a spectral 'black friar', who local legend suggests to be the ghost of Abbot Moon, the last abbot in charge before the brethren were evicted by Henry VIII. One of the most vivid descriptions of the ghost was recorded by the then Marquis of Hartington in the early 1900s, which was subsequently included in *Lord Halifax's Ghost Book* of 1936. The young Marquis recounted how, late one night in August during a holiday stay at Bolton rectory, he was disturbed by a 'bright-eyed old man' of some sixty-plus years. The rough-shaven man wore a long dark ankle-length robe topped with a grey hood, and appeared to be looking past the Marquis and down a corridor which led into the room. The Marquis was determined that the rector should see the apparition for himself, and he left his room to fetch him, only to find that the man had vanished without trace when he returned. Around this time, local people regularly encountered the ghost of a 'black monk' who wore a 'strange pointed hat', and subsequent sightings by visitors told of a man wearing a black cassock and a flat black hat. During the 1970s the congregation of the abbey church themselves witnessed an unaccountable black-robed figure in the old choir stalls, and on one occasion the organ was heard to 'play itself' despite the organ room being locked at the time. The then rector and his family saw a spectral monk on numerous occasions, and once saw two robed figures together, which were seen to walk straight through a wall.

In the early 1970s, an excavation of the tomb of nobleman John de Clifford was undertaken by archaeologists. When the

The Scrope family arms.
Mary Queen of Scots was once the reluctant guest of the Scropes of
Bolton Castle

team involved suffered numerous misfortunes and even illness while working on the project, 'the curse of the Cliffords' was popularly held responsible. Several archaeologists felt a sinister 'presence' in the abbey, and others saw what they described as 'an Augustinian monk' in the same location as Abbot Moon is legendarily believed to appear. When certain team members began to experience the paranormal in their own homes, feeling presences and 'seeing ghosts', they drew a link with their work at the abbey. One archaeologist refused to return to the de Clifford tomb, blaming 'the curse' for the flu-like illness he had suffered throughout the dig. Although this beautiful ruin is today renowned for its peaceful atmosphere, there have been a number of sporadic sightings of a party of black-robed monks seen passing silently through the grounds.

Scarborough Castle

Bolton Abbey estate is administered by the Trustees of the Chatsworth Settlement, and is open to the public throughout the year.

SCARBOROUGH CASTLE
Scarborough

The extensive ruin of this twelfth-century castle sprawls out along the eroding cliff edge overlooking a magnificent coastal view. The site is believed to have been occupied since the Bronze Age, and features a 'sacred' well whose waters were once held to have miraculous powers of healing. The remains of Scarborough Castle's keep today still stand over three storeys high, despite being attacked as late as the Civil War with blasts of cannon-fire. The castle is said to be haunted by the headless spectre of the unfortunate Piers Gaveston, who was betrayed and executed after being promised his freedom in return for surrendering the building. His headless ghost has reputedly been seen parading the remaining battlements late at night. Although there have been no recent sightings of this ghost, the following story was recounted in 1996 by a couple who had visited Scarborough Castle knowing nothing of its history, haunted or otherwise.

Janet and Steve McDonald took their two children to Scarborough Castle during the school holiday in the summer of 1983. In the courtyard at the top of the path which leads past the keep is an old cannon which once played a part in the defences of the castle. The children leaned against the cannon while their parents stood close by, until Janet warned them to move away because an old woman was watching them. Janet had seen her staring out from the open doorway of a nearby stone cottage. Steve, who had been looking at the keep and had his back to the cottage, turned around to look, but the door was closed and the area seemed to be empty. Out of curiosity, the McDonalds walked towards the cottage, wondering where the woman had disappeared to, and peered in through the windows. They were surprised to find themselves looking in on an uninhabitable interior, with rooms full of builders' rubble. The door, which Janet had previously seen open, proved to be securely locked when she tried it. Although the experience was somewhat puzzling, the McDonalds were not unduly concerned, although on their way out they did ask the gatekeeper if by any chance, the castle was haunted. He remarked that Scarborough Castle 'used to be haunted', and informed the McDonalds that the ghost of an old lady in grey had been seen many times in and around the small cottage which once belonged to the castle gun keeper. The woman was believed to be his wife. Her appearances had been so frequent and disturbing that some form of 'exorcism' ritual was eventually performed, leaving staff convinced that her ghost had been successfully 'laid'.

Scarborough Castle is maintained by English Heritage, and is open to the public daily until 4 p.m.

BYLAND ABBEY
near Thirsk

The ruin of the Cistercian-built Byland Abbey languishes in lush meadowland at the foot of North Yorkshire's Hambleton Hills. Byland is a setting often used for historical re-enactments performed by visiting societies from all over the country; on the last Bank Holiday weekend in May 1996, the abbey was visited by a group called Horrarium who re-enacted a day in the life of a fifteenth-century abbey. The role-playing monks and nuns planned to camp at the abbey on Sunday night and continue their re-enactment on Bank Holiday Monday. Unfortunately, the rainfall on Sunday was so heavy that Horrarium were unable to pitch their tents, and, as their Cistercian robes were dripping wet, they decided to spend the following day as Benedictines! Although some of the group offered to spend the night in their cars, others asked permission to sleep in the abbey museum, which was duly granted.

Bill Greaves, a member of Horrarium who had travelled from Sheffield, set up a camp-bed on the left-hand side of the museum. He placed it next to the wall to enable him to tuck his blankets tightly between this and the bed, so as not to shake them off in the night. The group settled down to sleep. Bill was woken in the dead of night by the sensation that somebody was trying to wake him quietly. He became aware that a hand, the heel of the palm on his buttock and the fingers curled over his hip, was rocking him gently and soundlessly to and fro, from behind. It took Bill a few moments to orientate himself as the museum was in total darkness. He felt that the time was somewhere between 2 and 3 a.m., and realised that he had woken up with his back to the wall, making it impossible for somebody to be trying to wake him from behind. Bill slowly moved his free hand to feel for where the arm of the person behind him should be, and felt the hand gently removed from his hip. There was nobody there, so Bill, who recalls being more puzzled than frightened, fell back to sleep. The following day, members of Horrarium visited the adjacent Abbey Inn, whose landlord enquired matter-of-factly whether they had 'seen the ghost'. Bill related his experience, and the landlord remarked that 'it sounded about right!' Bill later discovered that, during the fifteenth century when Byland Abbey was in service, the first prayer meeting of the day, known as Vigils, took place around two thirty each morning. A member of the brotherhood would silently wake his colleagues by rocking them gently to and fro.

Byland Abbey is administered by English Heritage, and is open to the public daily from 1 April to 31 October between 10 a.m. and 6 p.m.

BOLTON CASTLE
Leyburn

'One of our best preserved castles, grey and forbidding, vener-able with all the centuries,' recorded the seasoned traveller and diarist Arthur Mee of his visit to Bolton Castle in Wensleydale. The building of Bolton was begun in 1379 by Sir Richard Scrope, and it was originally known for its comparatively lavish comforts. Its ancient sewerage system was considered so advanced for the age that it continued in use until the Victorian era! Mary Queen of Scots spent six months in custody at Bolton during 1568, during which time it is thought that she lodged in Lord Scrope's private quarters. Local legend tells how Mary made a bid for escape, being recaptured in a matter of hours on a part of Leyburn Shawl now known as the Queen's Gap. She was eventually transferred to Tutbury in Staffordshire. Bolton Castle remained remarkably undamaged until the Civil War period, during which time it housed a garrison of Royalist soldiers. The besieging Parliament forced their surrender, and in the eighteenth century the north-east tower finally collapsed as a result of damage sustained during the attack. The greater part of the castle still remains largely unaltered, and today's resident Orde-Powlett family are direct descendants of its founder.

The Hon. Harry Orde-Powlett notes that his ancestor the 1st Duke of Bolton is notorious for having sold his soul to the Devil during the second half of the seventeenth century. According to family legend, the Duke refused to go abroad in daylight and only ever hunted at night. He also reputedly enjoyed bacchanalian banquets at a hall in the woods, where his guests gorged themselves and slept in their seats until daybreak. The Duke is said to have been buried alive and to this day still hangs out of his coffin in the family vault. His wife Henrietta, the illegitimate daughter of the Duke of Monmouth, is buried alongside him, with her heart in a small lead casket on top of her coffin. According to local legend, the Duke's ghost is still believed to haunt Hellgill near the castle where, Mr Orde-Powlett notes, 'at strange times in the middle of the night, hounds can be heard in full cry'.

A woman wearing a long dark cloak was watched crossing the courtyard and walking towards the gatehouse by a custodian who was locking up one evening in 1995. The figure disappeared without trace, and the witness later discovered that she was not alone in her sighting, for the cloaked woman had been seen by another member of staff on a separate occasion, in the same area. The chapel is the site of another unidentified ghost, this time a gentleman who, one midsummer afternoon in broad daylight, disappeared through a doorway into a room with no other exit which was found to be empty when checked. Bolton Castle often plays host to visiting historical societies, and one such group recently overnighting here heard the sounds of horses in the dead of night, with bits jingling and male voices chatting and laughing.

Bolton Castle is privately owned, and is open daily to the public between March and November, 10 a.m. to 5 p.m. Since winter opening hours may vary, potential visitors are advised to contact the castle direct.

WHITBY ABBEY

The majestic ruin of Whitby Abbey, overlooking the small fishing town of Whitby nestled in the bay below, dates back to the late twelfth century. The first Christian monastery which stood on this site was founded by Abbess Hilda in AD 657. The original abbey was plundered by marauding Viking raiders, remaining in ruins for many years until Reinfrid, a knight of William the Conqueror, visited the site on a pilgrimage and pledged to rebuild it. On Christmas Day, the sound of a ghostly choir has often been heard drifting across the harbour, along with the eerie tolling of a non-existent bell. Bram Stoker, author of the novel *Dracula*, immortalised the ruins of Whitby Abbey when he set several sinister scenes among them, since filmed on location here. In this tale, the vampire first came to shore in the form of a black dog. Interestingly, the Kettleness area was reputedly haunted by 'a huge black dog' until it was exorcised by a local clergyman in 1950. The phantom was seen on numerous occasions prowling the point of Kettleness and running ashore from the sea, not unlike the dog in Stoker's story. The Dracula Experience, a museum in the town below the abbey, tells his famous story, and visitors can also enjoy a choice of Whitby Ghost Walks, which include the abbey.

Whitby Abbey is administered by English Heritage, and is open all year round, with car-parking in the town below. Due to the setting of the abbey, wheelchair access is not possible. The Dracula Experience is open daily between 10 a.m. and 8 p.m. throughout the tourist season.

The head of St Hilda, founder of Whitby Abbey, presides over its
haunted remains

THE CITY OF YORK

York, formerly the Roman city of Eboracum, began its life in
AD 71 as a fortress erected by the invading Roman 9th Legion
to withstand the Celtic Brigantes tribe. This beautiful and
historic city is today the capital of the North of England, whose
Mayor stands second only in the realm to the Mayor of
London. York also proudly boasts its claim to being the 'most
haunted city in the British Isles', having recorded over a
hundred and forty sightings of ghosts within its walls in recent
years. Roman and medieval remains still stand tall among the
more modern buildings in and around the city centre. One of
York's outstanding features is the restored pale stone medieval

wall which almost completely surrounds the city, a circumference of almost 3 miles, and which possesses many of the Roman foundations of the earliest city wall. Under the Vikings, the city they named Jorvik became a flourishing centre for national and international trade. Excavations within the city walls have revealed a wealth of information about Viking occupation, which is today displayed for visitors in the Jorvik Centre.

The Treasurer's House in Minster Yard proudly claims to have the oldest ghosts in the country, in the form of a Roman legion witnessed by a young plumber named Harry Martindale in the early 1950s. Harry was working in the cellar one afternoon alone when he thought that he heard a trumpet sound from a great distance. As the sound got nearer he turned to see the helmeted figure of a Roman soldier walking straight out of the wall and along an excavated section of the cellar floor under which archaeologists involved in a survey had discovered a Roman road. Although this was a number of inches lower than the cellar floor as it stood, the spectral Roman soldier appeared to be walking on the old ground level. Mr Martindale promptly fell from his ladder, and continued to watch as an enormous heavy horse followed the first soldier, and was trailed by a line of several more 'bedraggled' soldiers. They were small in stature and each sported a plumed helmet and a round shield, which experts were later most impressed to identify as the standard uniform of the 9th Legion. Harry Martindale was not the only person to witness the phantom soldiers, as a curator of the Treasurer's House around the same time regularly encountered the phantom procession in the cellar along with other members of her family. A most amusing tale is recounted by staff of the Treasurer's House, who note that, when the house was owned in the early 1900s by a Mr Frank Green, one young lady attending a fancy dress party here remarked on the rudeness of

Bootham Bar, medieval gateway to York,
one of the most haunted cities of the north

a gentleman dressed as a Roman who had barred her entrance to the cellar with a spear. Nobody could account for the identity of the mysterious soldier.

York Minster, the dominating cathedral which took over two hundred and fifty years to build, finally being completed in 1472, hit the headlines in the summer of 1984 when a sudden blaze reduced it to a shell of stonemasonry. Despite the fact that the minster had been the victim of several serious fires throughout its history, caused by both sabotage and natural disaster, something about the 1984 fire excited public speculation, and the tabloid press soon began to circulate stories from eyewitnesses who felt that the cause of the fire was far from explicable. A taxi driver from Haxby had noticed a 'cigar-shaped object' hovering over the minster shortly before the blaze began, and watched as it appeared to project an orange-coloured ray from the air on to the top of the building. Independently, a local van driver made a sketch of a similar object from his York home, detailing how it glowed bright orange and left a trail of white vapour on moving away from the minster. Although the authorities attempted to discredit these accounts, shortly after the two original statements became public knowledge, several more witnesses came forward to tell similar tales. Eventually, with no evidence of arson and no further clues forthcoming, the Home Office was forced to consider unlikely possibilities before filing its obligatory report on the minster fire. Further to taking advice from experts at Leeds University, they noted as a possible cause 'St Elmo's Fire', a ball-shaped, electrically charged cloud sometimes encountered at the top of ships' masts, which is similar to lightning although not accompanied by thunder. The electrical charge generated by this rare and unusual 'fireball' would certainly have been enough to spark the old dry timbers of the historic minster, to devastating effect.

The Cock and Bottle public house, on Skeldergate, is connected with a man whose infamous history is believed to be the source of its haunting. George Villiers, the 2nd Duke of Buckingham, was a notorious courtier and a favourite of Charles II. Buckingham was an alleged alchemist, said to possess the fabled knowledge of turning base metals into gold, and his chemistry workshop during the mid-1600s was supposedly the Plumber's Arms, a building dating back to 1575 which stood on the site of the Cock and Bottle inn until 1962. Modern visitors to the latter will be delighted to notice that, despite the building having been demolished to make way for a road-widening scheme, many of the original features of the Plumber's Arms have been incorporated into the Cock and Bottle, including the dark wooden panelling and beams, windows and fireplaces. Several previous tenants noted plummeting temperatures within the building, and objects such as keys and knives often disappeared without reason, before coming to light in unexpected places. There were also numerous reports of the materialisation of a figure with long, dark curling hair wearing a wide-brimmed hat. Since some irresistible force also seemed to be at odds with the exhibition of crucifixes, removing them without warning from customers who wore them, the legendary Duke of Buckingham's dabbling with magic was called to mind, and he was soon blamed for any such activity. In 1994, a gentleman filming a video for schoolchildren was alarmed to feel himself being pushed out of a corner recess at the top right-hand side of the bar, where the original dark wooden seating is situated. In 1996 bar staff experienced beer taps turning themselves on and off at will, and kitchen utensils moving when their backs were turned.

The latest sighting of a mysterious figure is even more baffling, because, rather than the spectre being the expected period-costumed gentleman in a wide-brimmed hat, a member of a local band saw a man in shirt and tie appear by the doorway behind the bar. He mistakenly assumed the figure to be the landlord, until he noticed that the landlord was, in fact, sitting in the bar behind him! The men's toilet door has been known to lock itself from the inside, forcing staff to reopen it by pushing a broom handle through the tiny window at the back of the Cock and Bottle. Locals also speak of the legend of a 'face in the wall', which, hidden behind a picture which bar staff will remove for the curious, appears to be imprinted on the interior of one of the stone walls.

The Treasurer's House is maintained by the National Trust, and is open daily. York Minster is accessible to the public throughout the year (certain areas are subject to an entry charge).

LANCASHIRE

CHINGLE HALL
Goosnargh, near Longridge

Chingle Hall may not be the easiest place in the country to find, languishing on a private estate on the outskirts of the former Viking settlement of Goosnargh, but visitors from near and far overrun this ancient medieval manor several days and nights each week, drawn as much by its great history as by infamous tales of its hauntings. The original moated manor house was built in 1260 by Adam de Singleton, who inherited land formerly awarded to a forebear for service to King Harold. Much of the original building still remains, notably the squat, sturdy main door of tarred oak, although its original drawbridge was removed and many later Tudor additions are visible.

Traditionally, any person on the wrong side of the law in times of old could flee to Chingle Hall for protection, providing they approached the main door wearing white clothing and used the 'Sanctuary Knocker' three times. The hall priest would

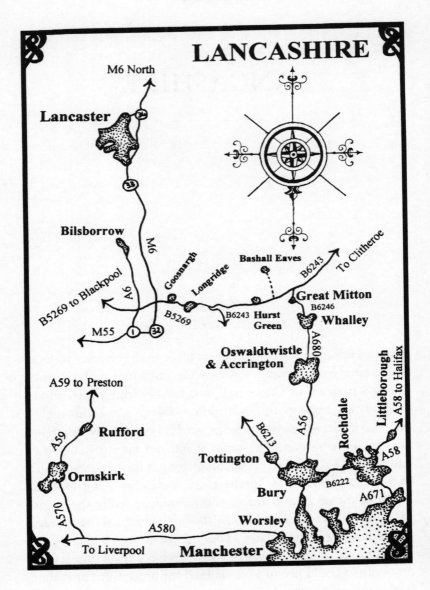

LANCASHIRE

M6 North

Lancaster

Bilsborrow

B5269 to Blackpool

M6

A6

Goosnargh

Longridge

Bashall Eaves

B6243

To Clitheroe

Great Mitton

B5269

B6243 Hurst
Green

B6246

Whalley

M55

**Oswaldtwistle
& Accrington**

A680

Littleborough
A58 to Halifax

A59 to Preston

A56

Rochdale

A59

Rufford

B6213

A58

Ormskirk

Tottington

Bury

B6222

A671

A570

A580

Worsley

To Liverpool

Manchester

then receive them at the main door and hear their confession, which allowed them nine days' respite untouched by the authorities ... during which time many doubtless made their escape! Chingle's seclusion rendered it a successful Catholic stronghold during Protestant reigns, for those who attended its secret Masses knew that they were unlikely to be stumbled across by the authorities. The hall is consequently associated with four martyred Catholic saints, and is riddled with secret priest holes, of which a number have been discovered to date which are today displayed to visitors. The great hall's original darkened beams proved on analysis to be Scandinavian oak impregnated with sea salt, and must therefore have been segments of a Viking longboat recycled by the original builders.

Chingle Hall's guided tours provide a wealth of historic and paranormal information, as every guide and inhabitant of the house seems to have had a brush with the supernatural at some

Chingle Hall, a former Catholic stronghold

point, along with many of those who have chosen to overnight here. Numerous visiting psychics and mediums have added their impressions to a catalogue of supernatural events, and upwards of twenty ghosts are believed to have been identified in and around Chingle Hall. Spectral monks, a ghostly nun, a Grey Lady, Victorian children, a Roman centurion, a Cavalier, a knight in armour, a colonel and even a phantom cat, to name but a few, have all been noted around the premises. Visitors' cameras occasionally refuse to work in certain areas of the house, but those which do sometimes produce prints showing coils of white 'vapour' which are not visible to the human eye when the photograph is taken. Several such photographs are on display in the great hall, and experts from Kodak recently gave the opinion that an inexplicable form of 'electrical energy' was to blame. The figure of a monk has also appeared on photographs taken both in and outside the house, and both residents and guides have had their own encounters with the spectre, who has been noted walking through the garden and standing in the small chapel. (The chapel, which possesses its own priest hole, often mysteriously smells of incense despite none having been burned here since 1788.)

A common occurrence which visitors and guides note at Chingle is the sensation of being pinched, pushed or having their hair pulled, with ladies occasionally even having their handbags tweaked from their shoulders. Heavy footsteps often ring out over unoccupied parts of the wooden-floored building, and mysterious ringing bells have been noted coming from an area between the chapel and the porch, on the latest occasion being heard by several visitors in January 1996. In February of the same year, resident Jason Karl was sitting in the great hall with a group of friends when he noticed a large, black figure with a solid outline, which appeared to be wearing some kind of uniform with epaulettes judging by the angle of its shoulders,

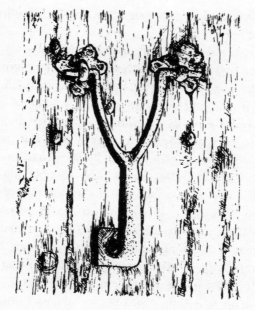

Chingle Hall's rare Sanctuary Knocker

walking through the open doorway. Although the figure disappeared in an instant, Jason had a second encounter in the same room with the strange apparition within weeks of the first, describing it as too large to be an ordinary man. This ghost had so far been uncatalogued at Chingle, so it was with great interest that Jason showed around a Dutch medium soon afterwards who declared that the great hall was haunted by a colonel, resplendent in a red jacket with striking epaulettes, who had died at Chingle during a visit here. Although the psychic was convinced that the spirit's name began with J, he could offer no further information at the time, except to describe the colonel as drunk! Perhaps the discovery of this military ghost could be linked to the sounds of a phantom swordfight which were heard twice during the summer of 1992, coming from the empty great hall.

The inexplicable scent of lavender (supposedly associated with former resident Eleanor Singleton, whose portrait today hangs in the great hall), has often filtered through the manor house, and it is said to be Eleanor's hand which has occasionally gently stroked the heads of visitors and guides. In the summer of 1995, the current owner's mother looked out of one of the great hall windows to see two ladies approaching the house with a little girl in a yellow dress, who was playing by the side of the moat. The women arrived at the door but there was no sign of the little girl, of whom, on being asked, they had apparently been unaware. The owner's mother had no idea at the time that this young female ghost had been seen before. Shortly afterwards, a visiting medium declared that a little girl had been drowned in the moat many years before.

Local legend tells that a still-born child was interred underneath the flagstone floor of the great hall centuries ago, and although attempts have been made to locate the grave, they have so far been unsuccessful. Chingle guide Anna, along with a number of others, has heard the mysterious crying of a child in this room, and has experienced regular drops in temperature whilst sitting by the large log fire. A gentleman who arrived at Chingle to clean the great hall fireplace with a sandblaster during the 1980s was horrified to see the room become enveloped in increasing darkness before an invisible hand took hold of his shoulder ... He left without completing the work, and was found by a guide shortly afterwards smoking a cigarette with a shaking hand from the safety of the moat bridge. Consequently, the fireplace remained uncleaned for several years.

In November 1995, members of the Aphelion Ghost Research Society arrived at Chingle Hall ready to undertake an all-night vigil. It was already dark as their president, Paul McKinley, took photographs of the outside of the building, although once inside the great hall his camera flash refused to function. This being quite a common phenomenon at Chingle, Paul commented that he hoped whatever was messing about with his equipment would stop, and the flash instantly triggered itself without human aid. Within a short while of entering Chingle, three of the group members complained of the sudden onset of oppressive headaches. Kerry-Anne Marjerrison was later alone in the St John Wall Room at around 11 p.m., when the silence was broken by a loud scratching from the area of exposed brick near the door, where a priest hole is today uncovered for visitors. After a few seconds' pause, the scratching began again; its source was never traced. The St John Wall Room is thought by some to be the most haunted room in the building, the figure of a monk having been noted by several visitors here over the years. Paul McKinley believed he could well have seen the same figure briefly in the darkened outside corridor at around four the following morning, as he experienced a sudden drop in temperature and watched a dark shape move towards him before it vanished underneath the chandelier.

Robert Appleton, a ghost-hunter of thirty-plus years' experience and one-time voluntary guide at Chingle, is the veteran of over a hundred all-night vigils at the hall. He feels that its haunted history owes much to the fact that it is built over crossed ley lines, paths of magnetic earth energy believed to attract spirit activity. Robert's first paranormal encounter at Chingle was on the night of his first vigil here in July 1993, when he encountered the rough outline of an Elizabethan lady on the stairs. On a subsequent occasion, his hand was grasped in an icy grip by an invisible force on the 'haunted' corridor, and further vigils provided him with a wealth of photographic evidence suggesting that spirit energy can indeed be captured on film. His collection of photographs taken in and around Chingle displays materialisations ranging from the ghostly white 'vortexes' of 'spirit' energy, to strange forms akin to grotesque faces, and even the manifestation of what appears to be a cloven hoof.

Chingle Hall is privately owned, being open for guided tours at weekends, and for overnight stays for keen ghost-hunters on Thursdays, Fridays, Saturdays and Sundays. Booking well in advance is advised. For bookings: Chingle Hall, Whittingham Lane, Goosnargh, Preston, Lancashire PR3 2JJ.

THE PUNCH BOWL
Hurst Green, near Clitheroe

The Punch Bowl, a beautiful and historic pub which fronts the winding B6243 road leading into Clitheroe from Longbridge, is a welcome respite for visitors to the Pendle area. This public house was formerly a coaching inn, which in the last century, was frequented by a local highwayman named Ned King. King picked his victims from the unwary travellers who stopped here to refresh themselves and their horses, before continuing on their journeys. The landlord was reputedly as guilty as King, advising him of the richest pickings and pointing out likely visitors for robbing. King fell in love with the landlord's daughter, and for a while the rich pickings were divided between the conspirators. However, the highwayman was captured by a band of redcoats one night, and was taken to the top of Gallows Lane close by, where he was hanged. The Punch Bowl is said to be haunted by Ned King's restless spirit, which some visitors believe they have seen leaning over the balcony observing the diners below. A visiting psychic in the 1990s was convinced that there were two ghosts here; one she believed to be that of Ned King, the other she declared was female, possibly King's long-dead sweetheart, the former landlord's daughter.

BRANDLESHOLME OLD HALL
Tottington, Bury

Brandlesholme Old Hall was once the family seat of the Greenhalghs, who, after many generations in residence, eventually sold the property in 1728. Brandlesholme is believed to have Norman foundations, and much of the structure is known to date at least from the fifteenth century. In common with many historic Lancashire houses, Brandlesholme was once a Catholic stronghold complete with its own secret priest hole, in which an unfortunate man became trapped during the Civil War period. He consequently died of starvation, and so began a well-documented haunting which continued for over two decades. Unexplained noises in the form of banging and moaning were accompanied by 'an emaciated figure pointing a fleshless finger' towards the priest hole. The poor man's skeleton was finally recovered in 1763, and after the remains had been laid to rest the haunting ceased. The location of the priest hole was once again forgotten until the 1950s, when it was inadvertently set alight by the then occupiers on lighting a new fire. In the near future, Manchester University Archaeology Unit and English Heritage hope to open the priest hole with the approval of the Kaufman family, who occupy the house today.

An unknown grey-haird White Lady has long been rumoured to walk the minstrel gallery, although no sightings have been recorded in recent years. The ghost is believed to have been 'laid' following the visit of an American descendant of the Greenhalgh family during the 1950s. The house is also connected with a now-forgotten brotherhood who once resided here, and whose ancient bell until recently hung on a wall overlooking the garden. A small sewing room is still known as the Monk's Cell, and is the site for a flight of currently unexplored steps which are rumoured to enter a subterranean tunnel. Locals of the area are aware of the legend of a ghostly monk said to haunt the premises. This ghost has never been encountered by the Kaufman family who bought the property in 1994, although Stuart Kaufman notes that a 'sensitive' friend had an unusual encounter whilst baby-sitting here one night. This lady felt a presence in the great hall which she described as 'following her' from room to room, touching her foot at one point. Another house-sitter told the Kaufmans on their return from holiday that he had seen the figure of a monk pass by an outside window.

Stuart Kaufman notes that his own strangest experience regarding Brandlesholme Old Hall is the story attached to its purchase. The house had been on the market for four years when the Kaufmans heard about it and arranged an exterior viewing, on 15 October 1994, followed by a full viewing on the 16th. Mrs Kaufman was expecting a baby at the time. The names decided on for the new baby were Amelia Sophia if a girl, and a middle name of Mortimer if a boy, after Mrs Kaufman's maiden name. Shortly after agreeing to the purchase of Brandlesholme, the Kaufmans visited Blair Castle in Scotland (home of the Dukes of Atholl), where the first portrait they saw was of James Stanley, 7th Earl of Derby. Stanley had been a frequent visitor to Brandlesholme Old Hall during his lifetime, and was the patron of Sir John Greenhalgh whom he appointed Governor of the Isle of Man between 1640 and 1651. Next to his portrait was that of his daughter, who was named Amelia Sophia. Close by there was a display of various relics including Stanley's speech prior to his execution, which had taken place on 15 October 1651. When the Kaufmans returned to Manchester they discovered that the previous owner had died on 16 October and that his middle name had also been Mortimer, after his own mother's maiden name. Moreover, he had moved into the house on 16 October twenty years previously. Stuart Kaufman feels certain that it was not a matter of his family choosing the hall, but rather, it was the hall that chose them!

Brandlesholme Old Hall is a private residence. Guided tours, conducted by Mr Kaufman, are available by written request only at certain selected weekends throughout the year. For enquiries: Brandlesholme Old Hall, Brandlesholme Road, Tottington, near Bury, Lancashire BL8 4LS.

GUY'S THATCHED HAMLET
St Michael's Road, Bilsborrow

This unusual row of renovated and redesigned buildings today houses a number of different establishments under the umbrella of Guy's Thatched Hamlet. A restaurant, a stone-flagged tavern known as Owd Nell's, overnight accommodation facilities and craft shops open to visitors are arranged in two main blocks situated adjacent to the beautiful Lancaster Canal. Part of the main bar of Owd Nell's dates back to the seventeenth century, and was formerly School House Farm, being owned in the early 1900s by a Mr and Mrs Firth. Mr Firth was described as a 'travelling swine slaughterer' by trade, and local legend tells how his unfortunate wife was literally scared to death by a swine which escaped into the walled yard when she was alone one day. Ghostly activity at Owd Nell's is consequently blamed on the spirit of the unfortunate Mrs Firth, several staff reporting cold spots in the oldest part of the bar, with others declaring that a hand has occasionally been felt brushing the tops of their heads. Several fishermen who frequent the Lancaster Canal have mentioned to staff that they have seen 'a strange figure' walking along the canal bank by the tavern. Intriguingly, in Guy's itself, according to the current manager, a former member of staff reported seeing a 'little pixie-like figure sitting watching him clean' one day. A member of the management team was later working late at night in the same area when he witnessed the same 'little figure, sitting on the cashier's desk watching' him. This gentleman immediately left the building by the nearest fire exit and drove home, averting the mirror in his car so that he had no rear view.

Guy's Thatched Hamlet offers overnight accommodation (booking preferred but not necessary), with food available in Guy's Restaurant and Owd Nell's Tavern. For bookings: Guy's Thatched Hamlet, Canalside, St Michael's Road, Bilsborrow, Preston, Lancashire.

MITTON HALL
Mitton, Whalley

Mitton Hall was built at the turn of the sixteenth century close to the banks of the River Ribble, and is today run as a sister establishment to Guy's Thatched Hamlet, providing overnight accommodation and featuring a family pub and an all-day restaurant. The hall was once a Catholic stronghold, and its formerly secret priest hole is today visible in the restaurant along with a historic minstrel gallery. The current owners took over the hall in the early 1980s, and were soon made aware of unusual activity which seemed to focus on one of the children's bedrooms. Objects were regularly moved around and the child was often disturbed during the night feeling a 'presence' and on one occasion even witnessing a figure here. The room often became noticeably cold, although over time the strange phenomena ceased to occur, and the family remain happy here after many years, feeling their 'ghost' to be 'mischievous' rather than harmful. The managers note that supernatural activity at Mitton Hall is occasional but ongoing. A lady visitor once looked up into the gallery from the restaurant to see an unidentifiable figure walk directly through it. One gentleman swore that he had seen the spectre of a Cavalier at Mitton, and a regular lady visitor refuses to sit at a certain table underneath the minstrel gallery because she remains convinced that she has felt her hair being tampered with from above.

Mitton Hall is privately owned and run, featuring en-suite bedrooms (guests pay by the room and not by the person). Breakfast is served from 6.30 a.m. onwards each day. For bookings: Mitton Hall, Mitton, Whalley, Clitheroe BB7 9PQ.

PENDLE WITCH COUNTRY

The Pendle area of Lancashire draws tourists intrigued by its seventeenth-century history of witchcraft, although its wildly beautiful undulating scenery, high winding roads and small scattered villages today bear little resemblance to the poor and peasant-ridden Lancashire of the past. Pendle's infamous associations could well owe much to the outlawing of the 'old religion', instigated by laws passed by Elizabeth I and subsequently James I, banning the practising of 'magic'. The inhabitants of Pendle were not the only folk in England to be branded 'Satanists' for their superstitious beliefs and incessant inter-family squabbling. The cause of witchcraft was cried many times over in feuds and neighbourly disputes. More often than not, such cases were taken so seriously that witch-mania spread rapidly, leading to the torture and hanging of many innocent people for their alleged crimes. The tragedy and trial of the Pendle witches found its place in history due to clerk Thomas Potts, who produced the most detailed account of a seventeenth-century English witch trial on record.

The story began when a Pendle girl named Bessie broke into the Malkin Tower and stole food and clothing which were later discovered to be in her possession. Committed to prison, she accused her prosecutors of witchcraft, in particular Alison Device, who promptly admitted to the fact. Alison had allegedly caused a local man to suffer a debilitating fit when he refused to fund her begging, although to the modern eye it would appear that this gentleman chose an unfortunate moment to have some kind of seizure. The Justice of the Peace, having already noted the witchcraft accusations, doubtless decided that this was all the evidence he needed to question the entire Device family. Counter-accusations soon began to fly between Bessie's family and the Devices, and the courts were intrigued by statements of sickening cows, souring ale and the making of clay dolls to effect curses. Much damning evidence came from nine-year-old Jennet Device, who named friends and relatives as witches with devastating results, soon widening the net beyond the squabbling peasants to include the gentlewoman Alice Nutter of Roughlee Hall, under the tenuous charge that she had attended a sabbat. Within weeks, the witch-hunt had spread to nearby Samlesbury, and a total of nineteen individuals were incarcerated in Lancaster jail awaiting trial at the August Assizes.

The chief witness in the Samlesbury trials was a fourteen-year-old girl named Grace, whose wild and fanciful accusations were finally revealed as lies by the judge on cross-examination. Grace had been instructed in her testimony by a local Catholic priest who probably wished to take revenge on a number of lapsed Catholics who had transferred to the Protestant religion. Accusing them of witchcraft must have seemed the most appealing route to revenge at the time, although Grace faltered in her testimony and the truth was soon discovered. All seven of the accused Samlesbury witches were therefore acquitted. The Pendle witches were not quite so lucky, the damning testimony of the child Jennet alone being enough to commit several to the gallows. Eleven so-called witches were found guilty, ten of whom were hanged and one of whom was imprisoned, with only one woman (Alice Gray) being acquitted. On 20 August 1612, a crowd of thousands gathered on the moors above Lancaster Castle to watch the bodies of the eight women and two men declared guilty of witchcraft swinging from the gallows.

The Pendle Heritage Centre, set inside a range Grade II listed buildings known as Park Hill in Barrowford, offers a wealth of information regarding the Pendle witch trials; there are also woodland walks and a traditional seventeenth-century cruck barn, where seasonal events such as sheep-shearing, sheepdog handling, dry stone walling and traditional hay-making are exhibited to visitors.

Written Stone Lane in Longridge is the site of an archaic-looking carved stone over 8 feet in length which lies longways on the ground, underneath the outer hedge of Written Stone Farm. It was placed here in 1655 by Ralph Radcliffe 'To Lye For Ever'. Local tradition states that the stone was laid some time after a particularly fiendish murder, following which locals were plagued by a ghoulish spirit which haunted the spot. Whether the stone was set here following a ritual performed to 'lay' the ghost is unknown, although local superstition still holds that the Written Stone is cursed and must not be moved. A new tenant of Written Stone Farm in the last century is alleged to have removed the stone to use for building, a task which required many men and horses. Such ill fortune followed in the household that within days the Written Stone was returned to its original spot, although on its return journey only a single horse was needed to haul it away. Some years later a local doctor, disbelieving the old superstition and determined to prove that the stone was no longer a sinister object, rode towards it and scoffed out loud. A formless object is said to have risen from the stone and sent his horse into a frenzy, throwing him into a hedge and almost crushing him to death. The horse galloped for nearly 2 miles before being finally recaptured.

The Pendle Heritage Centre, just off Junction 13 of the M65 between Burnley and Colne, is open daily from 10 a.m. to 4.30 p.m. The Written Stone can be visited via the track to Written Stone Farm, Longridge.

The enigmatic Written Stone

LANCASTER CASTLE
Lancaster

The site of the oldest sitting court in the country, Lancaster Castle houses the small cell in which the Lancashire witches were incarcerated in dreadful conditions for almost a year, prior to their trial. The infamous Witches' Tower hides this dark, deep recess which still possesses the iron rings believed to prevent the escape of witches and the casting of magic spells. Lancaster Castle was primarily a legal and administrative centre rather than the home of a monarch, and became noted as a strict prison during the time of Henry VIII. Some visitors are alleged to have encountered something other than the human in the depths of the Witches' Tower itself, and members of staff tell how a parapsychologist who visited the castle in the summer of 1995 was convinced that 'the spirit of a mistreated child' was earthbound here. When the well-known 'sensitive' and author David Icke visited Lancaster Castle in 1995, he declared himself unable to venture far inside, receiving intense feelings of suffering related to the castle's past. Around the sitting of today's modern court, staff operate a chilling tour which includes the cells and hanging rooms; they are also expert on the history of the old judicial system and its barbaric ways, painting a horrifically clear picture of what an accused criminal incarcerated in Lancaster Castle in days of old could expect.

Lancaster Castle is open every weekend and each day throughout the summer, with guided tours operated on a regular basis around the sitting court.

WARDLEY HALL
Worsley, Manchester

Known for over two centuries as the House of the Skull, Wardley Hall, the official residence of the Bishops of Salford, was built by the Tyldesley family in the mid-1500s on the site of an earlier house dating from 1300. The skull of St Ambrose, a Catholic martyr who was hanged, drawn and quartered in 1641 for refusing to renounce his faith, sits today in a secure niche within the house. Before his death and subsequent canonisation, Father Ambrose Barlow was a Benedictine monk who had been jailed many times over for his beliefs. Father Ambrose always somehow secured his release until the fateful day in April 1641 when he was seized by a fanatical Protestant mob whilst saying Mass at Morley Hall near Astley in Lancashire. Thrown into Lancaster Castle dungeons before his execution, but still refusing to abandon his faith, Ambrose was tortured and beheaded, after which his head was displayed on a pike outside a Manchester church. A family friend soon removed the grisly relic and stowed it away secretly in Wardley Hall, where for over a hundred years it remained concealed and guarded. Former Bishop's secretary Father Mark Davies told how, in the late 1700s, 'according to legend, the skull was thrown into the moat which still surrounds the house. From that moment on, the whole area was filled with disturbances. Thunderstorms raged, and screaming could be heard all through the house. The troubles continued until the moat was dragged – and the skull was recovered.' Thereafter, the skull was kept inside the house in an open niche close to the stairs.

Manchester antiquary Thomas Barritt noted his own encounter with the Wardley skull, when he visited the hall together with three friends. At this time it was kept in an open niche which the tenants never glazed, believing that the skull would be 'unruly and disturbed' if not open to view. Barritt recounted how an unnamed member of his party removed the skull from its hole, hiding it in a dark niche in the same room before leaving the building. According to his account, two days later 'such a storm arose about the house, of wind and lightning, as tore down some trees, and unthatched outhousing'. When his father visited a relative the following week he returned to testify to the havoc the storm had wreaked on the surrounding countryside. Barritt concluded that 'all this might have happened had the skull never been removed; but, withal, it keeps alive the credibility of its believers.'

Following the theft of the Wardley skull as recently as 1930, local people claimed that there were storms across the sea which raged for days. Late one night soon after the theft, the then Bishop Thomas Henshaw is reputed to have heard a noise at his window, which he opened, to be confronted by the thief who had suffered so much misfortune as a result of his actions that he could not wait to hand the skull back again! Thereafter, peace is said to have reigned, and today the skull of St Ambrose sits in a glass case on the right of the landing inside Wardley Hall, set into the wall where nobody can remove it. The current secretary to the Bishop of Salford neither admits to nor renounces the supernatural properties of the skull, feeling instead that 'the stories and legends attributed to the relic arise not so much out of superstition, but of spiritual appreciation for the holy relic, and its veneration thereby giving greater glory to God'.

Wardley Hall is a private residence, although group visits may be organised by written arrangement with The Reverend Secretary, Wardley Hall, Worsley, Manchester M28 5ND.

STUBLEY OLD HALL
Littleborough near Rochdale

During the reign of Richard the Lionheart, Sir Ralph de Stubley, founder of Stubley Hall, took up the cross and followed his King to the Crusades. Whilst away from English shores, it is said that Sir Ralph became deeply involved with a Saracen girl, named Fatima, to whom he promised himself before his return to Lancashire. Legend tells how Fatima resolved to follow Sir Ralph, stowing herself on a ship disguised as a travelling musician, accompanied only by her harp. Fatima died of the plague before ever reaching England. It is said that Sir Ralph, during a feast following his wedding to a Norman noblewoman, heard a harp playing in the grounds of Stubley Hall. He went outside to investigate and collapsed from shock on encountering the ghost of his former love.

Today, a commissioned painting above the fireplace of the oak-beamed public house and restaurant at Stubley Old Hall commemorates the story of tragic Fatima, whose ghost has been encountered here on a number of occasions. Sightings of Fatima occur mainly over the Christmas period, when staff note that she is most often to be seen in the top part of the restaurant. And after closing time, when the premises are empty, lights previously turned off upstairs are found to be mysteriously switched on again.

Stubley Old Hall public house and restaurant is situated on Featherstall Road, Littleborough, Manchester.

RUFFORD OLD HALL
Rufford, Ormskirk

This beautiful timber-framed Tudor hall, built in late medieval style and resplendent with a traditional black and white exterior, is considered to be one of the finest historic buildings in Lancashire. Legend tells how a young woman who stayed here during the sixteenth century was celebrating her betrothal to a local soldier, when an urgent message arrived telling him to leave immediately to quell an uprising nearby. The soldier never returned, and, since no messenger arrived at Rufford to inform the waiting party of his death, his bride-to-be watched for him ceaselessly from the windows, eventually pining away. Her ghost is traditionally to be seen wandering the grounds of Rufford Old Hall. Although the current custodian notes that there have been no reported sightings of the ghost in recent years, she has been approached by a number of visitors who have experienced a strong and yet invisible 'presence' in certain rooms, along with an unaccountable 'cold draught' which seems to have no source.

Rufford Old Hall is administered by the National Trust, and is open from 2 April to 31 October, Saturday to Wednesday between 1 p.m. and 5 p.m., with the gardens open additionally on Sundays between 1 p.m. and 5.30 p.m.

THE RED PUMP
Clitheroe Road, Bashall Eaves

The Red Pump public house, a former farmhouse situated in the Ribble Valley village of Bashall Eaves, is today run as a freehouse and restaurant. In 1989, former landlord Jim Fenton had decided to build a small patio at the back of the pub. While digging one afternoon he unearthed a cube of sandstone approximately 12 inches square, which appeared to be uneven on one side. The stone was cleaned to reveal the carving of a goat's skull with ears of corn hanging down on either side. The moment Jim saw the stone he recalls disliking it, and instinctively wanted nothing more to do with it, deciding to leave it in an outbuilding. However, staff and locals soon heard of his unusual find, and Jim was frequently asked to bring the stone head from the outhouse into the bar for the curious to see for themselves. Eventually he decided to leave it in the kitchen. Several members of staff felt uncomfortable with the stone and requested that it be removed, and Jim noted that there was a sudden and inexplicable increase in sick-leave. When a child of one of the staff fell ill with a particularly unpleasant virus, Jim's wife suggested that perhaps the stone head should be returned to its former resting place, as popular superstition began to earmark the object as 'cursed'.

With local curiosity aroused, the *Clitheroe Advertiser* picked up the story and the ensuing publicity sparked many theories as to the origin of the stone head. Some people felt that the archaic carving was a 'witchstone', traditionally set close to the stables of a property to prevent witches from riding horses to death in the dead of night. Others believed that the head could once have been set in the lintel of an old fireplace as a decoration, stemming from the Celtic tradition of using carved heads to aid prosperity and afford protection to a household. Jim Fenton eventually decided to reinter the stone in a plastic bag at the spot where it had been unearthed. When he and his wife left the Red Pump in 1991, they did so knowing that the stone head was once again underground. However, a subsequent landlord had heard much of the tale, and was determined to unearth the stone to use it as a feature within the Red Pump. He asked a colleague to visit Jim one afternoon to find specific details of its whereabouts. Soon afterwards, the stone was dug up again. Within eighteen months the landlord was forced to leave the Red Pump amid financial trouble. Perhaps he too was convinced that the carved head had something to do with his bad luck, for it was eventually sold to a hospital consultant. Whether this gentleman still has the head in his possession today is unknown.

During their tenancy at the Red Pump, the Fentons were troubled by a mischievous ghost which could often be heard moving around in unoccupied areas of the building. The pub as it stands today was built in two main stages, with the old kitchen exit door being close to the area of the modern toilets. On many occasions, customers and staff heard somebody unknown leaving through the door, on the route of the old exit. Jim Fenton and his son-in-law took a regular weekly stock count in the cellar before reordering, and often noted that they had run out of drinks which would suddenly reappear in the racks after the new stock had been ordered. In 1989, Jim approached a medium who visited the Red Pump and identified the playful spirit as that of a young girl named Ruth, who was apparently delighted that the Fentons were taking care of the property so well. On the medium's advice, Jim and his wife fixed a sprig of rosemary to one of the beams in the barn (the area at which the ghost's presence was felt to be strongest), as a mark of remembrance. Thereafter, activity in the building quietened down. However, it would seem that the Red Pump could well be haunted by more than one apparition, since a local lady drinking here one afternoon saw the dark figure of a man leave the men's toilets and head straight into the ladies'. Although she had not looked at the man closely enough to give a detailed description, she assumed him to be a customer who had taken a wrong turning, and followed him into the toilet. When she entered, the man had vanished. Severely shocked, she rushed into the bar, pale and shaking, for a medicinal brandy!

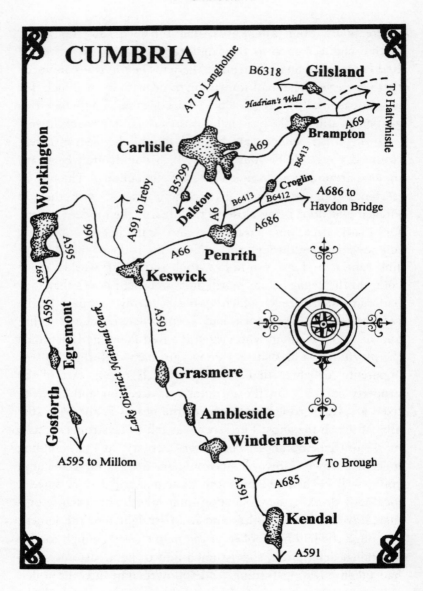

CUMBRIA

WORKINGTON HALL

Workington

During a period in history when frequent Scottish raids rendered timber houses easy to attack and burn, Gilbert de Culwen founded the first all-stone building on the site of Workington Hall. The year was 1362, and further fortification of the original pele tower continued under Gilbert's descendants for the next two centuries. In 1568 the captive Mary Queen of Scots stayed in the north wing of the hall, and shortly after this date Sir Nicholas Curwen transformed the ancient fortress into an impressive Tudor mansion. Under the direction of John Christian, who married the last Curwen heiress, Workington Hall reached its current proportions around the turn of the nineteenth century. The hall was vacated by its resident family around 1929, in preference for an estate in Windermere, and, after being used as billets for troops during World War II, it was left to the local council and eventually deteriorated into ruin.

The haunted staircase at Workington Hall

The infamous Henry (Galloping Harry) Curwen was murdered at Workington Hall in 1725, and it is to him that the
ghostly presence at the hall's ruin is today attributed. Henry was
nicknamed for his love of horses and horse-racing, and was
instrumental in the breeding of the 'Curwen Barb' strain. According to J. F. Curwen's recorded history of the family, Henry was

already very ill and close to death when a 'French lady' (whose identity is unknown) and her maid dragged him by his heels down the stairs into the Justices Hall. Here they sat him in a chair and removed his jewellery, telling servants that Sir Henry's condition was improving and that he had asked not to be disturbed. By the time the servants found him, Henry was already dead, and the Frenchwoman and her maid had long since set sail. The tale did not end there, however, for fifty years later an old lady visited the hall and described how she had been maid to a French lady at the time of Henry's death. According to her story, the ship on which she and her mistress escaped with their stolen property had been wrecked off the Scilly Isles. Her mistress had drowned, the jewellery was lost, and she herself had been picked up by a French fishing boat. After many years in a convent, the maid felt compelled to revisit the scene of her earlier crime when her conscience proved impossible to ignore.

Henry Curwen was a very unpopular figure during his lifetime, particularly within his own family. He was a staunch Catholic who supported the exiled Catholic James II, deposed his family from the Curwen estates on returning from his own exile in France, and willed Curwen property to a Catholic cousin. Perhaps this would have been reason enough for his own family to have conspired to murder him. The tale of the mysterious French lady and her maid dragging the dying man by his heels downstairs is recalled in the haunting of Workington Hall, for the ghost of Galloping Harry is reputedly to be heard rather than seen, as his head bumps over the stairs. J. F. Curwen recalled the haunting in a poem dated 1927 which noted how '*that awful noise is heard, which starts you from your bed, that awful bumping down the stair of Henry's dying head!*' The narrow turning steps of what is still known today as the 'haunted staircase' end underneath an intact stone archway, and are the focus for modern guided tours.

Derek Woodruff is the warden and guide at Workington Hall, and has located a number of newspaper articles (dating from the time Workington was occupied) which detail sightings of Galloping Harry's ghost. This was witnessed by both the resident family and their visitors. Derek has also been visited by old soldiers billeted here during World War II who themselves encountered the ghost of Galloping Harry during their stay. Today, certain visitors have described feeling a strong 'presence' in the house and their canine companions are apt to behave strangely.

A number of local people in recent years have reported sporadic sightings of 'spectral children', who appear to be playing in the courtyard. In 1606 over a hundred men, women and children were held in the hall's tiny dungeon prior to being transported to the wastes of Roscommon in Ireland. The monarch James I had ordered the families of thirty-five border reivers out of the country, never to return. The concentration of prisoners kept in such a small area would undoubtedly have led to several deaths. All records of this event were purposely omitted from the Curwens' recorded history. Perhaps this offers one possible explanation for the spectral children in the courtyard.

The pub at the foot of the hill on which the house is built is situated in a corner of Workington's original parkland and is known as the Henry Curwen after the infamous squire himself. Its placard is taken from a portrait of Henry dated *c.* 1688, the same portrait, it is said, which the family 'always turned to the wall'. Derek Woodruff notes that, over the years, the original portrait has had a habit of disappearing from the family's hands and becoming temporarily and mysteriously 'lost'.

Workington Hall is administered by Allerdale Borough Council, and is open to the public from Easter to the end of October,

Tuesday to Friday 10 a.m. to 5 p.m. and weekends 2 p.m. to 5 p.m. Guided tours are always available, and since the hall has a resident theatre group (Curwen Heritage Theatre), costumed activities and plays are regularly advertised locally.

THE KIRKSTONE PASS INN
Kirkstone Pass, Ambleside

In the autumn of 1996, the Kirkstone Pass Inn, famous for standing at the highest point of any public house in the Lake District, celebrated its five hundredth birthday. A true old-world inn, the Kirkstone Pass is not supplied with electricity, using instead a generator by day, and car batteries to supply its power after dark. Tenant Tracy Collings notes that visitors who choose to stay in the historic four-poster beds, which are built into the three guests' rooms, find the place very atmospheric indeed!

Local legend tells how, during the eighteenth century, a former innkeeper was hanged here by local villagers following the mysterious death of his twin baby boys. The Kirkstone's resident ghost, however, is unrelated to the legend, being believed to be an old coachman known as Nevill. A visitor who had taken a photograph of his family in the porch developed the film to find that, in the background of this particular snapshot, was a male figure who had not been present at the time. A member of staff saw the apparition of a 'large man' here in the summer of 1996, and only weeks later a woman overnighting in Room 2 experienced what she described as 'an ice cold thing' moving across her feet as she lay in bed. Although Tracy has never encountered the ghost herself, she notes that, after closing one night, a glass flung itself from the back of the bar, landing at her feet several yards away as she was clearing up.

For bookings: The Kirkstone Pass Inn, Kirkstone Pass, Ambleside, Cumbria.

OVERWATER HALL HOTEL
Ireby, Keswick

In the early 1800s Overwater Hall was built around a previously modest manor which had occupied the site since 1780. This beautiful area has been settled for much longer, however, as no more than 200 yards from the hall is the site of a Roman encampment which is believed to have housed holidaying troops relieved from their duties at Hadrian's Wall. During the 1950s, Overwater Hall was owned by Charles de Courcy-Parry. He was infamously known as 'the man who shot Percy Toplis' (the subject of the BBC's *The Monocled Mutineer* series), a label which dogged him until his death in 1988, and which he hotly disputed. De Courcy-Parry investigated the haunted history of Overwater Hall during his time here. On his purchase of the house, he was assured that it was 'haunted by the ghost of a black woman, who had met her sad ending by being drowned' in Overwater Tarn close to the hall. The woman was supposedly murdered by her own husband, who tipped her over the side of a boat. When she clung to the side to save herself, he hacked off her hands with a 'chopper'. Her ghost is reputed to have terrified a great number of people by roaming the interior of Overwater Hall; its most notable feature is that it has no hands. The ghost's appearances were so regular that domestic staff at one time refused to stay in the house itself, and eventually had separate cottages built at the end of the drive.

De Courcy-Parry encountered a ghost one summer evening just after midnight, although, in his own words, he was 'very surprised . . . to see not a negress at all, but an Indian princess in a sari passing noiselessly up the stairs'. The spectre drifted into the 'best bedroom' without opening the door, directly through the panelling . . . and de Courcy-Parry noted that she had no hands. Modern encounters with the ghost are significantly less detailed, although staff and visitors continue to report unusual phenomena on a regular basis. In the summer of 1996, a relative of one of the hall's managers was sleeping in a room which is today part of the original 'best bedroom' described by de Courcy-Parry, somewhat altered in recent years. She witnessed an apparition in the form of a 'glowing iridescent outline of a figure', although its features were indeterminable. Another member of staff who lives on the premises described encountering a similar vision in her own bedroom one night.

For bookings: Overwater Hall Hotel, Overwater, Ireby near Keswick, Cumbria CA5 1HH.

LAKE WINDERMERE

For well over a century people local to Windermere have sporadically reported strange, howling cries which seem to come from the lake and its surroundings after dark. During one extreme winter in which the lake froze over, locals noted a continuous moaning sound which was heard here after dark for several consecutive nights. Although it seems highly likely that the winter wind, carrying with it the sound of cracking ice, was responsible on this occasion, Lake Windermere has long been associated with ghostlore and legend. The phantom Crier of Claife, who is said to make himself heard by wailing and moaning over the waters of Windermere, is believed to be the spirit of a Furness Abbey monk. Legend tells how he became involved with one of the destitute women whom he was pledged to help, and, after being rejected by her, died on the heights of Claife raving and howling with grief. A local ferryman once mistakenly assumed that the ghostly cries were a call for his services, and duly took his boat out across Windermere. He returned without a passenger, speechless and shocked, and died within a matter of days. According to local belief, neither man nor beast would venture close to the Crier's haunt, day or night, even during the nineteenth century. The uneasy spirit of the Crier was eventually exorcised by a local priest, and 'laid' in an area still known as the Crier of Claife Quarry (Grid Ref. SD 384 981). Lake Windermere is also associated with a ghostly white horse, which is said to gallop across the surface of the lake as a warning of impending doom for the beholder.

Windermere Tourist Information Centre can provide details of steamboat trips, cruises and rowing-boat hire on the lake.

WARDREW HOUSE
Gilsland, Carlisle

'Wardrew' is believed to translate as 'watch tower', and, on the site at which a building of this name has been recorded since 1300, stands the base of an ancient pele tower which was incorporated into a larger building in 1750. The Gilsland area was once disputed borderland, whose residents were prone to raids and skirmishes. The resident Wade de Thirlwall family built the watch tower in the late thirteenth or early fourteenth century, following which they built nearby Thirlwall Castle. Their new pele tower replaced an earlier wooden building which had been burned down by the Prioress of Lambley's shepherd, following a dispute over local grazing rights. From the late

1700s onwards, Wardrew House was a family-owned mansion with an attached farm. Robbie Burns visited friends here, and it was at Wardrew House that Sir Walter Scott met his future wife. The house was partly demolished during the 1960s and was renovated in the 1970s to the same ground plan, but one storey shorter. Today, this historic building is owned and run by Sue and Robin Rew, a retired couple who cater for bed and breakfast guests.

When the Rews first moved into Wardrew House, they were told of a vague legend concerning a Grey or Green Lady who was believed to haunt the house, although the details of her haunting were rather scant, and they believed that she had not been seen for many years. However, a local lady recounted a story to Robin of her own experience at Wardrew House shortly after World War II. This lady entered an upstairs room and as she did so felt an enormous gust of air, like a powerful draught. She became aware of what she felt to be 'green curtains, lace or cloth' brushing and billowing around her. Her first thought was that the windows must be open but once she had focused on the interior of the room she discovered that they were tightly shut. In a state of terror she left the room, and remains most vehement in expressing her experience in the same detail and with the same conviction to this day, more than forty years later. Although neither Robin nor Sue has ever encountered any such visual manifestation, they have both heard what they described as a 'disembodied' female voice on two separate occasions in 1995 and 1996. Both times the voice was heard by the pair simultaneously, in an area within the confines of what would once have been the former pele tower, today close to the office door. Robin described the voice as very clearly female, although on both occasions it uttered one single word which neither of the Rews could quite discern. The experience did not disturb the couple, who feel that Wardrew House is a very benign place despite its turbulent history as a border reivers' stronghold.

The Gilsland area is legendarily haunted by the spirit of a young boy known locally as the Cauld Lad, whom some believe to be connected with the Cauld Lad of Hylton Castle. Barely dressed in rags and shivering and gibbering, the ghost is said to utter the phrase 'Cold for ever more!' before disappearing with a sob. On occasions he is felt rather than seen, in the form of a 'cold spot' or the icy touch of an invisible hand. The Cauld Lad is rumoured locally to have been the orphaned son of a nobleman, who was left in the care of an evil guardian. Determined to have the child's inheritance for himself, the guardian turned his ward out on to the moor during a blizzard. The boy's body was discovered frozen solid underneath a mantle of snow the following day.

Robin and Sue Rew offer bed and breakfast throughout the year. For bookings: Wardrew House, Gilsland, Carlisle CA6 7EW.

LEVENS HALL
Kendal

The Elizabethan Levens Hall is world-famous for its unusual award-winning topiary gardens, which were first laid in 1694 and are kept to their original design to this day. The hall is still home to the Bagot family after several generations in residence, and is the subject of an unusual legend said to date back to the early 1700s. A travelling gypsy woman requested alms from staff at the main entrance and was turned away and told to use the servants' entrance at the rear of the house. Weak and half-starved, the woman collapsed and died before she reached her destination. She did, however, manage to curse the resident family, declaiming that no son should follow to successfully inherit his father's estate, unless a white fawn was born in the park and the nearby River Kent ceased to flow. Levens Hall did indeed pass by inheritance through an indirect line for a number of generations until the birth of Alan Bagot in 1896, when the River Kent froze over and a white fawn was found on the estate, born to one of the herd of dark Norwegian fallow deer who wander the parkland.

The current owner of Levens Hall, Hal Bagot, noted that on the year of his birth in 1946, the River Kent once again froze over and a white fawn was again born on the estate. Moreover, when his own son was born in December 1981, the same thing happened. Intriguingly, Hal Bagot's sister witnessed a ghostly woman outside Levens Hall when she was seven years old, and accurately described the appearance of an early eighteenth-century gypsy woman with 'hair like bootlaces', a straw hat, short skirt and heavy shoes. The woman appeared to walk straight through the wall of a building, and has been noted on a number of occasions on the back drive and on the bridge over the river. Two further ghosts seen here over the years by visitors and members of the Bagot family are the unidentified Pink Lady, a woman in a pink dress with a mob-cap always seen in the main hall of the house, and the ghost of a small black dog (described by a member of the family as 'small and woolly, like an unclipped poodle') which often runs past visitors' legs up the main stairs, and has even mysteriously appeared on a family photograph.

Levens Hall is privately owned, and is open to the public between 1 April and 30 September from noon until 5 p.m.,

Sunday until Thursday. The gardens open additionally on weekdays throughout October.

THE VILLAGE OF CROGLIN
approx. 10 miles SE of Carlisle

The origin of the legend of the Vampire of Croglin is shrouded in mystery. One form of the story suggests that a travelling tinker laid a curse on the village of Croglin around the turn of the eighteenth century after he was attacked by a local mob; he vowed that local folk should shortly see such misfortune as they had never known, and thus unleashed the legendary blood-thirsty beast. Other accounts tell how stonemasons renovating a nearby church in Renwick in 1733 had freed a hideous winged creature from the vaults, which one valiant man had either beaten back inside and bricked in, or killed with a club. Stories of the vampire, an inhuman creature which drained the blood of its victims in order to survive, were doubtless terrifying and very real to many folk in days of old.

In the early 1700s, a local girl named Amelia Cranswell is said to have been attacked by what she later described as a 'cloaked man' late at night whilst lodging at the old hall. Amelia was taken abroad by her two brothers to recover from the ordeal. According to the story, on her return, she decided that the fiend responsible must be caught, and with her brothers hatched a plot to lure the cloaked man to his capture. Amelia waited in her bedroom with the curtains wide open until the small hours, and sure enough she was disturbed by a human form approaching her through the darkness. On her cue, her brothers entered the room and shot at the intruder, who made his escape through the open window, a dark cape trailing behind him. The following day, a posse of locals armed with guns followed a trail of blood into the crypt of the local church. There they met a disturbing scene, for every tomb but one had been desecrated, and smashed coffins and remains were scattered over the floor. Only one tomb was undisturbed; when it was opened, a recently laid corpse with either blood around its mouth or a bullet wound to the leg was found. Some accounts of the story suggest that Amelia drove a stake through the heart of the corpse, others that the body was burned in the churchyard.

Bram Stoker is said to have used this folk-tale as an inspiration for his novel *Dracula*. No recorded account of the story from the time of its supposèd happening has ever been found. It was first committed to paper by a diarist who heard it from a retired army officer, whose father had lived at Croglin Grange during the mid-1800s. There has been much dispute over the supposed time of its happening, since the tale was passed down by word of mouth over several generations, and probably elaborated over the years. Thus the story of the Vampire of Croglin could well be a completely fictional piece of 'horror' which somehow found its way into oral folklore. However, the curious legend of the tinker's curse and promise of ruin is made more intriguing by the fact that the original church of Croglin disappeared for an unknown reason at some point after the episode. The site of this church, whose crypt is believed to be the one featured in the vampire legend, is only remembered locally in the name of Church Field. The privately owned hall in which Amelia Cranswell and her brothers lodged still survives, and features a bricked-in window which tradition asserts was the point of entry used by the vampire.

The tenants of Croglin's Robin Hood Inn today keep a file behind the bar which contains much material regarding the vampire story, and, on the wall by the front door, two newspaper cuttings detailing an earlier investigation into the story. Eminent researcher Charles Fort noted that a mysterious beast terrorised Ennerdale, Cumbria, in the early 1800s, its trademark being that it killed sheep by 'biting into the jugular vein and sucking the blood'. As far as the mythical winged creature of Renwick church is concerned, local researcher Gerald Findler noted that 'an enormous black bird-like figure' had caused much consternation after being spotted in the Renwick area as late as the 1980s. Although there has naturally been much speculation as to the authenticity of the vampire tale, Croglin and its legend continue to draw visitors.

Croglin is situated just off the B6413, 10 miles SE of Carlisle. The Robin Hood Inn, Croglin, caters for bed and breakfast.

CASTLERIGG STONE CIRCLE
Keswick

The breathtaking sight of this circle of misshapen grey stones, set on a natural plateau surrounded by towering Cumbrian fells, has held a sense of mystery and intrigue for centuries. The circle is believed to be one of the earliest examples of its kind to have been constructed in Cumbria, and is thought to date back as far as 3000 BC. Professor A. Thom located what he believed to be two 'sighting stones' which could have been used during neolithic times to mark the sunrise of an ancient festival, which later became Christian Candlemass, and sunset on the winter solstice. Superstition holds that the stones can never be counted more than once to reveal the same number, and indeed, it is noticeable that several contemporary sources of information on the circle all quote a different number of stones!

Castlerigg Stone Circle

Castlerigg Stone Circle is maintained by the National Trust and English Heritage, and is open to the public free of charge throughout the year, at all reasonable times.

DALSTON HALL HOTEL
Dalston

The crenellated battlements of the fifteenth-century Dalston Hall successfully withstood centuries of siege and rebellion in this historic borderland setting. Roman remains still visible in the grounds hark back to the days of occupation, when a road from Carlisle existed to supply the garrisons at Hadrian's Wall. During the Jacobite rebellion of 1645, the hall, with its fortified pele tower, became the headquarters of General Leslie. Today, Dalston welcomes visitors in its capacity as a historic country hotel, set in beautiful grounds on the northern edge of the Lake District National Park.

Little is known of the Grey Lady of Dalston Hall save that

she is said to have been a teenage maidservant who fell in love
with a married estate gardener, and died a mysterious death as
a result of their passionate affair. A member of the management
team who arrived at Dalston in 1995 named the ghost The Lady
Jane, and was most surprised to be told many months later that
the Grey Lady's name, according to local legend, had indeed
been Jane. Many of the supernatural happenings noted by staff
and visitors at Dalston are consequently attributed to the restless
spirit of the young maidservant. However, according to the
account of a workman involved in renovations here in the
1960s, there would appear to be at least one more ghost
attached to the property. This gentleman was servicing the
boilers in the cellar when he stopped to chat to another fellow
who helpfully passed him tools until the job was completed.
When the workman visited reception to tell them he was ready
to leave, he thanked the staff for sending somebody down to
help him. Reception, however, were unaware of the presence of
any other person in the area, and nobody could account for his
mysterious helper.

In 1996 a guest staying in the new wing came down for
breakfast after a disturbed night's sleep, and asked if there were
wooden floorboards close to his room. As the entire new wing
is carpeted it caused a great deal of curiosity when the guest
declared he distinctly heard 'something being dragged across
the wooden floor' in the small hours. He also heard noises
indicating that a staircase was close by, although he had no
knowledge that, as his bathroom was in the tower, it was
surrounded by a locked and unused staircase. Staff checked to
ensure that nobody had broken in during the night, and found
that the staircase had not been used at all. Another guest resting
in his room before dinner awoke to find a lady reclining on the
bed next to him. He later recounted to staff that, when she
began to talk, her voice appeared to be coming from somewhere

behind him and not from her mouth. The guest was left with no recollection of what the woman had said and without a clear description of what she looked like, although he recalled experiencing no fear.

During October 1996, staff noted a sudden onset of activity within the building. Each Saturday night a medieval-style banquet is held at Dalston, and a number of large ornamental candles are used to light the baronial hall. They are all carefully extinguished afterwards. Three days after one such banquet, two staff in the baronial hall watched astonished as one of the candles flared up in front of their eyes. Due to the time-lapse involved, during which the candle had not burned down at all, they felt it was impossible that it had been smouldering all the while. The previous day, a member of the management team had been most surprised to hear a glass smash itself in the empty kitchen; on investigation, it seemed to have landed feet away from the shelf it came from. Within days, the library (whose windows always remained closed) was found with its windows wide open, the bookcase open, and an old encyclopaedia lying on the sofa at the opposite end of the room. In the bar, two staff looked on as a pint glass rose slowly off the bar top and dropped to the floor without breaking. During all this activity, which continued for several days, the night porter was also disturbed after dark by the unexplained sound of what he described to be 'wooden planks' banging together. On each occasion he failed to locate the source of the sound as it always seemed to come from behind him. The activity culminated in a fire in the restaurant after it had closed one night, which was believed to have been caused by a guest's smouldering cigar stub. The fire brigade was called in the small hours and the fire, which had been focused on one particular table, was extinguished within seconds. A member of the management team noted that despite the table being destroyed, a heavy lace drape next to it had somehow remained untouched by the flames. She commented that, with hindsight, the spate of activity had somehow been directed at staff as a 'warning' of impending trouble in the form of the unexpected fire. The ghost, she noted, seemed to be happiest when the hotel was busy and thriving, and manifested itself most often when any type of disruption loomed.

Exactly a year earlier the telephones throughout the hotel had begun ringing incessantly every ten minutes. When they were answered, there was nobody on the line. A management meeting had been scheduled to take place in the library, and it was decided that this should go ahead regardless. As the meeting began, the library lights began to dim and flicker. This was followed by the fire alarm triggering itself. When staff checked to see which zone the sensitive electronic system had highlighted as the location for the fire, they were amazed to watch every zone flashing on and off repeatedly. No evidence of a fire was found. This spate of activity was later noted to have preceded management restructuring crucial to the future of the hotel, after which it ceased immediately.

Several witnesses have noted a female figure walking through the gardens of Dalston Hall at night, and a 'strong presence' can be felt, according to staff, in the same area. There have been many incidences of footsteps being heard in corridors which upon investigation prove to be empty, and electrical items such as televisions and kettles switching themselves on and off in the middle of the night. The minstrel gallery is also a favourite spot for the sensing of a 'presence' assumed to be that of The Lady Jane, along with Room 4, aptly named The Lady Jane Suite.

Dalston Hall Hotel caters for short breaks, medieval banquets, corporate and private functions. For bookings: Dalston Hall Hotel, Dalston, Carlisle, Cumbria CA5 7JX.

BROUGHAM HALL
Penrith

The Eden Valley hides the remaining outer wall and outhouses of the once prosperous Brougham Hall, whose substantial remains are currently the subject of a restoration programme. Brougham (pronounced 'broom') was recently created a centre for local self-employed and self-contained craftspeople, who are housed in the array of small buildings attached to the boundary wall. A small museum portrays the history of the site, including antiquated photographs which show the former splendour of the once magnificent crenellated hall with its richly tapestried, armoured and panelled rooms. Sadly, little of this remains, although under the direction of Christopher and Alison Terry, who have been involved in a rebuilding programme since 1985, the surviving remains and workshops are today open to the public.

Brougham Hall was long believed to house the skull of a warrior killed at a long-forgotten period in history, which, it is said, was bricked into one of the walls after his death to ensure good luck and prosperity for the household. A paper written by the 2nd Lord Brougham details his discovery of a skull, sword and spur said to belong to the medieval warrior Gilbert de Burgham. Whether this is in fact the skull referred to in the legend can never be known for sure. However, early sources detail how the skull's removal from its resting place had, in the past, been accompanied by an unpleasant haunting featuring 'diabolical and unearthly noises' which reverberated through the house in the night, similar to the haunting of Burton Agnes Manor (see the section on East Yorkshire). On each occasion the skull was returned and peace reigned once more at Brougham, the tale being retold until it seemed no more than a fireside anecdote.

The haunted remains of Brougham Hall

Then, during renovation work, Christopher Terry unearthed an ancient human skull from a wall. In his own words: 'When the skull was in my hands, I noticed that it had three equidistant holes in the top of its head, about 2 inches from each other, which were almost certainly the cause of the unfortunate fellow's death. He had an excellent set of teeth so he can't have been very old. Perhaps he was aged somewhere between twenty and thirty because his skull was fully formed and that of an adult rather than a child. The skull was situated at the corner of a massive stone tower. I know, having been an archaeologist, that it was a Roman habit to place infants on the corners of buildings ... some of the Roman suspicion may have survived into medieval times and may account for our skull which is only just above ground level at the corner of a massive building.' Mr Terry noted that the injury could have been caused by a spiked mace, according with the legend that the unknown soldier had died in battle. Since superstitious belief affirms that removal of the relic will trigger a very unpleasant haunting, Mr Terry was unwilling to risk any such manifestation and decided to honour the legend that the skull must never be removed. He placed it inside a ceramic casket, before cementing it securely into a secret niche within a renovated wall, the whereabouts of which he refuses to reveal. A stone epitaph including all the details known about the warrior was carved in memoriam, and is today visible set into the wall of a small room adjoining the museum. The inscription, copied from one of an earlier and unknown date, reads: '*Unknown Soldier from a sunlit shore, Who paid the price in an unknown war, For an unknown God in an unknown time, May peace eternal now be thine. Pray lie within this ancient wall, And guard that it should never fall.*'

Brougham Hall is open to the public daily from 10 a.m., throughout the year.

GOSFORTH HALL HOTEL
Gosforth

The builders of Gosforth Hall resourcefully took timbers from a shipwreck off the West Cumbrian coast with which to beam this splendid mid-seventeenth-century manor. The house was built for Robert and Isabel Copley, and is almost entirely intact three hundred and fifty years later, minus one wing which was destroyed by fire in the last century. The Copley family history does not show any arms since Robert is reputed to have refused to pay the herald's fee in 1665. He designed his own coat of arms instead, still to be seen in Gosforth's bar today.

The hall has known several uses throughout its history,

although at present, under the management of Chris and Jean Thorpe (who are undertaking extensive interior restoration work) Gosforth is run as a hotel and restaurant. A particular feature of interest within the building is the original 'nowel' staircase, a winding staircase made of solid stone, which dates from *c.* 1658. Chris Thorpe notes that several members of staff have heard what they describe as a 'baby crying on the stairs', although investigation always proves the area to be empty. Chris also described another most unusual phenomenon linked to the staircase: 'There is an awful smell which occurs quite regularly on the stairs, lasts for about twenty to thirty minutes, then disappears. It is very powerful and does not "build up", it just arrives and disappears as fast. We have called in a drainage expert who inspected the drains, and all were perfectly normal. We then called in Rentokil to inspect the roof spaces (the floors are solid), and they could not find anything at all.' The staff and management of Gosforth Hall are resigned to the continued appearance of the mysterious smell.

The beer cellar which supplies the bar is situated across a small yard and is always kept locked, with only Chris Thorpe having access. He notes that on many occasions the gas taps have been switched off (sometimes just one or two, sometimes all of them) without human aid. Chris has noticed that this usually occurs between 10 and 11 p.m., and points out that it could not happen accidentally, since the taps are heavy and stiff to operate. Room 1, situated just above reception overlooking the car-park, is also the focus for unexplained occurrences. The morning cook has on several occasions heard movement in this room despite the hotel being empty of guests. On 29 December 1995, the local milkman was delivering at around 4 a.m. when he saw a figure in the window of Room 1. Assuming this to be Chris Thorpe, he waved but received no response. He later discovered that Chris had not in fact been standing at the window of Room 1 at the time, because the Thorpes' living accommodation is on the ground floor at the back of the house. Neither had anybody else been in Room 1, since Gosforth is closed to the public between Christmas and the New Year. The figure was never successfully identified.

The Thorpes also possess what they believe could well be a 'haunted' rocking chair. There is no logical explanation for the chair's movement, for it has been witnessed to regularly rock backwards between fifteen and twenty times of its own accord. The Thorpes have tried to set the chair rocking on their own to test the possibility that the phenomenon is natural, but when they do this the chair only moves up to four times before stopping.

For bookings: Gosforth Hall Country Hotel and Restaurant, Gosforth Village, Cumbria CA20 1AZ.

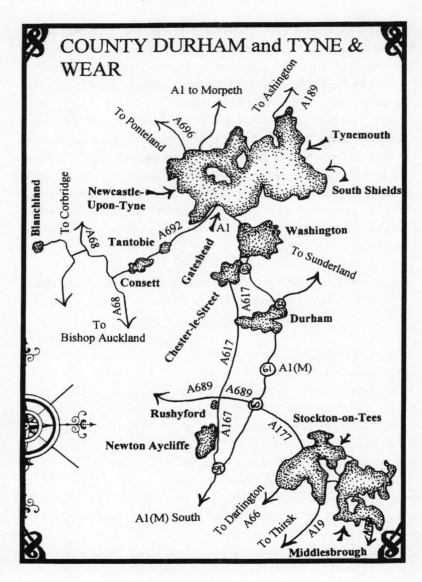

COUNTY DURHAM and TYNE & WEAR

A1 to Morpeth

To Ponteland

A696

To Ashington

A189

Tynemouth

South Shields

Blanchland

To Corbridge

A68

Newcastle-Upon-Tyne

Washington

To Sunderland

Tantobie

A692

Gateshead

A1

Consett

A68

Chester-le-Street

A617

A617

Durham

To
Bishop Auckland

A1(M)

61

A689

A689

Rushyford

A167

Stockton-on-Tees

A177

Newton Aycliffe

A1(M) South

To Darlington

A66

To Thirsk

A19

Middlesbrough

COUNTY DURHAM
and
TYNE AND WEAR

REDWORTH HALL HOTEL
Newton Aycliffe

Redworth Hall was home to the Crosier and Surtees families from when it was built in 1693 until it was finally sold in the 1950s. Anecdotes recorded through the ages indicate that certain family members were colourful and eccentric, with an impeccable history of martial service stretching from the medieval Battle of Crécy to the Boer War. Crosier Surtees, grandson of Redworth Hall's builders George and Eleanor Crosier, regularly entertained onlookers by twisting metal horseshoes with his bare hands. He also indulged in drinking sessions where several of his companions ended up under the table before he did, a party-trick for which he was well known. Crosier's brother James was considered a giant at 6 feet 3 inches tall, and thus enlisted in Churchill's Dragoons and fought at the Battle of Dettingen. Tragically, he collapsed and died at a Redworth inn after a hard drinking bout following his return. A generation later, Jane Surtees married her cousin Crosier, described as 'a designing, artful man, a bad character', and was made so utterly miserable by her husband's behaviour that she fled Redworth Hall in 1800 and never saw it or her husband again. Crosier himself died three years later, freezing to death in a ford on Linburn Back after falling, probably drunkenly, from his horse following a visit to Raby Castle. The last resident member of the Surtees family decided to sell Redworth in the 1950s, after which it was purchased by Tomorrows Leisure plc and restored and extended in 1990.

With such a long and lively history it is almost to be expected that the old house is haunted, and a great variety of reports indicate the existence of a plethora of ghosts within its walls. The hall has been visited on a number of occasions by paranormal investigators who recorded inexplicable sounds in certain areas, including footsteps and sobbing. An experienced ghost-hunting team visited in the summer of 1900, and monitored erratic cold spots in a number of bedrooms. They also witnessed the appearance of the outline of a female figure in the Blue Room lounge, at around two forty-five one morning, which was accompanied by a rapid temperature drop and the 'very strong feeling of a presence'. The team left convinced that Redworth was a very haunted place indeed.

In 1990, a bounty of £5000 was offered by Redworth's management to anybody who could prove the existence of the paranormal within the building. On Hallowe'en of the same year, a team comprising a medium, two paranormal investigators and a journalist rose to the management's challenge, and spent the night in the hall in an attempt to gather evidence. On their arrival, the medium immediately sensed that a man had committed suicide by hanging himself in the tower, a feeling which became stronger as they approached. This was confirmed later when the team were informed that the hall had once been a home for 'maladjusted' children, and a member of staff had indeed hung himself here. A seance ensued, and the medium made contact with the ghost of a Lady Catherine (possibly Surtees) whom he felt to have committed suicide two centuries previously. Everybody present heard the sound of footsteps crossing the floor of an empty room at one point during the investigation, and cold spots and phantom humming were experienced on the ground floor, with the 'sensitives' in the group declaring the 'vibrations' to be strongest in the banqueting hall.

As part of the investigation, statements were also collected from a number of staff. Two members of the senior management team had heard a piper playing (the hall has no resident or local piper). Waitresses who had slept in Room 26, in the tower staff quarters, refused to be housed there again after being awakened every hour throughout the night by slamming doors, footsteps and banging noises. A waiter heard the cries of a baby and the sound of coughing coming from empty rooms. In Rooms 5 to 9, rattling china ornaments and other mysterious noises were commonly noted. One member of staff, who had previously been sceptical of Redworth's rumoured haunting, heard what he described as 'a noisy phantom party taking place' one night when the hotel was supposedly empty, and a former receptionist even claimed to have seen a ghostly figure sitting in front of the fire in the lounge.

Despite the wealth of data collected by the ghost-hunting team, it was generally felt that none of the evidence was solid enough to merit the £5000 bounty. Although many anecdotal accounts of paranormal activity had been compiled, hard and fast evidence such as photographs and video footage was never achieved. Local legend says that Redworth Hall is haunted by the spectre of a Grey Lady, who is said to walk the oldest wing of the building following her suicide leap from the clock tower. This was the very location at which the medium made contact with the spirit of Lady Catherine on Hallowe'en in 1990. Folklore records that the Grey Lady flung herelf from the tower after being betrothed against her will, although the spirit contacted at the Hallowe'en seance apparently referred to herself as having been unhappily married. Redworth Hall today invites visitors to partake of its overnight 'Haunted Breaks', where, according to the enormous variety of paranormal experiences recorded at the hall, almost anything could be expected.

Redworth Hall's 24-hour Haunted Breaks take place on certain selected nights only throughout the year, and include pre-dinner drinks, a candlelit meal, a late-night showing of a ghost film and overnight accommodation in the 'haunted' wing. Redworth also offers regular theme banquets and conference facilities. For bookings: Redworth Hall Hotel, Redworth, Newton Aycliffe, County Durham DL5 6NL.

THE COOPERAGE
The Quayside, Newcastle-upon-Tyne

The thirteenth-century wooden-timbered Cooperage, a former medieval barrel-making establishment situated on the Quayside, is one of Newcastle's most historic surviving buildings. Its exterior has changed little throughout the centuries, and many of the original interior beams remain within. For as many years as people can remember, staff and management of the Cooperage have believed the building to be haunted by several ghosts. The current general manager, Clive Gibson, had himself noted footsteps pacing up the old staircase in the small hours of the morning, and has had the regular sensation of glimpsing 'something' on the periphery of vision which quickly vanishes. However, his most chilling experience occurred in the summer of 1996 whilst alone in the pub with a plumber who was at work in the toilets. Clive was preparing to leave and called the plumber through the wall to let him know. The toilet appeared to be empty so he went upstairs to look for him. On his way past the restaurant Clive saw a man standing in the corner by the window. The man raised his hand and suddenly vanished, just as Clive realised that, in a grey jumper and brown trousers, he did not answer the plumber's description. The pub was empty of all other people at the time. The restaurant had long been rumoured to be haunted by the ghost of an unknown man, and also, it is said, by a woman, although her ghost has not been encountered for some time. The wooden-panelled disco room on the first floor of the Cooperage is the location of a ghostly figure which was seen to materialise and 'change colour' by a former member of staff. A disused, well-rusted barrel hoist in one of the old lofts began to operate itself one afternoon and was overheard by a member of staff, who left the area immediately. The ghost of a young girl in a silver dress, combing her long blonde hair, also appeared to a former cleaner in one corner of the middle bar.

Newcastle's Quayside is renowned locally as a 'very haunted' area indeed, where never a year goes by without several reports of supernatural phenomena being added to the ever-growing catalogue. The small alleyway at the side of the Cooperage is said to be the site of a terrible murder undertaken by a press-gang in the sixteenth century. The gang plucked out the eyes of a local cooper who refused to be taken to their ship. His ghost has been noted shambling around the Quayside, with empty sockets where his eyes should be. Two different stories attempt to explain the ghostly sound re-enactment which is to be heard around the steep Dog Leap Stairs on the Quayside. The first version tells how a young Tudor girl was forced to leap up this steep area to escape from an attacker. Unfortunately she failed and was brutally murdered, despite a horseman hearing her screams and galloping to her rescue. The second version suggests that a local girl, Bessie Surtees, eloped with her young lover on horseback in the late 1700s, being pursued up Dog Leap Stairs by her father's horsemen and hunting hounds. All accounts seem to agree on the fact that the distant sound of hoofbeats and the screams of a girl have been heard here at obscure times of the day and night. A local man who regularly jogs around the Quayside says he himself has heard 'strange, eerie noises' which have occurred in the vicinity of Dog Leap Stairs around seven o'clock on a Sunday evening and as late as three in the morning.

LUMLEY CASTLE HOTEL
Chester-le-Street

Lumley Castle gained its fortified status in the fourteenth century, having been remodelled by Lord Ralph Lumley from a manor house built by his forebears, a task for which permission was granted by King Richard II. Through the changing fortunes of the resident family, the castle was often left uninhabited, and by the early 1800s circumstances had forced the sale of many rare paintings and other valuable artefacts. A century later, Francesca, Countess of Scarborough made the castle her home, and began to recreate the interior splendour of the building. Today, Lumley Castle's crenellated battlements stand proud amid landscaped grounds, welcoming visitors in its capacity as a hotel and conference centre, still featuring many of the original hidden corridors and secret passageways of earlier times, and once again richly furnished with a great variety of antiques.

Lumley Castle possesses its own tragic legend concerning 'the Lily of Lumley', the first wife of Lord Ralph Lumley, who was

King James' Suite, Lumley Castle, where 'the Lily of Lumley' walks

so called because of her great beauty. According to local legend, the lady had broken away from the Catholic faith to become an ardent follower of the religious reformer Wyclif. When Lord Ralph was called away on duty as Governor of Berwick, two local priests visited Lady Lumley in an attempt to persuade her to rejoin the Catholic faith. Being unsuccessful, the priests, determined to save her soul, decided that murder was the only alternative, and lured her into a bedroom where they brutally killed her. Afraid of discovery, they dragged the body down the mural staircase to the castle basement, and threw it into the well. The pair then took a fatally ill young woman from the village and installed her in a nearby convent, telling the Mother Superior that this was Lady Lumley. When she died soon afterwards, the priests informed Lord Ralph of his 'wife's' death.

When the River Wear rises, the Lily of Lumley legendarily rises from her watery grave to walk the endless rooms and corridors of the castle. The Lumley family archives, however, do not record any other marriage of Lord Lumley apart from that to Eleanor Neville, sister of the 1st Earl of Westmorland, and an overnight vigil on Hallowe'en in 1995 by a ghost-hunting local radio station failed to reveal any new sightings of the ghost.

Lumley Castle hosts regular medieval banquets, Medieval Memories weekends and Murder Mystery weekends. For bookings: Lumley Castle Hotel, Chester-le-Street, County Durham, DH3 4NX.

TYNEMOUTH PRIORY AND CASTLE
Tynemouth

Situated on a headland at the entrance to the Tyne estuary, against the backdrop of a beautiful sea panorama, Tynemouth Priory and Castle is a rare example of a fortified priory, common in Europe but extremely rare in the British Isles. A party of Scouts overnighting here in 1993 saw the figure of a 'black monk' drifting through a solid wall in the grounds. According to the custodian, the visitors had no idea that the coastguard, resplendent in a long dark raincoat, had just passed by and made his way through a small gate in the wall which was hidden from their view. As a result of their supposed sighting, the custodian notes, avid ghost-hunters from as far afield as Australia are on the trail of the mysterious black monk! However, many years earlier, in 1979, a group of more than thirty visiting local schoolchildren and their teacher were adamant that they saw a figure in black walk *through* the main gate . . . which was closed and locked at the time.

Tynemouth Priory and Castle is administered by English Heritage, and is open to the public between 1 April and 31 October, 10 a.m. to 6 p.m. daily, and between 1 November and 31 March, Wednesday to Sunday 10 a.m. to 4 p.m.

HYLTON CASTLE
Durham

The final part of the fourteenth century saw the building of Hylton Castle by Baron William Hylton, of which a fragmentary ruin and a surprisingly intact tower house still remain, set into a modern landscaped park. Geophysics equipment has been

Tynemouth Priory and Castle where walks a figure dressed in black

able to plot traces of earthworks today invisible to the human eye, which suggests that the area was once graced by formal gardens of seventeenth-century design. The surviving tower house was formerly flanked by two huge wings which were demolished in the 1860s, leaving the central structure as it stands today. At the turn of the seventeenth century, the Lord of the Manor was Sir Robert Hylton or Hilton, who according to local folklore was notoriously bad-tempered. Sir Robert allegedly murdered a young stable-boy with a hay-scythe for falling asleep in the stable after being asked to saddle up one of the horses. Sir Robert is said to have removed the body under cover of darkness and tipped it into the local pond, ensuring that all the evidence of his deed had been removed. The nineteenth-century historian Surtees discovered that a free pardon was obtained by Robert Hilton for the manslaughter of one Roger Skelton with a 'Syth', details of which are given in the Episcopal rolls of September 1609. Whether the pardon was given due to the absence of a body is unknown, although according to Surtees' *History and Antiquities of Durham* (1820), after drainage of the local pond, 'the skeleton of a boy was ... discovered in the last Baron's time', and was reburied elsewhere shortly afterwards.

There are many different stories attributed to the ghost of Hylton Castle, popular folklore suggesting that the Cauld Lad, as the spirit became known, was a helpful 'brownie' who did tasks for serving staff and played tricks in the kitchen. He was reputedly 'exorcised' when staff left him a little green cape and hood with which to cover his nakedness, prompting him to leave one night for ever. In this version of the story, the Cauld Lad appears as one of a breed of pixie-like spirits which were popularly believed to occupy domestic buildings in the fifteenth and sixteenth centuries. However, the ghost of the Cauld Lad is also connected with poor Roger Skelton, who some believed returned to haunt the scene of his murder, teeth chattering and dripping wet. Another version of the tale, noted by traveller William Howitt in the 1840s, was told to him by a local woman. According to her story, a young boy had once been imprisoned in Hylton Castle in a small cupboard in a now demolished chamber. He had suffered terribly before dying as a result of his incarceration. The combination of truth and legend surrounding the story of the Cauld Lad has rendered it a popular if confused tale, which doubtless tangles the threads of several different stories under the one heading.

As late as the 1970s, a local newspaper reported that unexplained voices had been heard near the castle after dark. A local man witnessed a spectral form which 'called out' to him and then followed him for some distance as he made his way home after a late shift one night. During the 1980s, a team of local ghost-hunters including a medium stayed overnight at the castle, and experienced a great variety of supernatural phenomena. They noted the sounds of phantom music, a sobbing voice (perhaps recalling the Cauld Lad's legendary wailing and crying), and the presence of a number of 'dim figures' shrouded in what appeared to be mist. In the late 1980s, radio presenter and author Alan Robson masterminded two separate night-time vigils, during which local volunteers used a live link-up and relayed their experiences directly to him. On both occasions, towards the conclusion of the vigil, the participants independently reported the strong feeling of a 'presence' close behind them.

Hylton Castle, maintained by English Heritage and Sunderland City Council, is situated in the centre of the Hylton Castle estate 3 miles W of Sunderland. It is accessible to visitors at any reasonable time.

THE THEATRE ROYAL
Grey Street, Newcastle-upon-Tyne

The historic Theatre Royal is believed to be haunted by a Grey Lady who appears in the auditorium, sometimes carrying a lit candle, often manifesting herself as a faint shadow accompanied by the scent of roses and mothballs. As far as can be ascertained, the Grey Lady was seen for the first time within living memory in 1990 when a number of theatre staff were working through the night to install the set of a new show. A lighting engineer working high up in the gallery witnessed a shadowy figure carrying a light, following a stage-worker across the stage as he swept up. It was around three in the morning, and the stage-worker had previously felt extremely tired; although he was unaware of the 'shadow' he suddenly felt overcome by cheerfulness for no apparent reason and began to sing out loud to himself! Security guards at the Theatre Royal have since remained convinced that the Grey Lady appears as a good omen. Several other staff have encountered the smell of 'old mothballs' in the auditorium, which appears and vanishes for no apparent reason. Naturally, the unexpected appearance of a ghost aroused the curiosity of the theatre staff, and the two gentlemen involved in the original sighting undertook some research to ascertain whether the ghost could be 'explained'. They uncovered an intriguing story which is today repeated to any curious visitor to this beautiful old theatre.

In the mid-1800s, the theatre was very popular with the working classes, who regularly took cheap seats in the gallery at weekends. One such lady, who attended every weekend, developed a crush on a London actor who had arrived to star in a Victorian melodrama. She attended his every performance, and, after she had waited by the stage door to meet him one evening, they began a very public affair which, given the climate of the times, caused a great deal of scandal. The pair decided to elope after the final matinée performance of the play. The lady arranged to meet the actor by the stage door, but on her arrival he confessed to being married and declared their relationship to have been nothing but a fling. Heartbroken, the betrayed woman stayed for the final evening performance of the play, during which she is said to have thrown herself from the gallery and hurtled to her death in the stalls below.

THE OAK TREE INN

Tantobie, near Stanley

During the seventeenth century, a member of the wealthy Newcastle Liddel family lent the overspending monarch Charles I a substantial sum of money. When the loan was conveniently 'forgotten' about, the grateful King bestowed the title Lord of Ravensworth on his loyal subject in return. Ravensworth Castle thereafter became the family seat of the Lords Ravensworth, with a smaller manor house in nearby Tantobie housing the 'lesser' members of the Liddel family. The manor later became the Oak Tree Inn. Today, a coating of red brick on the exterior partially conceals the building's great age, for it dates from 1700, and there is evidence of earlier, medieval remains.

Sylvia Hurst bought the Oak Tree in 1977. During the early days of her tenancy, she and a number of regular customers were in the downstairs bar when they heard heavy footsteps pounding across the floor above. Suspecting an intruder, several of the men armed themselves with brooms and anything else which came to hand, and made their way upstairs with Sylvia. Each of the rooms in the first floor was still locked, however, and when opened their windows were found to be secure. During her twenty years here Sylvia has heard these mysterious footsteps only twice, although she recalls that a previous tenant refused to stay in the building at night after encountering 'strange noises' himself.

In 1996, the young daughter of a regular customer watched a man walk behind the back of the bar, towards the stairs which lead to the restaurant. When time elapsed and he did not reappear, she alerted staff. The stranger was never accounted for, and although he never made an exit through the bar, nobody was found upstairs. This unexplained episode was consequently attributed to the ghost of an unidentified man who, over the years, has been most commonly noted sitting on a corner seat next to the open fire. Although certain witnesses have described the 'funny hat' he wears, others have been more specific and noted that it is a tricorn. At first glance, the ghostly gentleman has been assumed to be a customer, since, to all accounts, he appears to be enjoying a drink . . . until he vanishes into thin air!

As well as tampering with the gas supply in the cellar, moving stacks of bottles around, and on one occasion even turning the bar stereo on full blast, the ghost has been blamed for playing a particularly unpleasant trick on men visiting the toilet. In November 1995, landlord Peter Lynch was trapped inside when the outer toilet door refused to open. At first he assumed that another member of staff was holding it closed, although he noted that, as he pulled, the door began to warp in its frame. After being trapped for a number of minutes, Peter was suddenly released, and narrowly escaped knocking himself out as he pulled the door sharply towards him. During the following summer, the mischievous ghost was to claim another victim, this time bar manager Paul McConnell. Late one night the inn had been emptied of customers, and the only remaining staff were Paul, and Peter and Pat Lynch. Paul found himself unable to open the outer toilet door, and at first suspected that Peter and Pat were holding it closed. He began to tug at the handle, and became aware that he could hear Peter and Pat talking at the opposite end of the pub, nowhere near the toilet door. Paul managed to attract their attention and heard Pat shout, 'It's got him! He's trapped inside!' before the door was suddenly released.

The second ghost attached to the Oak Tree Inn is slightly more comical, being that of a little black cat which darts between the kitchen, the bar area and the front door, and disappears in an instant. When Sylvia Hurst first arrived at the Oak Tree, she commented to a member of staff that the cat she had seen dart past really ought not to come near the kitchen . . . and found all the surrounding doors closed and no sign of the animal anywhere. Many visitors have apologised profusely for 'letting the cat out' on entering the pub. In 1996, one female visitor even complained to the bar manager that 'cats shouldn't be allowed', after watching a small black cat run behind the back of the bar. A short while before, a visitor who was convinced that a cat had run underneath the seats was found crawling around on his hands and knees trying to coax it out, puzzled that it seemed to have vanished. In September 1996, Paul McConnell saw the cat twice in one week, running out of the front door as he opened it, and vanishing into thin air halfway across the road.

The Oak Tree Inn offers short breaks and bed and breakfast throughout the year, and is renowned for its Continental cuisine, under the direction of Sylvia Hurst, for which it features in a number of travel and food guides. For bookings: The Oak Tree Inn, Tantobie, near Stanley, Co. Durham DH9 9RF.

PRESTON HALL MUSEUM AND THE GREEN DRAGON MUSEUM
Stockton-on-Tees

The grounds of Preston Hall Park were first recorded in the twelfth century as farming land. During the 1650s the estate belonged to a Catholic family who were branded 'Papist delinquents', and consequently had their belongings seized and sold via the Treason Trustees. David Burton Fowler took over in 1820, and began to build Preston Hall as it stands today. He sold the hall to the Ropners, who mysteriously reversed its front and back entrances for an unknown reason. Preston Park was almost turned into a shopping complex just after the war, although thankfully it was bought by the local authority and opened as a museum and gallery. It is well known today for its 'period street', a Victorian recreation complete with public house, police station and a variety of shops featuring genuine antiques which are still being donated regularly by the public.

Museum staff have noted what they describe as a Grey Lady who appears in a display area known as the 'brown corridor', always at twilight. No associated legend which gives substance to the haunting is known to be attached to Preston Hall, although a local historian visiting in the early 1990s claimed to have an explanation. He recounted how a son of the resident family many years ago fell in love with a young working-class woman and sought her hand in marriage. His father refused point blank to bless the pair, and the young woman duly committed suicide in the park, although where and how are unknown. Other sightings around the museum include a cleaning lady polishing a display case, a small dog which was seen to walk through a cellar wall, and the ghost of a World War I soldier appearing on the armoury stairs. On a lighter note, one frightened lady visitor reported to a member of staff that she had seen a 'ghostly white lady' peering from a gallery window late at night. When she identified the window she was assured that she was mistaken as her 'sighting' occurred in the Wedding Dress room, where a white veiled dummy was positioned close to the window!

*

The Green Dragon Museum, in Green Dragon Yard near Stockton's one-time quayside, occupies a complex of antiquated cottages and small warehouses dating from the 1700s. Its name is taken from the next-door Green Dragon Inn (a licensed premises since 1700) and reputedly indicates that an alchemist was once at work nearby. A former member of staff was convinced that a 'presence' could be strongly felt in the two second-floor rooms, which today act as a museum costume store. Adjacent to the museum is a former Georgian playhouse which was opened in 1766, becoming a music hall during the mid-1800s before being taken over by the Salvation Army. In the early 1900s there were several reports of a ghostly choir being seen here late at night, and locals passing the building after dark testified to hearing choral singing within.

Preston Hall Museum and Park are open to the public throughout the year. The Green Dragon Museum is open Monday to Saturday between 9 a.m. and 5 p.m., excluding Bank Holidays; both are maintained by Stockton-on-Tees Borough Council.

THE LORD CREWE ARMS HOTEL
Blanchland, Consett

'*The most obvious thing about Blanchland*', wrote the late G. W. Addleshaw, former Treasurer of York Minster and Dean of Chester, '*is its remoteness.*' Blanchland took its name from the white-robed Premonstratensian canons who settled here to build their abbey in 1165. The tiny village which grew around the remains of the monastery centuries later remains remarkably unchanged, many buildings having been constructed on the original monastic foundations. Blanchland Abbey was indeed extremely remote in its functioning years, with perhaps only a dozen or so canons at any one time, the last of whom were eventually dispersed by the Dissolution in 1536. The Lord Crewe Arms is the surviving abbot's lodge of the monastery, today a beautiful hotel resplendent with original stonework, huge medieval fireplaces, and featuring the original crypt now transformed into a bar.

The Lord Crewe who gave his name to this historic building was a Prince Bishop, and the hotel's resident ghost is believed to be his young niece Dorothy Forster, whose portrait today hangs in the residents' lounge. Dorothy's brother Tom was captured during the Jacobite Rebellion of 1715, and taken in chains to London to await his uncertain fate. Dorothy, on hearing of his capture, disguised herself as a peasant and travelled to London with the local blacksmith to free him. How she achieved her aim is unknown, but Tom was certainly freed, for the pair returned to Blanchland in disguise. The Lord Crewe Arms features a priest hole in the chimney of the Hilyard Room, in which Tom was able to remain undetected until his family smuggled him to France. Here he lived in wait for the signal from Dorothy that it was safe to return. Before her letter arrived, Tom died. Legend suggests that the ghost of Dorothy haunts the old building pining for her beloved brother, forever trying to reach him with the message that it is safe for him to return.

Although there have been no recorded sightings of Dorothy for some time, visitors and staff note that on occasion, a 'presence' can be detected around the older parts of the building, especially in the Bamburgh Room above the bar, which was once Dorothy's bedroom. The current owners took over the management of the Lord Crewe Arms in the late 1980s, and had only been in residence for a short while when a daughter of one of the partners was passed whilst walking up the stairs by a 'black shadow'. An American woman overnighting with her husband in the four-poster Radcliffe Room, situated in the oldest wing of the building, awoke in the middle of the night to see the figure of a monk dressed in white kneeling by her bed. Hardly believing her eyes, she reached out to touch it and with horror found the vision surprisingly solid. The guest turned to wake her husband, and the monk began to fade before her eyes. This lady had no previous knowledge that the monks of Blanchland had indeed worn white habits.

For bookings: The Lord Crewe Arms, Blanchland, Consett, County Durham DH8 1SP.

THE EDEN ARMS SWALLOW HOTEL
Rushyford

On the completion of the Durham to Darlington railway line in the 1840s, the Eden Arms, formerly a busy seventeenth-century coaching inn, was closed down and converted into a residential manor house which was lived in for many years by the Eden family. Today, this historic building is run by the Swallow Hotel group and once more welcomes visitors. According to staff, Room 19 is the site of many unsettling experiences reported by guests, and is believed to be haunted by a Grey Lady whose identity is disputed. A gentleman staying in this room in the early 1990s spent his first night at the Eden Arms with the night porter, claiming to have seen the ghost here, accompanied by an extreme drop in temperature which prompted him to vacate the room quickly. Although staff offered to change his room, he declined, putting the experience of the night before down to a fertile imagination. However, his second night was again spent with the night porter after a further similar experience.

A number of guests and housekeeping staff have witnessed

'spectral children' playing on the corridor between Rooms 1 and 7. Their identity is unknown, although local legend suggests that a number of children died in a fire at some point during the coaching inn's history. The ghost of a gentleman has been encountered wandering around reception, and although many details of his story have been lost with the passage of time, it is believed that during Lady Eden's lifetime the pair had an unresolved feud. Lady Eden has herself been seen at various points around the Eden Arms, dressed in grey, although she is believed by staff to be the hotel's second Grey Lady, the presence in Room 19 being different entirely. Lady Eden's ghost was 'contacted' in 1995 by a visiting medium who declared that she 'didn't like all these strange people staying in her house', adding that despite this, she had no intention of harming anybody. Her presence has also been noted by chamber-maids who have seen her whilst on their rounds, and have also witnessed toilets flushing themselves.

For bookings: The Eden Arms Swallow Hotel, Rushyford, Co. Durham DL17 0LL.

THE DORMAN MUSEUM
Middlesbrough

The Dorman Museum was founded following the Boer War by Sir Arthur Dorman, as a memorial to his son and other victims of the conflict. In 1923 the renowned northern archaeologist, geologist and naturalist Frank Elgee was appointed curator. Elgee's life was devoted to the excavation and cataloguing of sites of archaeological importance throughout the North, and he avidly publicised the Dorman Museum as an institution of educational importance. Elgee's work continued long after his resignation due to ill health in 1932, although five years later a deterioration in his condition forced his wife Harriet to largely direct the excavation of Loose Howe burial mound in his stead. Frank Elgee died in 1944, having never lost touch with his archaeological interests. Today, the Dorman Museum occasionally echoes with the sound of a person unknown moving around in one of the upstairs rooms, always late in the evening, and always when the area is supposedly empty. Staff are notably reluctant to remain here after dark. The current curator and her staff believe that a ghostly male figure sighted by a cleaner in the early 1990s, at the back of the building, could well be that of Elgee. The curator on one occasion left the museum immediately when she heard 'something' moving around upstairs, knowing full well that she was certainly alone in the building at the time.

The Dorman Museum is situated on Linthorpe Road, Middlesbrough, and is open to the public between 10 a.m. and 5.15 p.m. Tuesday to Saturday, and between 2.15 p.m. and 5.15 p.m. on Sundays.

WASHINGTON ARTS CENTRE
Fatfield

Washington Arts Centre is situated in a yard of historic former farm buildings, which have been carefully remodelled to include exhibition facilities featuring work by local and international artists, a theatre, a public bar, and work space for a variety of community and education groups. Local legend tells that many years ago a woman committed suicide by hanging herself from a beam in the theatre, and her ghost has reputedly been seen by several independent witnesses, sitting at the back of the auditorium. Staff have also encountered an unidentifiable form mounting a main staircase, although on inspection the area has proved to be empty. The cleaning staff have seen a figure walking through the brickwork of one particular wall which is known to have replaced a former staircase. Intriguingly, during the 1990s, local residents made a series of complaints of 'excess noise' coming from the arts centre late at night, having no idea that the building was empty and locked at the time.

Paranormal activity at Washington Arts Centre was consequently attributed to the legendary ghost of the unknown woman who had been seen in the theatre, until a medium visited the centre on Hallowe'en in 1994. Her visit was part of a 'haunted sit-in' masterminded by a local radio station, who set up a live radio-link to their studio. The medium informed the staff present that they were haunted not by one ghost but by two, one male and one female. She felt that the woman had died not in the theatre, but in a workshop which was once part of the stable block, and that she had met an untimely death, possibly connected with the male spirit whom the medium believed to be more malefic. Throughout her visit the inexplicable smell of roses was detected by staff, a sensation which is still reported today. When the medium went on to describe that the male ghost wore 'uniform', it was noted that a regular customer of the upstairs public bar had twice followed a man in a long dark trench-coat up the stairs, to find that he was nowhere in sight once she reached the top. On several occasions unexplained activity occurred in the public bar, with bottles being hurled from their shelves, and a one-armed bandit appearing to operate itself without human aid. Electrical phenomena, such as the radio changing channels and beer taps being tampered with, were also noted here. As well as the inexplicable scent of roses, a variety of phantom smells have been encountered in the centre. In the summer of 1994 two formerly sceptical local reporters, involved in writing a feature for the *Sunderland Echo*, were amazed to walk through a 'spotlessly clean' area which smelled strongly of cow manure, only to be told that this area had formerly been a cow byre when the building was a farm.

However, the most intriguing event to have occurred at the arts centre concerns a display of large wooden puppets which were exhibited here in the mid-1980s. Each puppet performed a movement when a coin was inserted into a slot. One puppet was fitted with a Polaroid camera which featured a delay mechanism to take a photograph of whoever was inserting money. Staff set up the equipment one evening and the following morning unlocked the centre to find that the camera had been activated during the night, and the puppet's timing device had automatically taken a photograph. Although there was no money in the machine, the Polaroid had recorded what appeared to be a misty-looking female face, similar to a translucent colour 'hologram'. The photograph, which was published in a local newspaper, is today part of a private collection and has never been released for scientific study. Staff note that the activation device which had triggered the photograph was immediately sent to a local university for testing, although no fault was found. A number of interested researchers have examined archive material in an attempt to uncover a murder or suicide at the former farm which could lend substance to the haunting, or could even possibly authenticate the visiting medium's impressions, although all such efforts have so far failed to reveal any further information.

Washington Arts Centre, situated on Biddick Lane, is administered by the City of Sunderland Council, and is open to the public from Monday to Saturday, 9 a.m. until variable times (depending upon activities at the centre). The arts centre also hosts the largest craft fair in the region on the first Saturday of each month.

NORTHUMBERLAND

BAMBURGH CASTLE

Bamburgh

The famous and much-photographed silhouette of Bamburgh
Castle, resplendent with its many restored walls and battlements, dominates the Northumberland coastline. The Anglo-
Saxon Chronicle records that the site on which the castle stands
was originally fortified by King Ida in AD 547. Its position was
doubtless chosen for the prominent rocky outcrop here, the
seaward side of which is blessed with the natural protection of
a sheer drop. Bamburgh was rebuilt by the Normans after the
Conquest, and in the following century, Henry II added a keep
which proved vital to its defences. Until the advent of the
cannon, the castle was considered impenetrable. Bamburgh is
today the home of Lady Armstrong, and its sprawling fortifica-
tions, which incorporate many rooms open to the public
including a museum, an aircraft section and domestic areas, are
the result of many years of expansion and careful restoration.

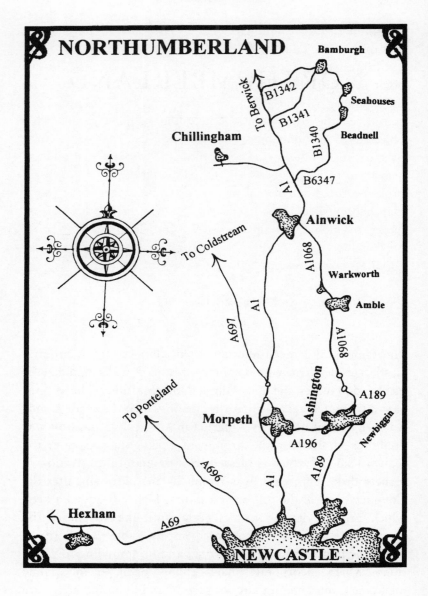

Bamburgh Castle's most celebrated ghost is considered to be that of the Pink Lady, who has her own legend. Around AD 700 a royal residence stood where Bamburgh's keep is today. At this point in history the Northumberland kingdom stretched from the Humber to the Forth, and the city of Bamburgh was considered the royal capital. According to the tale, the King objected to his daughter's suitor, and sent the young man overseas for seven years. During this time he prevented messengers from travelling between the pair, and eventually told his broken-hearted daughter that his spies had discovered the young man had married abroad. The princess was distraught, and her father, overcome with pity, asked the castle seamstress to make his daughter a new gown of fine material in her favourite colour – pink. When it was finished the princess dressed herself, walked

Bamburgh Castle

up to the highest battlement, and threw herself over the edge. When her beau returned, he was, needless to say, unmarried. The ghost of the Pink Lady is said to walk every seven years through the oldest part of the castle, through the grounds and down to the beach, waiting an eternity for her lover's ship to return to shore. Despite the legend having an unreal, fairy-tale ring to it, the housekeeper of Bamburgh Castle has seen a young and 'extremely beautiful' spectral woman dressed in pink many times during her employment here.

In May 1996 a visitor who had paused to look at three small pictures on a wall opposite a flight of stairs near the library was tapped on the back. She turned around, but was puzzled to see nobody there; she recounted her experience to her husband, who suddenly became very pale and decided to leave the castle immediately! A few days later, a member of staff watched a teenage girl suddenly and unaccountably begin to shake, her eyes watering, when she stood in exactly the same place. The young visitor noted that she detected 'a lot' of presence here, and continued into the next room where her shaking stopped immediately. Present on both these occasions was a member of staff who recalled that when, a year earlier, he had shown his cousin through the same area, she had paused against an archway and had almost passed out, commenting on the 'very nasty feeling' in this particular place.

Member of staff Keith Campbell has collected a dossier of paranormal experiences at Bamburgh over the years, which have either happened in his presence or been related to him by visitors. He recounted: 'Some years ago, a colleague was on duty at the entrance to the interior. It was very quiet, and no one was about. He was facing the first room, when he heard the wooden chair to his left being dragged along the floor. He looked and saw that it had been moved, but being such a laid back chap, he just said: "You are supposed to lift furniture, not drag it!" A few days later I saw a young man, wearing a soldier's uniform – English, eighteenth century – with his hand on the back of the chair. He was only visible for a few seconds, but was very clear; perhaps it was a case of "It was me!"' On another occasion Keith was taking a party of visitors through the castle when he felt a hand brush up against the back of his neck as he mentioned one particular ghost. There was no reaction from the visitors, who had obviously seen nothing, and Keith turned to find nobody behind him. Unafraid, he remarked quietly over his shoulder, 'Oh, behave!'

One terrified lady visitor witnessed a piano playing itself, its keys moving seemingly of their own accord, and staff are quick to point out that the instrument in question is not a pianola, and therefore cannot be 'self-operated'. Two members of staff have on separate occasions seen the 'shadow' of a man they were able to identify as Dr John Sharp, the original restorer of the castle in the eighteenth century. Another member of staff heard hushed male and female voices coming from a locked room before it was opened up, the sounds ceasing suddenly when the key was put in the lock. Witnesses have also reported ghostly children running along the corridor of the Outer Lodge, switching lights on and off, and a little girl in the ticket office itself, which was formerly the spare bedroom of the Outer Lodge. In the Armstrong Museum, there have been sightings of a man thought to be an Elizabethan naval gunner who is noted to have a 'cheeky grin'. Unexplained phenomena have even been known to occur outside the boundary walls of Bamburgh Castle. A former gatekeeper was awoken at three one morning by the sound of a huge posse of horses galloping up the hill. Supposing there to be as many as fifty from the noise, he looked out of his door and saw nothing at all. Intrigued, he continued to listen, and heard the horses ride *through* the locked gates and directly past him.

Northumberland

Bamburgh Castle is privately owned, and is open to the public between Easter and the last Sunday in October from 11 a.m. onwards (closing times are variable).

BEADNELL HOUSE
Beadnell, Seahouses

The Victorian mansion Beadnell House, today a sister hotel to the Bamburgh Castle Hotel, is set amid beautiful grounds a short walk from the sea in the coastal village of Beadnell. The house has long been reputed to be haunted by a White Lady, although the story attached to her ghost, and indeed her identity, have been all but forgotten with the passage of time. Consequently, the ghost seems to have faded somewhat, and, to the knowledge of the current proprietor, has not been encountered in recent years. However, on a number of occasions staff working alone in the building have been disturbed by mysterious noises coming from supposedly empty rooms. In 1995, a guest reported seeing a ghostly gentleman wearing naval uniform at the top of the main staircase. The guest was unaware that the house had been previously owned by a ship's captain, at the turn of the century.

Beadnell House is normally open for bed and breakfast guests from Easter to October. For bookings: Beadnell House, Beadnell, Seahouses, Northumberland.

Beadnell House, Seahouses

WARKWORTH CASTLE AND WARKWORTH HERMITAGE
Warkworth, near Amble

Shakespeare immortalised Warkworth Castle in scenes from *Henry IV*, which portrayed the life of this rather unpopular fifteenth-century King who took the English throne in 1399. Above the River Coquet, the eight-towered keep of Warkworth stands impressively intact, its pale stone walls providing the ideal backdrop for the variety of historic re-enactments and medieval-style entertainments which take place here each summer. Warkworth's former resident Percy family were once the unconquered Earls of Northumberland, driving the invading Scots away on behalf of the English Crown. In return, the

Warkworth Castle

Percys enjoyed royal favour and a great deal of status and notoriety. Sir Henry Percy, who earned himself the nickname of Harry Hotspur, helped to remove Richard II from the English throne in 1399 along with his father the Earl of Northumberland. Here the Plantagenet dynasty ended, and the House of

Lancaster came to rule under Henry IV, who was personally aided in his claim to the throne by the Percys. However, within a few years their new King had displeased them, and the Earl and his son became set against him. During this time Warkworth played host to the plotters of Henry's overthrow. Unfortunately Hotspur and his father both overestimated their capabilities, and consequently met a bloody end on the battlefield during the ensuing rebellion of 1403.

The banks of the River Coquet have long been believed to be haunted by a hermit, a member of the Bertram family, who once lived in a cave close to the castle. Before taking his pledge of solitude the hermit had been an eager young knight, and fought alongside Harry Hotspur against the Scots. On the eve of an important battle he was promised the hand of a young noblewoman if he acquitted himself well the following day. Desperate to prove himself, the young knight inadvertently felled his own brother, who was disguised as a Scot. He pledged to live out his remorseful life in seclusion. Popular local folklore tells that the ghostly figure of a hermit kneeling in prayer is occasionally to be seen by the banks of the river. Unfortunately, records indicate that the member of the Bertram family to whom the legend is attached was actually twice married, and that the brother whom he supposedly killed never existed! Visitors can, however, take a trip to the legendary hermitage, which is cut into the rock-face of the river cliff, situated upstream from the castle.

On Hallowe'en in 1994, Metro Radio's *Night Owls* programme featured a live radio event at the castle which attracted over six hundred people from the surrounding areas. Around three hundred of the crowd who were stationed outside the castle saw the face of a man appear in one of the windows, in an area of the castle closed to the public and known to be empty. The face was widely felt to be that of Harry Hotspur.

Warkworth also hosts another ghost, that of the legendary Grey Lady, who is believed to be Harry's mother, Margaret Neville, who died of the plague in the 1400s. Her ghost has been seen walking from the Grey Mare's Tail Tower, which was once a prison. Within this tower, visitors can see carvings of the twelve apostles which date back to 1536 and were carved by prisoners incarcerated in the Catholic uprising of the same year. The current custodian notes that visitors are most likely to feel an 'eerie' presence in one of the wine cellars which was formerly used as an overflow prison when the number of captives exceeded the resources of the castle. Canine visitors are also greatly disturbed in this area, often refusing to venture inside.

Warkworth Castle and Warkworth Hermitage are maintained by English Heritage. The castle is open to the public daily throughout the year from 10 a.m. until dusk. The hermitage is accessible to visitors between 1 April and 30 September, Wednesdays, Sundays and Bank Holiays, between 11 a.m. and 5 p.m.

MELDON PARK
Morpeth

Nothing is now left of Meldon Tower, the medieval structure built by the Heron family of Ford Castle, a branch of whom lived in Meldon between the fourteenth and sixteenth centuries. The original tower was believed to have been situated a mile from Meldon Park, which had remained as an estate of over 460 acres with only a deer-keeper's cottage on site. In 1832 Isaac Cookson III purchased the park, and commissioned the building of the beautiful mansion which stands here today, and is still the family home of the Cooksons.

The legendary Meg of Meldon, Margaret Selby, who was the daughter of a Newcastle money-lender and whose husband owned the Meldon estate in the seventeenth century, is believed to haunt the moonlit banks of Wansbeck River. It is said that her dower on marrying Sir William Fenwick was a large mortgage on the Meldon estate, which effectively prevented the rightful heir of Meldon from inheriting, as he was unable to repay the debt. Michael Cookson, the current owner of Meldon Park, notes that a portrait of the lady hung in the now-ruined gallery of Seaton Delaval as late as the 1930s, picturing her resplendent in a heavy ruff, 'vandyked' sleeves and a broad hat tied down at the sides over her ears. Meg was renowned for her greed, and her artful dealing and unsympathetic attitude to the less fortunate peasants on her estate aided her overspilling coffers. Doubtless the tale has grown in the telling, for there are even rumours that Meg had her own private underground coach-road via which she could hurtle to and fro unseen to conduct private business! It is rumoured that she was eventually forced to store her masses of gold at secret locations throughout the Meldon estate. Following her death, as Michael Cookson related, 'Men whispered to each other when the burial was over that Meg of the Moneybags was doomed to wander in strange shapes to and fro between the secret places of her hoards, flitting here and there for seven long years, then resting seven, only to begin the dreary round once more . . .'

Near the south-east tower of Meldon there was formerly an ancient well, which had supposedly been used by Meg to secrete a bullock's hide stuffed with pieces of gold. After her death, her ghost was often seen sitting or kneeling, peering into the depths of the well. It is said that a local peasant dreamed that he was summoned to recover the wealth within, and set off one night without a word to anybody, convinced that he could retrieve it. Armed with hooks and chains he fished the depths and hauled up the heavy bundle. As the peasant let out a cry of excitement the parcel slipped back into the depths of the well and was lost. Unfortunately for the ghost of Meg, it was believed that she would be condemned to haunt this and the other places where she had hidden her ill-gotten gains until every piece of gold had been recovered and used by the needy. An antiquated local schoolhouse was another site for part of Meg's hoard. Many years ago, a group of rowdy schoolboys romping around the room in the absence of their master loosed boards on the ceiling which fell away to reveal a shower of dusty gold coins amid the plaster.

The only hoard which today still remains unaccounted for is that of the now gone Meldon well, which slipped through the fingers of the poor peasant. It is widely said that the little ghost dog which once regularly scurried across Meldon Bridge was Meg's alternative form. After crossing either one way or the other, the ghost would assume the form of a beautiful but sad young woman. The ghost of Meg was also seen sitting on a huge stone horse trough (possibly an antiquated and unused stone coffin) at Newminster, causing no fear to the locals who were obviously familiar with the supernatural. It seems likely that several local supernatural legends were blended together at some point, each being later attributed to the widely known Meg of the Moneybags.

Meldon Park is privately owned, and is open to the public during the final week of May, the first three weeks in June, and August Bank Holiday weekend (Saturday to Monday) between 2 p.m. and 5 p.m.

BROOMLEE LOUGH
near Hexham

This wide expanse of water surrounded by bleak Northumberland hills is said to be the lake in which the dying King Arthur flung his sword Excalibur. Legends of concealed treasure lurking undisturbed in the murky depths of Broomlee Lough are a popular part of the local folklore. It is said that the former lord of a castle which once stood on Sewingshields Crag hastily deposited a treasure box in the lake whilst fleeing for his life. A spell supposedly prevented the discovery of the box, the only loophole being that it could be found by twin youths with a team of twin horses, twin oxen and a chain forged by a 'smith of kind' (a seventh-generation smith). Legend tells how one such team located the treasure box by trawling the lake, and attached the chain to drag it to shore. The chain snapped when the task was almost completed, and the treasure box sank back into the depths, where it has remained. Since the oxen, horses and youths were indisputably twins, it was assumed that the seventh-generation smith's pedigree had been compromised somewhere along the line, preventing the enchantment from being broken. The waters of Broomlee Lough are still today said to possess powers of healing, prompting at least one modern local woman to suggest that wading into the waters had cured her of a non-serious ailment!

CHILLINGHAM CASTLE
Chillingham

Chillingham Castle, site of many a bloody borderland feud during its vast history, began life in the twelfth century as a small stronghold, and was then built up as a castle and finally fully fortified in 1344. Since the 1200s, this magnificent castle, often visited by the Kings of England has been owned by the family of the Earls Grey, and today remains in the hands of their relation Sir Humphry Wakefield and his wife the Hon. Lady Wakefield. Both the castle and its surrounding parkland have historic connections with such great battles as Crecy and Agincourt. Here also are the last surviving herd of wild cattle in the British Isles. These shaggy white animals have grazed this parkland since pre-history, being descendants of the pre-Roman herds once common throughout the British Isles. Legend asserts that they were a breed which had belonged to the fairies, and that anybody daring to harm them is inviting retribution. During a radio phone-in on Alan Robson's Metro *Night Owls* programme in 1988, a Durham man told how he had chased the cattle as a boy on a visit to Chillingham. As he ran across the field towards the herd, he felt something unknown and invisible grasp at his foot, causing him to fall and break his ankle.

The most famous haunting at Chillingham Castle in former times was considered to be that of the 'radiant boy', or Blue Boy. Leonora, Lady Tankerville wrote extensively of her own and others' paranormal experiences at Chillingham during the 1920s. Of this particular ghost, she noted that his appearances were confined to the Pink Room, where, on the stroke of midnight, 'the cries and moans of a child in pain and in an agony of fear' were often heard. The sounds were always noted to come from a place nearest to a passage cut through the wall, which is 10 feet thick, leading into the adjoining tower. The cries eventually died away, leaving a bright halo of light near the old four-poster bed. Guests who slept in this room also encountered the ghostly figure of a young boy wearing blue and 'bathed in light'. The bones of a child were eventually discovered along with a fragment of blue cloth in a niche in the wall. Lady

Tankerville recorded that the 'poor remains were reverently removed and decently interred in consecrated ground', which she believed laid the ghost to rest. However, Sir Humphry Wakefield recently noted that guests staying in this room often complain of 'a blue light' flashing over one of the walls, prompting them to warn him the following morning of a possible electrical 'short'. There are no electric fittings in this wall; Sir Humphry concludes that one day he may well unearth 'a sliver of the poor boy's bone to quiet the blue flash for ever.'

In the autumn of 1996, a team of ghost-hunters visited Chillingham for an all-night vigil. Whilst in the oldest part of the castle, to which the legendary Blue Boy is attached, a member of the group described how he saw the small figure of a boy with a knife in his back. With the child was a little girl, who told the ghost-hunter that their mother had escaped but that her brother was still being held. This information seems to complement what little is known about the murdered child, and perhaps gives further insight into his plight, despite the fact that his name and story appear not to have been recorded in any written account of the castle's history.

Lady Tankerville's writings indicate that she herself was a 'sensitive' observer, who had several strange encounters throughout her years at Chillingham, including the following vision, which she recorded in her diary: '*One morning, after an exceptionally busy time, I sat down for a few moments' rest in a room facing the Cheviot hills. Very soon I could not help noticing that the gale sounded in the wide old chimney like the distant boom of cannon and as I looked out on the usually restful formal garden there too, wavering branches and heavy drifting clouds assumed a menacing and warlike aspect. As I looked, the form of a woman seemed to take shape before me, walking on the parapet of a tower apparently as solid as that wherein I sat. She was in the garb of a Dominican Abbess, and after looking eagerly towards the hills of Scotland she knelt beside the battlements as if in prayer. A man stood beside her proudly erect, handsome and richly dressed; he too was scanning the horizon towards the enemy country. A few paces behind were two men in velvet court dress of the time of King Henry VIIIth. They were chatting in subdued tones. In the background on the further parapet a halbardier paced up and down on sentry duty. I got up to watch the scene from the window, thinking I was about to witness some tragedy of former times. Presently, I called to my son in the next room, but he was out; then a housemaid came in to close the shutters and asked a couple of questions. I thought surely it will have disappeared – but no! I saw another woman bring the Abbess an ermine cape, and the man's rich dress was covered now by a surcoat. The atmosphere was tense with a feeling of impending danger, of fighting about to begin! I spoke to them twice, and asked if I could be of any service, when the man, (who was now pacing back and forth) stopped and looked at me. It was the face of my husband, but the garb of France of four centuries ago! Then who was the Abbess? Was that myself? And, why the anxiety? What was about to happen? If it was I, what was I praying God to avert? It was not long before we knew, not long before the din of battle sounded in our twentieth century ears, and official directions were sent to us in case of an invasion! I had, inadvertently, 'tuned in' as it were to a similar moment [of] long ago.'*

The castle is also believed to be haunted by Lady Mary Berkeley, wife of Ford, Lord Grey and Earl of Tankerville, who eloped with Mary's sister Lady Henrietta in the time of Charles II, abandoning his wife and baby girl. Today, the rustle of Lady Mary's skirts along certain corridors and stairs at Chillingham is said to precurse a sudden chill of cold air which Lady Tankerville experienced herself and noted 'seems to sweep through one's very marrow'. Certainly, there are regular reports of pattering footsteps throughout the castle. Following a Northumbrian pipe evening in the summer of 1996, Adrian Phillips, the castle custodian, heard footsteps crossing the medieval courtyard before mounting the staircase and crossing the minstrel gallery. The time was 2.15 a.m. and the courtyard was in total darkness. Adrian knew himself to be alone in the area, and was aware that nobody could take such a route without the help of a torch. The Phillips' daughter Chloë also encountered hasty footsteps whilst wandering up a tower spiral staircase with a friend. She moved to one side to allow whoever was advancing upstairs to pass ... and the footsteps continued on their way although nobody was in sight!

Earlier this century it was rumoured that a ghostly woman regularly 'stepped out' of an old family portrait before walking the castle nocturnally. The picture was kept in the nursery where not only the Tankerville family but children of friends who stayed here witnessed the same phenomenon. A family nurse herself testified to having seen the ghostly woman 'step out of her frame' and frighten all present by following them. Lady Tankerville consequently arranged for a friend, who was a well-known psychologist, to stay for the night. He asked to be taken to the picture after everybody else had retired to bed and spent two hours alone sitting in front of the portrait. The following morning he declared that he had encountered 'nothing malefic'. However, the psychololgist did approach another, different painting and exclaimed to Lord Tankerville, 'That is the woman I saw last night!' Lord Tankerville maintained that this was not the ghostly woman who was rumoured to walk at night, but the psychologist was insistent. It was with a great deal of surprise that Lord Tankerville's old nurse identified this portrait as the same lady who was believed to 'leave her frame'. This second portrait had been painted several years later when she was much older, a fact of which Lord Tankerville had been unaware.

The earlier portrait was sold some years later, and in 1993 eventually found its way to Christie's in London for auction. Sir Humphry Wakefield decided that the picture should be returned to its original home, and requested that a director bid on his behalf. The picture, however, was unwittingly sold, and letters to the dealer who had purchased it mysteriously went astray. The portrait was sold to a private buyer, leaving Sir Humphry puzzled over the catalogue of mishaps which had prevented the portrait from returning to its former home. Almost, he later commented, as though it were not coincidental, and the picture did not want to come home!

Chillingham's 'inner pantry' was traditionally a store for the silver in use during the Victorian era, and a footman was therefore required to stay overnight there to safeguard its contents. During the lifetime of Lady Tankerville's father-in-law, the footman on duty was approached one night by a very pale woman dressed in white, who asked him for a glass of water. The footman at first assumed her to be a guest of the house, and turned to fetch a glass, before realising that he was locked in and nobody could possibly have entered the inner pantry. When he turned back, the woman had vanished. Years later, Lady Tankerville invited a psychic friend to Chillingham who saw the same pale white-clad figure despite having been told nothing of the castle's haunted history before her visit. The psychic described the ghost's 'longing for water', and concluded that she felt that this woman 'may have been slowly poisoned in olden times'.

One of the castle lodges also has a particularly unpleasant tale attached. It is here that either a nobleman or a reiver is said to have murdered a girl-child after stealing away her mother on a raid. The child's screams can reputedly be heard from time to time. Whether the legend has any basis in truth is unknown, although in 1977 a resident of the lodge described how 'on numerous occasions when my father was alive he would talk about a cat which he could hear crying. He would go to the door but never found anything. My mother heard it also. When my sister came home on one occasion the cat was heard crying again. She immediately identified the sound as that of a baby crying, and not a cat.' A little girl of seven years old who was a guest at the lodge one evening approached her mother and asked who was the small child sleeping on her bed. On investigation there was nobody there, and nothing which could possibly have been misconstrued as another child in her bed. Other experiences here suggest that the lodge plays host to another presence. A tall man wearing a top hat and a cloak was seen by the present resident to appear by the door in the living-room. His features were indistinguishable, and his identity remains unknown. On another occasion, the sudden manifestation of what appeared to be poltergeist activity disrupted a visitor's peace when loud noises from an untraceable source echoed through the lodge one night. By now wide awake, she watched her small bedside table move itself a considerable distance across the bedroom without human aid.

Although the castle is agreed by custodian Adrian Phillips and his wife Diane to possess an 'extremely friendly' atmosphere, it was noted that an overnight ghosthunters' vigil in the spring of 1996 was accompanied by an 'extremely oppressive atmosphere'. Cold spots, traditionally associated with supernatural activity, appeared at random throughout the castle. An experience of a totally different nature was recalled by Diane Phillips who, the following summer, was comforted by a gentle hand on her shoulder whilst having a particularly tiresome day! A busy decorator was once given an approving nod by a strangely dressed gentleman who appeared from nowhere to examine his handiwork, and disappeared just as suddenly. Diane has also noted a crying baby in the empty Dungeon Room, and the noise of a phantom party which seemed to be taking place in one of Chillingham's towers whilst she was accompanying a journalist up the spiral staircase.

Chillingham Castle is owned by Sir Humphry Wakefield, and is open to visiting groups at any time by appointment. The castle is regularly open between 1 May and 1 October (except for Tuesdays in May), from noon to 5 p.m. (5.30 p.m. throughout the summer months and on Bank Holidays). The castle is available for functions, and coach parties are welcomed by prior arrangement. Self-catering holiday or weekend apartments are available within. Dogs are sadly not permitted on the premises owing to the castle's own dogs and wild animals.

ACKNOWLEDGEMENTS

Many thanks are due to the following people for their assistance. From tenants, administrators and curators, to custodians, receptionists and complete strangers I approached in the street, from Northumberland to Nottingham – without their help, *The North of England Ghost Trail* would never have been completed.

Thanks to: Caroline Abrahams, Christine Abrahams, Vinty Ackrill, Reverend E. Adamus, Lydia Aers, Clive Alford, Wayne Anthony, the Aphelion Ghost Research Society, Robert Appleton, Julian Atkin and the staff of Branston Hall Hotel, Hal Bagot, Terry and Norman Baines, Karen Baker, A. Barbieri, Kerry Barnett, Barnsley Library information desk, Dr Nicholas Bennett, Alec Bettney, Charles Birdsall, Stephen Bore, the staff of Burton Constable Hall, James T. Butler, Brian Buttery, Aidan Caddick, Keith Campbell, the staff of Chingle Hall, Peter Chubb, David Clark, David Clarke, Mike Cooksley, Michael Cookson, Sybil Cox, the staff and management of Cromwell's Eating House and Restaurant, Annemarie Crouch, Patricia

Crouch, Heather Cummins, Keith Daddy, Hazel Davison, Margaret Doughty, Sally Dunbar, Robert Elwes, Richard Felix, Jim Fenton, Lord Feversham, John Ferguson, Reverend Hugh and Janis Gallagher, Eileen Garratt, Clive Gibson, Bettie Gilliatt, Bill Greaves and Horrarium, the staff of Gunby Hall, Catherine Hall, Les Hallford, Keith Hawkins, Cliff Hodgetts, Helen Hogg and the staff of Washington Arts Centre, Paul Hopper, Sylvia Hurst, Sir Thomas Ingilby, Stuart Kaufman, the staff of Lancaster Castle, Angela Leach, Pam Leng, the staff of the Lord Crewe Arms Hotel, Peter Lynch, Kerry-Anne Marjerrison, Mr and Mrs Marks, John Martin and the staff of Conisbrough Castle, Vicky Martin, Annie Melhuish, Callum MacAllistar, Jean Macmillan, Paul McConnell, A. McDonald FBHI of the British Horological Institute, Steve and Janet McDonald, Paul McKinley, Craig Monument, Steve Moore, Lizzie Neville, Donald Nutbrown, the Hon. Harry Orde-Powlett, Lady St Oswald, Robert Parker, John Parsons, Adrian and Diane Phillips, the staff of Redworth Hall Hotel, Robin Rew, Jan Rinvoluckri, Michael Rook, Ernest Rothery and the staff of Nottingham Castle, Steve Rudd, the staff of Rufford Country Park, Brian Rushworth, Paul Schofield, Dorothy Sewart, Danny Shaw-Andrews, Sheffield Paranormal Research Group, Debs Singleton, Arthur Skelhorn, Phil Skelton, David Spittal, Mark Stoneham, Sarah Swallow, Steve Taylor, Christopher Terry, David Thompson, Chris Thorpe, Ann Tick, Rob Turpin, Hilary Wade, Sir Humphry Wakefield, Brian Watson, Paul Weston, Andy Wills, Derek Woodruff, Joanne Worth, Charles Wright, Irene Wright, and Michelle Wright.

BIBLIOGRAPHY

G. Addleshaw, *Blanchland, A Short History*, Vaux and Associated Breweries Ltd, 1951

J. and C. Bord, *Atlas of Magical Britain*, Guild Publishing, 1990

D. Clarke, *Ghosts and Legends of the Peak District*, Jarrold, 1991

G. Dodd, *Ghosts and Legends of Brontëland*, Bobtail Press, 1986

K. Eyre, *Witchcraft in Lancashire*, Dalesman Books, 1986

A. Fraser (ed.), *The Lives of the Kings and Queens of England*, Weidenfeld and Nicolson, 1975

F. Green, *A Guide to the Historic Parks and Gardens of Tyne and Wear*, Tyne and Wear Specialist Conservation Team, 1995

J. Hallam, *Ghosts of the North*, Douglas David and Charles Ltd, Canada, 1976

A. Hamilton, *Nottingham's Royal Castle*, Nottingham Civic Society, 4th edition

R. Humble, *English Castles* (the English Tourist Board's Discover England series), Weidenfeld and Nicolson, 1984

Bibliography

J. Hunter, *South Yorkshire* Vols I and II, J. B. Nicholson and Son (out of print)

L. Linahan, *Pit Ghosts, Padfeet and Poltergeists*, The King's England Press, 1994

L. Linahan, *More Pit Ghosts, Padfeet and Poltergeists*, The King's England Press, 1996

Readers Digest Association Ltd, *Folklore and Legends of Britain*, 1973

A. Roberts, *Ghost and Legends of Yorkshire*, Jarrold, 1992

A. Robson, *Grisly Trails and Ghostly Tales*, Virgin Publishing Ltd, 1992

V. Salim, *A Ghost Hunter's Guide to Sheffield*, Sheaf Publishing, 1983

J. Toy, *The Fires of York Minster*, Pitkin Pictorials Ltd, 1985

M. Warren and T. Wells, *Ghosts of the North*, Broadcast Books, 1995

J. Westwood, *Albion, A Guide to Legendary Britain*, Granada Publishing Ltd, 1986

INDEX

Abbess Hilda, 194
Abbey House Museum, Leeds, 166
Abbot Moon, 187, 188
Ackworth-Pontefract Road, 158
Addleshaw, G.W., 266
Alan of Brittany, 184
Alford, Clive, 48–9
Alfreton, Wingfield Manor, 22–4
Amble, Warkworth Castle and
    Hermitage, 279–82
Ambleside, Kirkstone Pass Inn,
    229–30
Ancaster, 1st Duke of, 108
Anthony, Wayne, 32, 33
Aphelion Ghost Research Society,
    115–16, 206–7
Appleton, Robert, 207
Arbour Low Stone Circle and Gib
    Hill Barrow, Monyash, 36–7
Armstrong, Lady, 273
Ashover, 40–45
    Church of All Saints, 40–41
    Crispin Inn, 41–5
Atkin, Julian, 109
Aurelius Ambrosius, 114

Babington, Sir Thomas, 41
Bagot family, Kendal, 234–5
Baines, Norman and Terry, 21
Baker, Karen, 131
Bamburgh Castle, 273–8
Barn Gallery, Sleaford, 107
Barnett, Kerry, 78–80
Barritt, Thomas, 218–19
Bashall Eaves, Red Pump, 221–3
Batley, Oakwell Hall and Country
    Park, 163–5
Beadnell House, Seahouses, 278–9
Beeston-Mansfield Road, 77–80
Bellamy, David, 151
Beningbrough Hall, York, 181–2
Bettney, Alec, 21–2
Beverley, Yorkshire, 146–9
Bilsborrow, Guy's Thatched Hamlet,
    211–12
Black Canons, 80
Black Death, 19–20, 130
Blackfriars Art Centre, Boston, 94–5
Blanchland Abbey, Consett, 266–7
Blue Bell Inn, Chester, 61–2
Blue John Mine, 27
Bolton, Abbey, Skipton, 187–9

Castle, Leyburn, 192–3
1st Duke of, 192–3
Boston, Blackfriars Arts Centre,
94–5
Bourchier, John, 181
Bramall Hall, Stockport, 62–5
'The Maid of Bramall Hall', 64
Brandlesholme Old Hall, Bury,
209–11
Branston Hall Hotel, Lincoln,
108–11
Bratoft Castle, Skegness, 99
Brigg, Elsham Hall Country and
Wildlife Park, 145–6
Bright, John, 122
Steven, 122
British Horological Institute, 73–4
Brontes, 159–60, 163
Broomlee Lough, Hexham, 285
Brougham, Hall, Penrith, 243–5
2nd Lord, 243
Brown, Lancelot 'Capability', 124
Bull's Head, Eyam, 20–21
Burkes, Eddie, 91–2
Burns, Robbie, 233
Burton, Agnes Manor, Driffield,
135–8, 243
Alfred, 65
Constable Hall, Hull, 150–52
Fowler, David, 265
Bury, Brandlesholme Old Hall,
209–11
Byland Abbey, Thirsk, 190–92
Byron family, 80–81

Caddick, Aidan, 133
Campbell, Keith, 276–7
Canute, 95
Carbrook Hall Hotel, Sheffield,
121–4
Carlisle, Wardrew House, 232–4
Casson, Libby and Nick, 54–8
Castle Hotel, Castleton, 29–32
Castlerigg Stone Circle, Keswick,
238–9
Castleton, 26–32
Charles Birdsall's Parkside Inne and
Leisure company, 169

Charles I, 47, 262
Charles II, 29, 155, 199
Cheshire, map of, 46
Chester, Blue Bell Inn, 61–2
Higher Huxley Hall, 51–2
Llyndir Hall Hotel, 59–61
Chesterfield, Canal, 39–40
Ringwood Hall Hotel, 34–5
Royal Oak, 24–5
Chester-le-Street, Lily of, 254–6
Lord Ralph, 254
Lumley Castle Hotel, 254–6
Chichester-Constable family, Hull,
151–2
Chillingham Castle, 285–92
Chingle Hall, Longridge, 201–8
Christian, John, 225
Church Farm Museum, Skegness,
92–4
Clark, Dave, 83
Clarke, Samuel, 129
Clitheroe, Punch Bowl, 208–9
Clumber Park and Sherwood Forest,
70–73
Cock and Bottle, York, 199–200
Collings, Tracy, 229
Conan, Earl, 184
Congleton, Lion and Swan Hotel,
50–51
Little Moreton Hall, 53–4
Conisbrough Castle, Doncaster,
113–16
Consett, Blanchland Abbey, 277–7
Lord Crewe Arms Hotel, 266–8
Constable family, Yorkshire, 150–51
Cookson, Isaac III, 282
Michael, 283
Cooperage, Newcastle-upon-Tyne,
252–4
Copley, Robert and Isabel, 245
County Durham and Tyne and Wear,
map of, 248
Cranswell, Amelia, 236
Cresacre, Percival, 131
Crispin Inn, Ashover, 41–5
Critchlow, Mr and Mrs Butler, 22
Croglin, 236–8
Cromwell, 122, 178

Cromwell's Eating House,
    Doncaster, 128–9
Crosier, George and Eleanor, 249
Cumbria, map of, 224
Curwen, Henry, 226–8
    J.F., 226–7
    Sir Nicholas, 225

Dale, John, 183
Dalston Hall Hotel, 239–42
Davies, Father Mark, 218
De Bevere, Drogo, 144–5
De Burgham, Gilbert, 243
De Clifford, John, 187–8
De Courcy-Parry, Charles, 230–31
De Culwen, Gilbert, 225
De Gant, Gilbert, 83
De Lovetot, William, 75
Delves, Father Tony, 121
De Tateshale, Robert, 97
De Warenne, Earl John, 113–14, 162
Derby, 37–8
    Battle of, 37, 38
    George Inn, 38
    Ye Olde Dolphin Inn, 37–8
Derbyshire, map of, 18
De Singleton, Adam, 201
De Stubley, Sir Ralph, 220
Devonshire, Duke of, 34
Dissolution, 80, 84, 105, 124, 126,
    146, 166, 187, 269
Domesday, 51, 62, 116, 145, 168
Doncaster, Conisbrough Castle,
    113–16
    Cromwell's Eating House, 128–9
    Lindholme area, 132–4
Dorman, Museum, Middlesbrough,
    269–70
    Sir Arthur, 269
Doughty, Margaret, 94
Driffield, Burton Agnes Manor,
    135–8
Druidic rites, 32–3
Duncombe Park, Helmsley, 182–4
Dunham Massey Hall, Altrincham,
    47–50
Dunkerley, John, 89–91
Durham, Hylton Castle, 257–60

Earnshaw, James, 153, 155
Easby Abbey, Richmond, 185–6
Eden Arms Swallow Hotel,
    Rushyford, 268–9
Edward III, 82, 178
Elgee, Frank, 269–70
Elizabeth I, 213
Elsham Hall Country and Wildlife
    Park, Brigg, 145–6
Elwes family, Elsham, 146
Eyam, 19–22
    Bull's Head, 20–21
    Hall, 20
Eyre, Reverend Thomas, 33

Fatfield, Washington Arts Centre,
    270–72
Felix, Richard, 37
Fenton, Jim, 221–3
Fenwick, Sir William, 283
Ferguson, John, 34
Feversham, Lord, 183–4
    2nd Earl of, 183
Forest, Michelle, 108, 110
Fort Paull, Hull, 141–2
Fretwell, Ralph, 129

Gainsborough Old Hall,
    Gainsborough, 95–6
Gallagher, Reverend Hugh and Janis,
    171–4
Gaskell, Mrs, 163
George Inn, Derby, 38
George VI, 48
Gibson, Clive, 252–3
Gosforth Hall Hotel, 245–7
Grantham, St Wulfram's Church,
    100–103
Great Fire of London, 19
Greaves, Bill, 19
Greenhalgh family, Bury, 209, 210
Grey, Lady Jane, 47
    Thomas, 47
Griffith, Anne, 135–7
    Sir Henry, 135
Gunby Hall, Skegness, 99–100
Guy's Thatched Hamlet, Bilsborrow,
    211–12

Hallford, Les, 125
Hamelin Plantaganet, Earl, 113
Harrogate, Ripley Castle, 178–81
Hartington, Marquis of, 187
Hawkins, Keith, 137–8
Haworth, 159–61
  Black Bull, 159–60
  Brontes, 159–60
Heathercliffe Country House,
  Warrington, 58–9
Hellaby Hall Hotel, Rotherham,
  129–31
Helmsley, Duncombe Park, 182–4
Hengist, 114
Henry II, 273
Henry IV, 281
Henry VIII, 105, 141, 145, 146, 187
Henshaw, Bishop Thomas, 219
Heron family, Meldon, 282
Hessle, 138–41
  Admiral Hawke, 140–41
  High School, 139–40
  Marquis of Granby, 141
Hexham, Broomlee Lough, 285
Heywood, Oliver, 164
Hickleton Churchyard, Doncaster,
  121
Higher Huxley Hall, Chester, 51–2
Horrarium, 190–91
Hospitaller Knights of St John, 153
Howitt, William, 259
Hull, 142–4
  Admiral Hawke, 140–41
  Albion Street, 143
  Burton Constable Hall, 150–52
  Fort Paull, 141–2
  George Inn, 139–40
  Hessle, 138–41
  Marquis of Granby, 141
  Tranby House (later Hessle High
    School), 143–4
Hurst, Sylvia, 262, 264
Hylton, Baron William, 257
  Castle, Durham, 257–60
  Sir Robert, 258–9

Icke, David, 217
Ingham family, Leeds, 155–6

Ingilby family, Harrogate, 178–9
Irwin, Viscount, 153

James I, 213, 228
James II, 227
John of Gaunt, 105
Junction 31, M1, Sheffield, 131–2

Karl, Jason, 204–6
Kaufman family, Bury, 210–11
Keel, John A., 14
Kendal, Levens Hall, 234–6
Keswick, Castlerigg Stone Circle,
  238–9
  Overwater Hall Hotel, 230–31
King, Ned, 208–9
King Sweyne of Denmark, 95
Kirkby-in-Ashfield, Newstead Abbey,
  80–82
Kirkstall Abbey, Leeds, 166
Kirkstone Pass Inn, Ambleside,
  229–30
Knights Templar, 24, 153

Lake Windermere, 231–2
Lancashire, map of, 202
Lancaster, Canal, 211–12
  Castle, 217
  Thomas of, 113–14
Leeds, Abbey House Museum, 166
  Farsley Road, 167–8
  Kirkstall Abbey, 166
  Temple Newsam House, 153–8
Leigh, John, 64
Leslie, Mrs Jack, 105
Leslie-Melville, Hon., 108
Levens Hall, Kendal, 234–6
Leyburn, Bolton Castle, 192–3
Liddel family, Newcastle, 262
Lincoln, Branston Hall Hotel,
  108–11
  Castle, 103–4
  Cathedral, 103
  Imp, 103
  Stragglethorpe Hall, 105–6
  White Hart Hotel, 98–9
Lincolnshire, map of, 90
Lindholme area, Doncaster, 132–4

Lion and Swan Hotel, Congleton, 50–51
Little Moreton Hall, Congleton, 53–4
Llyndir Hall Hotel, Chester, 59–61
Lord Crewe Arms Hotel, Consett, 266–8
Lovett, Matthew, 81
Lumley, Castle Hotel, Chester-le-Street, 254–6
Lily of, 254–6
Lord Ralph, 254
Lynch, Peter and Pat, 263

Mam Tor Iron Age hill fort, Peveril, 27
Manchester, University Archaeology Unit, 209
Wardley Hall, 218–19
Marjerrison, Kerry-Anne, 207
Markham, Violet, 34
Marks, Mr and Mrs, 51–2
Martindale, Harry, 77, 196
Mary Queen of Scots, 22, 37, 122, 155, 188, 192, 225
Maskery family, Ashbourne, 25
Massingbird, Sir William, 99
McConnell, Paul, 263, 264
McDonald, Janet and Steve, 189–90
McKinley, Paul, 207
Mee, Arthur, 192
Meldon Park, Morpeth, 282–4
Melhuish, Annie, 140–41
Middlesbrough, Dorman Museum, 269–70
Milbanke, Anne, 81
Mitton Hall, Whalley, 212–13
Mompesson, William and Catherine, 20
Monyash, Arbour Low Stone Circle and Gib Hill Barrow, 36–7
Moore, Steve, 131
Morpeth, Meldon Park, 282–4
Mortimer, Roger, 82
Mosborough Hall Hotel, Sheffield, 116–18
Museum of Childhood, 35

Nantwich, Red Cow, 54–8
Napoleon, 141
Nevill, Charles, 65
Neville family, Sleaford, 107
Nevinson, Ben (John), 161–2
Newark, Upton Hall, 73–4
Newcastle, Duke of, 67, 70
Newcastle-upon-Tyne, Cooperage, 252–4
Theatre Royal, 260–62
Newstead Abbey, Kirkby-in Ashfield, 80–82
Newton Aycliffe, Redworth Hall Hotel, 249–52
Nine Ladies Stone Circle, Birchover, 32–3
Norbury Old Manor, Ashbourne, 25–6
Northumberland, map of, 274
Nostell Priory, 170–74
Nottingham, Castle, 67–70
Salutation Inn, 76–7
Ye Olde Trip to Jerusalem, 82–3
Nottinghamshire, map of, 66
Nutbrown, Donald, 118–19

Oak Tree Inn, Stanley, 262–4
Oakwell Hall and Country Park, Batley, 163–5
Olde Dolphin Inn, Derby, 37–8
Ollerton, Rufford Country Park and Abbey, 83–8
Orde-Powlett, Hon. Harry, 192–3
Ormskirk, Rufford Old Hall, 221
Otter, Tom, 89–92
Overwater Hall Hotel, Keswick, 230–31

Packman Lane, Rotherham, 126–8
Parker, Robert, 35–6
Parsons, John, 133–4
Peak Cavern (formerly called Devil's Arse), Peveril, 27
Pearoyd Bridge, Sheffield, 12
Pendle Witch Country, 213–16
Penrith, Brougham Hall, 243–5
Percy, family, Warkworth, 279–80
Sir Henry (Harry Hotspur), 280–82

Sir Josceline, 147
Peverel, William, 27
Peveril Castle, 26, 27, 28
Phillips, Adrian, 289, 291
Pontefract, Rogerthorpe Manor,
    168–70
Potts, Thomas, 214
Preston Hall Museum and The Green
    Dragon Museum, Stockton-on-
    Tees, 264–6
Punch Bowl, Clitheroe, 208–9

Queen Adelaide, 35

Rabbit Nanny, 142
Ralph, Lord Cromwell, 97
Ravensworth, Lord, 262
Rawstorne, Colonel Edward, 169
Red Cow, Nantwich, 54–8
Red Pump, Bashall Eaves, 221–3
Redworth Hall Hotel, Newton
    Aycliffe, 249–52
Rew, Sue and Robin, 233–4
Richard I (the Lionheart), 220
Richard II, 98, 254, 280
Richard of Glafsby, 114
Richmond, Castle, 184–6
    Easby Abbey, 185–6
Ringwood Hall Hotel, Chesterfield,
    34–5
Ripley Castle, Harrogate, 178–81
Robin Hood, 72–3, 168
Robson, Alan, 260, 286
Rochdale, Stubley Old Hall, 220
Roche Abbey, Rotherham, 124–6
Rogerthorpe Manor, Pontefract,
    168–70
Rook, Major Alan, 105
    Michael, 105–6
Rotherham, Hellaby Hall Hotel,
    129–31
    Hickleton Churchyard, 121
    Packman Lane, 126–8
    Roche Abbey, 124–6
Royal Oak, Chesterfield, 24–5
Rudston Monolith, 149–50
Rufford, Country Park and Abbey,
    Ollerton, 83–8

Old Hall, 221
Rushworth, Brian, 142
Rushyford, Eden Arms Swallow
    Hotel, 268–9
Rykenild Street, 126

St Ambrose, 218
St Oswald, Lady, 171-2
St Wulfram's Church, Grantham,
    100–103
Sallis, Dr Les, 143
Saltonstal, Samuel, 168
Salutation Inn, Nottingham, 76–7
Savile family, Nottinghamshire, 84
Saxilby, Sun Inn, 89–92
Scarborough, Castle, 189–90
    Francesca, Countess of, 254
    Lords, 124
Scott, Sir Walter, 233
Scrope, Sir Richard, 192
Seahouses, Beadnell House, 278–9
Selby, Margaret, 283–4
Sempringham monastery, 105
Sharp, Dr John, 277
Shaw-Andrews, Danny and Linda,
    76–7
Sheffield, Carbrook Hall Hotel,
    121–4
    Junction 31, M1, 131–2
    Mosborough Hall Hotel, 116–18
    Paranormal Research Group,
    115–16
    Pearoyd Bridge, 12
    Stocksbridge bypass, 11–12, 13,
    118–20
Shrewsbury, 4th Earl, 84
Singleton, Deborah, 157, 158
Skegness, Bratoft Castle, 99
    Church Farm Museum, 92–4
    Gunby Hall, 99–100
Skelhorn, Arthur, 39–40
Skelton, Phil, 123–4
    Roger, 259
Skipsea Castle, 144–5
Skipton, Bolton Abbey, 187–9
Sleaford, Barn Gallery, 107
Society for Psychical Research, 121
Spittal, David and Sue, 42–5

Stamford, Earls of, 47, 48
Stanley, Oak Tree Inn, 262–4
Stockport, Bramall Hall, 62–5
Stocksbridge bypass, 11–12, 13,
    118–20
Stockton-on-Tees, Preston Hall
    Museum and The Green Dragon
    Museum, 264–6
Stoker, Bram, 194, 237
Stoneham, Mark, 92
Stragglethorpe Hall, Lincoln, 105–6
Stubton Hall, 105
Stubley Old Hall, Rochdale, 220
Sudbury Hall, 35–6
Sun Inn, Saxilby, 89–92
Surtees, Crosier, 249–50

Tankerville, Leonora Lady, 286–90
    Lord, 289–90
Tattershall Castle, Tattershall, 97–8
Temple Newsam House, Leeds,
    153–8
Terry, Christopher and Alison, 243,
    244–5
Theatre Royal, Newcastle-upon-
    Tyne, 260–62
    York, 175–8
Thirsk, Byland Abbey, 190–92
Thom, Professor A., 238
Thompson, David and Kate, 91–2
    Ian, 115
Thorpe, Chris and Jean, 246–7
Three Houses Inn, Wakefield, 161–2
Tick, Ann, 97–8
Toustain, Baron, 147
Towndrow, John, 40–41
Trip to Jerusalem, Ye Olde,
    Nottingham, 82–3
Tynemouth Priory and Castle, 257

UFOs, 120
Upton Hall, Newark, 73–4

Villiers, George (2nd Duke of
    Buckingham), 199

Wade de Thirlwell family, Carlisle,
    232
Wakefield, Sir Humphry and the
    Hon. Lady, 286, 290
Wakefield, Sandal Castle, 162
    Three Houses Inn, 161–2
Wardley Hall (the House of the
    Skull), Manchester, 218–19
Wardrew House, Carlisle, 232–4
Warkworth Castle and Hermitage,
    Amble, 279–82
Warrington, Heathercliffe Country
    House, 58–9
Washington Arts Centre, Fatfield,
    270–72
Watson, Brian, 169–70
Whalley, Mitton Hall, 212–13
Whitby Abbey, 194–5
White Hart Hotel, Lincoln, 98–9
William IV, 35
William the Conqueror, 67, 103,
    144, 147, 184
Wingfield Manor, Alfreton, 22–4
Winnats Pass, 26–7
Woodruff, Derek, 228
Workington Hall, 225–9
Worksop, Clumber Park, 70–72
    Priory Gatehouse, 75–6
Wragby Church, Nostell, 173–4
Wright family, Eyam, 20
Wright, Irene, 30–31
Written Stone Lane, Longridge,
    215–16

York, 195–200
    Beningbrough Hall, 181–2
    Cock and Bottle, 199–200
    Minster, 198–9
    Theatre Royal, 175–8
    Treasurer's House, 196–7
Yorkshire, East, map of, 136
    North, map of, 176
    South, map of, 112
    West, map of, 154
Young, Arthur, 182